ASSASSINATION IN AMERICA

James McKinley

Assassination in America

HARPER & ROW, PUBLISHERS

NEW YORK, HAGERSTOWN, SAN FRANCISCO, LONDON

Most of the contents of this book originally appeared in somewhat different form in *Playboy* magazine.

ASSASSINATION IN AMERICA. Copyright © 1975, 1976, 1977 by James McKinley. All rights reserved. Printed in the United States of America. No part of this book may be used or reproduced in any manner whatsoever without written permission except in the case of brief quotations embodied in critical articles and reviews. For information address Harper & Row, Publishers, Inc., 10 East 53rd Street, New York, N.Y. 10022. Published simultaneously in Canada by Fitzhenry & Whiteside Limited, Toronto.

FIRST EDITION

Library of Congress Cataloging in Publication Data

McKinley, James.
  Assassination in America.

  Bibliography: p.
  Includes index.
  1. Assassination—United States. 2. Violence—
United States. I. Title.
HV6285.M23 1977   364.1′524′0973   76-9195
ISBN 0–06–012951–4

77 78 79 80 10 9 8 7 6 5 4 3 2 1

For Mary Ann,
who knows truth from falsehood

Contents

ACKNOWLEDGMENTS

There are too many to list, but a few of my most outstanding debts must be mentioned.

I owe great thanks to three editors—Geoffrey Norman, Laurence Gonzales and Buz Wyeth—for their inspiration, encouragement and editing skill as this book made the transition from idea to magazine series to finished volume.

I must thank, too, the many people at *Playboy* and Harper & Row—art directors, researchers, copy sleuths—who spent large amounts of time helping me assemble and verify the basic facts of this history.

Above all, my gratitude goes to Glenda McCrary, who as researcher, typist and auditor of the author's tirades did an immense amount of the hardest sort of literary work.

FOREWORD

A melancholy fact motivates this book: that of all living Americans only those born after 1975 have escaped the scarifying impact of politics by assassination. Singly and collectively, almost all of us have shivered in those dark winds. Moreover, as a nation we have lived with the threats, and with the terrifying actualities, of assassination since at least 1835, when an unhinged house painter confronted President Andrew Jackson with a brace of pistols. That time, luckily, they didn't go off—in other times and places the guns did—but from then on the course of politics in America was mightily affected by assassins.

This book seeks to create a sense of those periodic violent eruptions in our past, to generate an understanding of the causes and agents and effects belching out of our assassinations. The hope is that such knowledge might help us sift out a remedy, however partial, for the bullets which too often have pre-empted the ballots. Certainly the odds are long. Assassination has been with the world almost forever, and Americans came to it relatively late.

We also came to it differently. Before ours, for time nearly out of mind, assassins had been those who calmly killed a public figure out of a clear political motivation. Even the twelfth-century *hashashin*—that hashish-eating Syrian sect who, killing on order of the fabulous "Old Man of the Mountains," lent assassination their name—murdered solely for political reasons. They came to typify the Old World assassin: cool, relentless, often organized into terrorist teams, and perfectly willing to die for the cause.

But American assassins broke this pattern. They have not, it seems, habitually banded together for their task, just as they haven't much gone in for slaying low-level officials, a frequent phenomenon in other countries. They are attracted instead to the President or to similarly striking figures. They kill fairly seldom (from 1919 to 1968 one American President was slain as compared with thirty-nine heads of state around the world), and it seems by whim. Cases of conspiracy—so prevalent elsewhere in the world—are difficult to prove in most American assassinations. Nevertheless, this book assays those possibilities using the relevant data available, and trying both for accuracy and to avoid the cheap profit-and-publicity seeking that some conspiracy theorists have indulged in, especially with our recent assassinations.

Obviously, the subject is too important for any foolery. Assassination ordains the death of a leader. Assassination changes things. The people who govern us change, and our laws change, and policies shift, and the governmental system is re-examined, even modified. But most of all, the assassination—so sudden, so unexpected, so terrible—shocks us into new consciousness, and *we* are fundamentally changed.

That's the last reason for the book, the personal one. On November 22, 1963, at 12:30 CST, I was in the cannery-like corridors of the Procter & Gamble building in Cincinnati, earnestly pursuing the preparation of Big Soap's advertising copy and contemplating, with what seemed like joy, my eventual just deserts as a corporate success. Then down the beige halls, reverberating as though in a submarine, came the cry, "The President's been shot, the President's been shot." When, indecently soon, I learned John Kennedy was dead, his skull blown away, something seemed to happen to my head, too, something not as frightening or as final, but something still unmistakably and irremediably basic. Business no longer seemed so alluring. The New Frontier was closed. Large matters—security, success—shrank, and others, perhaps repressed before, took form and grew. Within three months, my family and I were jobless in Spain, where I tried to learn to write and to relax, and where I could weep and then consider what had happened to me and my country. All I could conclude was that we were changed utterly. Kennedy's aims, my life, the dreams of millions of others around the world, had been ruptured by a man with a gun. Or, as it seemed after more thought, by a monstrous and unstoppable force which had gotten to Kennedy, a President surrounded by guards, just as it earlier had gotten to Lincoln, Garfield, McKinley, Cermak, Huey Long, and afterward to Martin Luther King, and Robert Kennedy, and almost to George Wallace and Gerald Ford. How could that be, and can we ever understand this force of the assassin which changes things?

I wrote this chronicle of our assassinations largely to help me answer that question for myself. Yet in the end, I suspect and fear the mystery of why Americans kill their leaders is as nearly impenetrable as before, although I fervently hope not.

JAMES McKINLEY

INTRODUCTION

*"The essential American soul
is hard, isolate, stoic and a
killer."*

—D. H. LAWRENCE

When the first settlers came to America, they brought with them two fateful articles—a God-drunk dream of themselves as blessed and a gun. They believed they needed the dream to endure and the gun to impose their dream on a new world.

They were right, for with Scripture and shot and shrewd dealing, they spread the dream until, 169 years later, their rectitude was proved with the signing of the Declaration of Independence. That day, the citizenry ran home and armed itself to ratify, forever, the American dream, first with celebratory gunshots, then with the Revolution.

For the next two hundred years, wars were fought, Presidents assassinated, strikes broken, minorities persecuted and riots suppressed, and succeeding generations awoke to their horrors. Still, the dream persisted, inspiring and shaping each wave of Americans, until, in Dallas' Dealey Plaza, our turn came. The gun that killed John Kennedy shocked us awake, drove into our brains the fact that assassination was now, terribly, more than historical. Wide-eyed as horror-movie addicts, we then watched the murders of Malcolm X and George Lincoln Rockwell, Martin Luther King, Jr., and Robert Kennedy and an attempt on George Wallace—watched American assassins kill with perfect democracy, left and right alike, while we stuttered, "Can this be us? Who are we, to kill this way?"

Those who believe America is a more homicidal nation than others— who compare us with Imperial Rome and point to atrocities in Vietnam —can take special comfort in the legend that long before Jamestown, white men's blood had baptized the land. The story goes that in about 1000,

1

on one of the several Viking expeditions to Vinland, the explorer Thorvard was persuaded by his wife, Freydis—the bastard daughter of Eric the Red —to slaughter their companions. It seems that Freydis wanted their friends' larger boat and their booty. If true, Freydis' murders—she herself hacked down five women—are the first recorded instance of economic violence in American history.

Indeed, one of the remarkable facts of America's past is that not until the nineteenth century, well after our Revolution, that of the French and the one we call the Industrial, did political murder—assassination—become a native curse. It wasn't until 1804, when Aaron Burr killed Alexander Hamilton in a duel, that there was a sharply etched case of one-on-one killing over political differences, and it was 1835 before anybody tried to kill an American President. Nevertheless, it clearly was in the Colonial and Revolutionary periods that we first became aware of our capacity for murder and its varying causes. It surfaced early.

Not long after the Plymouth colonists landed, Miles Standish, the upright Pilgrim who was not nearly so reluctant in war as in love, felt his position threatened by a new boatload of settlers who didn't worship God the right way. With his fellows, Standish decided to solve two problems at once. They would liquidate some Indians who were menacing them, then warn the new arrivals that a similar fate awaited them. Safe in the conviction that they acted justly, they lured a Massachusetts Indian chief to their camp, hacked him and two of his braves to bits, then publicly hanged his eighteen-year-old brother before proceeding to attack the Indian camp and continue the massacre. Thereafter, Standish warned the new colonists away, proclaiming that the economy, not to mention the theology, couldn't support them all. The rival colonists decamped for Maine. Standish returned in triumph to Plymouth, put the Indian chief's head on a pike and settled down to some fur trading.

In these acts of the Pilgrims—and in their later battles over trade with the other "chosen," the Puritans, or in their "Hangman, do your duty" persecutions of the Quakers—we cannot know whether the motives were mostly economic, racial, civil, theological or, ultimately, personal. The violent usually have a smörgåsbord of rationalizations at hand. But we can, in those killings, detect the lineaments of a key question: Did Freydis' murders for booty and Standish's killings for God, territory and trade begin a tradition of *assassination* in America or merely one of violence?

To find an answer, we need some definition of assassination, and one peculiar to our national experience. Assassination? We can say it is the killing of a prominent person, rationally planned to advance or sustain a cause that most often is political—or, as is too frequently the case in our time, to secure notoriety, however temporary, for the assassin—that killing usually being carried out by an individual or a small group of conspirators. Accepting that, we have to excuse Freydis and Standish as our prototypal assassins. Killing solely for monetary gain is not assassination, nor is leading a bunch of crazed zealots against unsuspecting natives. Even so, the Viking lady and Pilgrim father foreshadow the age of assassination in America, and we can legitimately ask: What are the constituents of American assassination?

We can begin with what's least important, the myth of Americans as hand-to-hand killers, struggling like epic heroes against their opponents. It's true that those earliest Americans grappled directly with their adversaries, just as the assailants of Lincoln, Garfield, McKinley, Anton Cermak, Huey Long, Malcolm X and Robert Kennedy were belly-close to their victims. But, like the Greeks and Romans and the Borgias, who preferred slow poisons administered by servants, we have had our long-range assassinations—most recently, of John Kennedy and Martin Luther King. And lest we think those are twentieth-century technological aberrations, akin to fire bombing from five miles up, we should remember the apocryphal story that Lincoln, before he fell to the native-gun tradition, was the victim of a poison-kiss plot. Lincoln, who reportedly once said assassination was not an American crime, was bussed at a White House reception by a rebel lady whose lips were infected with smallpox germs. Whether or not this story is true, it tells us much about the American imagination and about the passions that swirled around Lincoln before he attended the last performance at Ford's Theater of John Wilkes Booth.

Assassination as a frontier-ethic facedown is not, then, peculiarly American. Nor is tyrannicide our invention, the Greeks having instituted it as early as the fifth century B.C. and the Romans having carried it to perfection. Europeans, beginning in the Middle Ages, assassinated Thomas à Becket, two Henrys of France, James I of Scotland, a number of the Medicis, and so on down to figures as diverse as Marat, Alexander II, Count Bernadotte, Trotsky and Admiral Darlan. In our time, assassination, as much as ever, crosses national and cultural barriers at random. The names Trujillo, Diem, Lumumba, Gandhi, Faisal and Zapata make the point.

Perhaps the unique characteristic of the *American* assassination is that the assassin misunderstands the nation in whose cause he thinks he kills. *He is a poor historian, though he believes otherwise.* In his linear and insular reasoning, things must proceed as fantasized in his own delusions.

Booth believes he eliminates the great threat to the South, but Lincoln's death brings on the tight-lipped Radical Reconstructionists, latter-day Puritans whose policies halve the nation for two generations.

McKinley's death, a sacrifice to the common man and to the end of Imperial America, brings on the Roughest Rider of them all, and Teddy Roosevelt acquires new dominions for us.

Huey Long's murder removes the populist dictator but clears the way for Earl and Russell Long to rule Louisiana.

Lee Harvey Oswald—or someone—destroys Kennedy the appeaser and Lyndon Johnson's bellicosity makes us war haters.

Martin Luther King's death brings not race war but gun-control laws and an avalanche of civil rights legislation.

Sirhan Sirhan slays Robert Kennedy and, while the Arab watches from his cell, the nation moves closer to Israel.

And the assassins, if alive, are bemused. Some have made yet another miscalculation. They've ignored the avenging angel: the sergeant who slays Booth, or Long's bodyguards, or Jack Ruby.

Yet the assassinations have had effects. Not always what the killers anticipated, not nearly so effective as those bloody but systematic coups in Europe and the East and Latin America, where power is usurped and governments toppled. But effects nonetheless, and conceived in a peculiarly American way. Our prototypal assassin—usually a spiritual isolate—believes with molish irrationality that one great deed will maintain or restore his perfect republic. Ironically, the assassin is both conservative and hopeful. He *believes* in the promise of America, believes he has been cheated of the dream's fruits, and so with gun in hand presents to his victim, to the individual he thinks has caused his woes, what amounts to a petition, a Magna Carta in murder. Our surviving assassins tell us their act righted a fundamental wrong, that they have behaved in accordance with America's ideals. Coupled with the toleration, even veneration, we have had for violence, that paradox beats deep in the secret heart of American assassins. In John Wilkes Booth it pulsed incessantly.

I

DEATH TO TYRANTS!

"Fellow-citizens, we cannot escape history."

—ABRAHAM LINCOLN,
December 1, 1862

Abraham Lincoln knew he was an assassination target. Like John Kennedy one hundred years later, he sometimes mused over the possibility of his death. On the Good Friday in 1865 when he was shot, Lincoln remarked to William Crook, his bodyguard, "I believe there are men who want to take my life. And I have no doubt they will do it."

Those intrigued by historical repetitions recall JFK's words that Friday morning in Dallas: "If anybody really wanted to shoot the President of the United States, it would not be a difficult job—all you have to do is get on a high building someday with a telescopic sight. . . ." Both Presidents agreed, too, that they could easily be slain if the killer was prepared to sacrifice his life. Perhaps our first and latest Presidential victims—whose murders are similar in several ways—meditated on their ends in this way because they were, unlike their assassins, good historians. They could keep time in mind, could see themselves as targets ordained by history, by war, by controversy, by great and conflicting interests within the country. It seems they knew they could not escape their assassinations.

It is also certain that Lincoln's death prefigures the assassinations of our time. Reviewing it, we shall see the similarities. There are the uncertain motives of the alleged assassins. Inconsistencies in physical evidence. Missing evidence. Contradictions or impossibilities offered as facts by the Government and its commissions. The odor of a governmental cover-up. Finally, the crucial specific questions, such as: Was Lincoln betrayed to Booth's fatal gunshot by someone in his Administration? By his Secretary of War and political rival, Edwin Stanton? In his home? In the South? In the Vatican? Or did the mad Booth act alone?

From the beginning of his term, Lincoln was shadowed by untimely death. In February, 1861, on his way to his inauguration, he was informed by superspy Allan Pinkerton that an attempt on his life might be made in Baltimore as he changed trains for Washington. Throughout the Civil War, Maryland seethed with Secessionists—the Booths were Marylanders—and it appears that in 1861 some six or eight conceived the idea of killing Lincoln in the confusion of a diversion staged at the train depot, then fleeing by ship to the South. Whether or not the plot existed is debated, but Lincoln *was* spirited to Washington by a secret route and arrived in semidisguise, huddled in an old overcoat, crowned by a rumpled soft hat, accompanied by only two trusted bodyguards (one of whom, Lincoln's former law partner, Ward Hill Lamon, was to lament being absent April 14, four years later). The cartoonists had a marvelous time depicting the new President skulking into his capital. Lincoln's own sentiments seem to have been uttered in Philadelphia, before his ignominious arrival in the city where he would finally be struck down. He said, "If this country cannot be saved without giving up that principle [the Revolution's prize: an equal chance for everyone] . . . I would rather be assassinated on this spot than surrender it."

In Lincoln's mind was our history. We were, after all, risen commoners. That forbade an imperial Presidency. Lincoln disliked guards and panoply, once said he couldn't be the people's President if he shut himself up for safety in an iron box and that an assassin had better be careful, because he might get somebody worse for the next President. Still, Lincoln knew we had a tendency to violence. He could look back to 1804 and see Aaron Burr prod his political opponent Alexander Hamilton to a duel. Some said Burr did so to rid the nation of a dangerously aristocratic and ambitious man; others that Burr had avenged himself for 1800, when Hamilton had thrown his support to Jefferson, thus defeating Burr in the House of Representatives for the Presidency. Lincoln knew, though, that this duel was emblematic of his own time: Hamilton's whiggish pragmatism versus the egalitarian absolutism of Burr.

Then Andrew Jackson had been threatened in 1835, when Lincoln was a twenty-five-year-old Illinois legislator. Old Hickory was strolling out of the Capitol when an out-of-work house painter named Richard Lawrence popped from behind a pillar, raised two pistols and pulled the trigger of one. Jackson heard the cap explode but felt nothing. He rushed Lawrence, his cane raised to thrash him to the ground. Lawrence pulled the other trigger, and that pistol also misfired. Jackson was lucky; but then he always had been. He'd killed Charles Dickenson in a duel in 1806 through the stratagem of wearing a loose frock coat that slowed his enemy's ball so that it wounded him grievously but not fatally. Andy then coolly shot Dickenson dead. As for Lawrence, Jackson suspected he had been part of a Whig conspiracy to murder him and not the lone, deranged man the failed assassin seemed to be.

So Lincoln knew history, knew about Burr, about Jackson, about the mobbing and killing of Elijah P. Lovejoy in 1837, when Lovejoy defended his abolitionist newspaper in Alton, Illinois, and by dying at the hands of angry proslavery men gave the cause its first martyr. Before Lovejoy's death, Lincoln had in the Illinois legislature counseled those very citizens that slavery was a grievous wrong. Slavery, he said in 1856, "debauches even our greatest men." He might well have been thinking of Kansas, where the issues had led to killings, rapes, burnings, as proslavers and free-soilers fought it out.

In 1858, Lincoln and Stephen A. Douglas debated for the U.S. Senate seat. Lincoln won the popular vote but Douglas the election in the legislature, so Lincoln stayed in Springfield while John Brown, the terrorist abolitionist, left Kansas bloody-handed to capture the Government's arsenal at Harpers Ferry in October, 1859. "God's Angry Man" hoped to pass out rifles to the oppressed blacks and spark a slave revolt. But Colonel Robert E. Lee and the Marines were summoned. They recaptured the Federal property and put down the rebellion, and on December 2, 1859, Lee gave the order and Brown swung at rope's end in the mild Virginia autumn. Among the onlookers, dressed fit to kill as a temporary member of the fashionable Richmond Grays, was a handsome actor, only twenty-one, second youngest of a famous family of thespians and now himself a budding idol of the Southern stage. John Wilkes Booth got sick after Brown was hanged and he later told his sister that "Brown was a brave old man." Certainly, Brown seemed braver than Booth, who had joined the Grays in order to see the hanging, then ended his enlistment the next day. He told all those, then and later, who asked why a man with his pro-South views didn't join the Army that he had promised his mother he wouldn't go to war.

Back in Illinois, Lincoln was preparing a speech that, within three months of its delivery at New York's Cooper Union in February, 1860, would make him the Republican Presidential nominee. Lincoln told the skeptical city slickers that Brown did not represent responsible antislavery Republicans—the radical abolitionists on the platform snickered—and that the South need fear no interference "with your slaves." It was a speech to placate everyone except the most fervent abolitionists. Yet such sentiments did not soothe Booth's histrionic secessionism and the actor slandered Lincoln in Southern salons with a ferocity that increased after Lincoln's election as our sixteenth President. Booth's rebel talk earned him the applause his acting did not, at least in the North, where his elder brother Edwin was king of the stage. John Wilkes's envy of Edwin's earnings and his romantic espousal of the South's cause combined in late 1860 and early 1861 when he went North determined to equal Edwin's fame and earnings in the cultural capitals. He was, after all, now a star—a commentator said, "A star is an advertisement in tights, who grows rich and corrupts the public taste"—and now he could bad-mouth the "damn Yankees" in their own territory. Unfortunately, he found little sympathy until he joined the Baltimore chapter of a secret racist society, the Knights of the Golden Circle, which intensified his hatred of the gangling Lincoln's preserve-the-Union talk. Unfortunately, too, Booth's acting was frequently panned, though he had the name, the physique and the looks: 5'8", but broad-chested and muscular. Black hair and flashing, imprisoning eyes. A good horseman, fine marksman, superb fencer, splendid gymnast.

But barely trained in theater; instead, making it on his looks and his physical abilities (he rewrote Shakespeare's scenes to include daring leaps and sword fights). He hadn't had Edwin's long, on-the-road apprenticeship with their father, Junius Brutus Booth, who had been the most famous Shakespearean actor in America. Nonetheless, John Wilkes had been quite successful with women in Richmond, Montgomery, Savannah, New Orleans, and now he went North to flaunt his abilities and anti-Union bravado. In Albany on February 18, 1861, he was playing, appropriately, in *The Apostate* when Lincoln's train came through on the way to his first inauguration. Booth first saw Lincoln then. He gleefully read the newspapers that ridiculed the President-elect's remarks as "inspired flatulence, slops and dregs," and that night played his role with a fury noted in the reviews. All the spring of 1861, Booth—or Wilkes, as he was called—loudly proclaimed in the dressing rooms, bedrooms, barrooms his admiration for Brutus and Charlotte Corday (Marat's assassin). He was prostrated when Fort Sumter fell on April 14, 1861. Four years later to the day, Abraham Lincoln was shot by Booth.

In the years from 1861 to 1865, we had come to know killing too well. The nation—North and South—was calloused to war's brutalities, to civil disorders (the Draft Riots in New York in 1863 killed and wounded almost a thousand), to brutalities in prison camps, to the savagery of guerrilla raids, to the terrible slaughter on the battlefield. Calloused, also, to military rule, directed since 1862 by Lincoln's pious, intolerant and fanatically abolitionist Secretary of War, Edwin M. Stanton—who allegedly schemed to keep the war going, to lose just enough so that the North would be turned to hatred of the South and of slavery. As Stanton saw it, the great aim of the war was to abolish slavery. General McClellan later reported that the Secretary of War believed "to end the war before the nation was ready for that would be a failure. The war must be prolonged and conducted so as to achieve that." If true, Stanton's desire was directly contrary to the sense-of-Congress resolution of 1861, which stated that the war was not to interfere "with the rights of established institutions of those Southern states."

It was also contrary to Lincoln's desires in the war's early phases. In 1862, he wrote to Horace Greeley, an adamant abolitionist: "If I could save the Union without freeing *any* slave, I would do it; and if I could save it by freeing *all* the slaves, I would do it; and if I could save it by freeing some and leaving others alone, I would also do that."

But Stanton, throughout the war, would maneuver against Lincoln and thwart his plans. He was a powerful and often devious man, who wanted to be President. He was in a splendid position to act against Lincoln in an ultimate way: either by organizing and directing a conspiracy to assassinate the President or by allowing an independent conspiracy to succeed. The evidence against him, as we shall see, is persuasive. Certainly the war bred both forgiveness and eternal enmity.

After the first years of defeats, the North's material and manpower had prevailed. At Appomattox on April 9, 1865, Lee had surrendered to Grant, who had stipulated generous terms, as his President wished. In Washington, the joy was boundless. Lincoln said, "I've never been so happy in my life." Torches lit the night, gunshots punctuated the cheers, bands paraded and played "Dixie" as though the ballad were a trophy of war.

On April 11, Lincoln addressed a crowd on the White House lawn. He carefully, wearily, laid out a plan for the reunion of the states. His tone was conciliatory. Later, he elaborated to the Cabinet that in dealing with the defeated South there would be "no bloody work." Twelve-year-old Tad Lincoln heard the people chant of the rebel leaders, "Hang 'em," and said to his father, "Oh, no, we must hang on to them," to which the President agreed fervently.

John Wilkes Booth, listening, was outraged. He muttered to an accomplice that that was the last speech Lincoln would make. He hated this "ape," this "Emperor," who wanted to install doulocracy. Lincoln had actually been to Booth's precious Richmond, had entered the conquered capital on April 4. Before that, he had been elected again, and Booth had been there on March 4 to watch him make that sickening inaugural speech about "malice toward none and charity for all." No, Lincoln would not really "bind up the nation's wounds," that was clear. With Lee beaten, Lincoln must be killed. Cut off the head and the body dies. The executioner as hero. As Booth put it in his diary for April 13, "Until today, nothing was ever thought of sacrificing to our country's wrongs. For six months we had worked to capture, but our cause being almost lost, something decisive and great must be done." (This messianic memorandum seems utterly familiar to us, who have seen Sirhan's confidences or read the journal of Arthur Bremer, Wallace's assailant. Booth was our first savior assassin.)

This decision to kill Lincoln was not Booth's first plot against the President. Before, he had wanted to kidnap Lincoln and exchange him for the thousands of Confederate prisoners Lee so desperately needed back in his armies. For that, he had assembled and subsidized a vaudeville troupe of conspirators. There was himself. He had some money, charm and contacts (his fiancée was a Senator's daughter, though his girlfriends were unconnected). And there were the others he'd enlisted to snatch the President:

•**LEWIS PAINE, alias POWELL and WOOD.** Aged 20. A Baptist minister's son and former Confederate soldier who had deserted after Gettysburg and later signed an allegiance to the Union. Handsome, enormously strong, stupid, a Negro hater (he'd been arrested for beating a black girl in Baltimore). Devoted to Booth after seeing him play in Richmond and meeting him in 1861. An absolutely reliable killer, trained for it in the war and out of place in a nonviolent world.

•**JOHN SURRATT.** Aged 20. A former Roman Catholic divinity student and currently a Confederate spy and dispatch carrier who knew the routes from Richmond through Washington to the Confederate underground in Montreal. Magnificent horseman and disarmingly convincing as a young clerk for the Adams Express Company in Washington.

•**GEORGE ATZERODT.** Aged 29. An illiterate, ferret-faced Prussian immigrant and coachmaker whose chief value was his knowledge of the roads south out of Washington, through Maryland, to Port Tobacco on the Potomac, and his skill and experience as a blockade runner who could cross the river with the captured President on board a chartered boat.

•**DAVID HEROLD.** Aged 22. Chief occupations: partridge hunter and drugstore clerk. A loyal, agile, chinless boy with few thinking abilities (estimated mental age of eleven) but with a profound knowledge of the back roads, swamps and houses along the likely escape route, south from Washington.

•SAMUEL ARNOLD. Aged 30. A former schoolmate of Booth's at the Catholic Saint Timothy's Hall in Catonsville, Maryland. Deserted Confederate soldier but brave, and smart enough not to take Booth's word in everything. Worked as a farm hand in Maryland.

•MICHAEL O'LAUGHLIN. Aged 24. Another childhood acquaintance and Confederate deserter who was captivated by Booth's brilliance. A Maryland livery-stable and feed-store laborer who drank too much and thought too little.

To these, when the conspirators' trial came, would be added two more interesting names: Mary Surratt, forty-five, a widow, the mother of John, who kept a Washington boardinghouse said to be the nest where the plots were hatched. Mrs. Surratt also had a tavern at Surrattsville, Maryland, on the Southern escape route. And Dr. Samuel Mudd, thirty-two, a physician charged with having introduced John Surratt and John Wilkes Booth, and who, after Lincoln's murder, admitted having treated Booth for the broken leg he sustained leaping from the Presidential box to the stage at Ford's Theater.

These were the principal players in the kidnaping-become-murder plot. There were many others, one in particular named Louis Weichmann—a pudgy, twenty-two-year-old former theology student who was a clerk in the War Department, an avowed Southern sympathizer, a boarder at Mrs. Surratt's and a fink.

Booth first planned to seize the President at Ford's during a performance of *Jack Cade* on January 18, 1865. He knew Lincoln went often to the theater. Indeed, in 1863, the President had seen Wilkes at Ford's in *The Marble Heart* and had admired his acting. That was the year Booth took to denouncing Lincoln's Administration from the stage—an act that got him arrested in St. Louis and released only when he signed an oath of allegiance to the Union. On another occasion, the President saw Booth perform a villain's role and noted that each malevolent speech seemed directed at him. He said afterward, "That fellow did look mighty sharp at me." Understandably, Booth's theatricalism would have made him perfectly satisfied to attack Lincoln in his box, singlehandedly truss him up, lower him to Herold, Arnold and O'Laughlin and escape through a door held open by another actor. In New York, Booth offered a stock player named Samuel Chester this latter role, but Chester refused, despite the assurance that "50 to 100" men were involved in the venture. Inevitably, Chester's recollection would lead to speculations after Lincoln's death about just who, and how many, had conspired to kill the President.

With Lincoln subdued, the kidnapers would head for the Navy Yard Bridge in a carriage driven by Surratt and escorted by other conspirators. Thence to Port Tobacco, Atzerodt's boat, Richmond and the presumed plaudits of a grateful Jefferson Davis. The plan failed when the weather turned bad and Lincoln stayed home.

While no evidence exists that Lincoln was aware of this Late Show plot, he certainly knew someone was after him. On March 19, 1864, the *New York Times* reported rumors of a plan, vetoed by Davis, to sent 150 Confederate raiders to kidnap Lincoln. In August of that year, a sniper plugged the President's top hat as he rode the three miles from the White House to his summer retreat at the Soldiers' Home.

Unabashed, Lincoln rode in and told the retreat's sentry, "Someone seems to have tried killing me." Who is unknown. It could have been a free-lance killer or one of Mosby's raiders (those irregulars were then operating in the Washington environs, to the consternation of officials) or merely a disgruntled citizen. Likewise, no one knows whether the attempt was premeditated or spontaneous.

Next came a report in November from Union spies that Confederates in Montreal were plotting Lincoln's death (Booth was then in New York, fresh from a Canadian visit, playing Marc Antony in *Julius Caesar* with his brothers Edwin and Junius Brutus, Jr.—during the star-studded performance, Canadian-based rebels made daring arson raids on several New York hotels and Union ships and docks, a coincidence that did not go unremarked). On December 1, 1864, an unsigned ad appeared in the Selma, Alabama, *Dispatch* soliciting funds to arrange the murders of Lincoln, Vice President Andrew Johnson and Secretary of State William Seward. Why Selma was chosen is unknown, unless the advertisers believed the town of eight hundred was especially ripe territory for such a scheme— an opinion Martin Luther King shared a century later. By April, 1865, Lincoln had numerous serious death threats filed in his desk under "ASSASSINATION."

Naturally, these reports brought efforts to protect the President, despite his dislike for bodyguards. Soon after taking office in 1862, Stanton had had his National Executive Police take over patrolling Washington from the small, badly manned Metropolitan Police. They were commanded by La Fayette C. Baker, later a prominent figure in the assassination saga. Baker formerly served the San Francisco vigilantes and he inclined to rough and immediate justice. He was described as sandy-haired, red-bearded, with "long, insatiate jaws." But his police did not guard the President. That was left to special detachments of cavalry (Lincoln complained that their jangling prevented conversation in his carriage) and to bodyguards either detailed by the Metropolitan Police or chosen by Lincoln's old friend Ward Lamon, marshal of the District of Columbia. Altogether, it was catch-as-catch-can.

Stanton often nagged Lincoln to increase his guard. But the President was obdurate, and so Stanton, Baker and Lamon did their best—or so it was thought. The result was a wartime President curiously open to threats, even from vainglorious actors.

Booth next planned to kidnap Lincoln on March 20, 1865. On the fourth, with most of the conspirators, he attended Lincoln's second inauguration. A photo shows Booth's hoboish underlings—so like the Dealey Plaza "tramps" of a century later—stationed at the foot of the speaker's platform, while the top hatted sinister dandy Wilkes peers down from a gallery at the President. Some historians speculate that Booth intended a flourish there and then, the whisking away of the President at his own inauguration. But Booth's men were not up to that stroke, even if the actor bragged later that he could have shot Lincoln where he stood. He didn't, either because the crowd would have torn him to fragments or because the conspirators' inaugural attendance was a scouting mission to see just how well protected the President was those days.

Apparently, not well enough that the group abandoned its plans. In mid-March, Booth and Paine supposedly laid in wait for Lincoln near the White House. They were frightened away when Lincoln strode into view surrounded by men. But with the South now tottering at Petersburg, it seemed to Booth they *must strike*, grab the President and use him as a towering pawn in the peace talks.

On March 13, Booth reassembled his band, which, following the inauguration, had scattered to prevent detection. They drifted into Washington, all making appearances again—as before the *Jack Cade* plan and the inauguration—at Mrs. Surratt's boardinghouse. All were duly noted by the observant Weichmann, who reported them to the War Department. The department did nothing about these callers. Perhaps they were thought too clownish for serious attention. But the inactivity provoked serious questions a few weeks later.

A number of the conspirators attended Ford's Theater on March 13 to reconnoiter (the Fords were Maryland friends of the Booths), and Wilkes urged again on them the ineffable *rightness* of grabbing Lincoln in a playhouse. At a dinner soiree that evening, after plenty of food and drink, Arnold and Booth argued over the plan. Arnold, supported by O'Laughlin, said even the newspapers were predicting the South would make some move against the President. They'd stay in for one more attempt, and in some sensible place, not a damned playhouse. Booth muttered that a man should be shot for backing out and Arnold retorted that two could play that game.

March 18 brought Booth's last full performance, again in *The Apostate*. From a stock player named John Matthews, Wilkes gathered that on the twentieth Lincoln would go to the Soldiers' Home retreat for a matinee of *Still Waters Run Deep*. That was the time. Again the conspirators gathered. Herold, Surratt and Atzerodt stashed carbines, rope and tools at the Surrattsville tavern, arranged for a boat, then returned to Washington. By the lonely road they waited. Surratt would seize the President's carriage. O'Laughlin, Arnold, Atzerodt would deal with the escort. Paine and Booth would handle Lincoln. The carriage clattered into view, alone. The conspirators surged forward . . . but it was not Lincoln in the carriage; rather, another person, whom Surratt later said was Salmon P. Chase, Chief Justice of the Supreme Court. Red with rage, the plotters returned to Mrs. Surratt's. Booth whipped his boots in anger. The group dispersed. Arnold and O'Laughlin said they were through and left for Maryland. Surratt went to Richmond to resume dispatch-carrying up to Montreal. Booth decamped for New York and a week of ladies and booze. Presumably, he suspected the Government knew something was afoot. And some officials did, if they were listening to Weichmann.

Nevertheless, Booth resolved to make one last try. On the twenty-ninth, the President would be at the theater. Booth wired O'Laughlin, but Michael was finished. Arnold wrote Booth the same. Cursing, Booth repaired on April 3 to Newport, Rhode Island, with an unknown lady. That day, Richmond fell to Grant. On Saturday, April 8, Booth checked into the National Hotel in Washington. On the tenth, the shouts in the streets told him Lee had surrendered. He began to drink heavily, to call at Mrs. Surratt's, searching for the remnants of his gang. Only Atzerodt, Herold and Paine were about. With Paine, or perhaps Herold, Booth heard that gentle speech on the eleventh. Booth railed about votes for niggers and drank on, especially the next day in John Deery's saloon. Like assassins of a later era—Oswald, Ray, Sirhan—he now seemed bent on mad public displays of his opinions, his intents, his skills. Whether Booth had gone mad or had chosen outrageous behavior as a protective device is moot, though a question we might ask of a contemporary expert such as "Squeaky" Fromme.

Lincoln not only spoke of his premonitions of death; he saw himself dead. Within a month of April 14 he'd had, and remarked on, a dream in which he saw a corpse lying in state in the East Room. The dreaming President asked a guard who was dead in the White House. He answered, "The President; he was killed by an assassin." Surely this was in the President's mind on the fourteenth, when he conducted his 11 A.M. Cabinet meeting. He listened once more to Stanton's urgings that parts of the defeated South be put under military rule and denied statehood. It's incontestable that in the afternoon Lincoln went to the War Department and requested that Major Thomas Eckert accompany him as bodyguard to the theater that night. Eckert, Lincoln said, could break iron pokers over his arm.

Stanton denied the request, saying he had pressing work for Eckert that evening. Lincoln then asked Eckert himself, who said he followed Stanton's orders. In fact, Eckert only went home that evening, while Stanton called on Seward and then went home himself. However many questions their excuses raised later, the President acquiesced that afternoon. He would have one Metropolitan Police Force bodyguard. In addition, Major Henry Rathbone and his fiancée, Clara Harris, would accompany him and Mrs. Lincoln. The Grants had begged off, pleading their desire to visit their children in Burlington, New Jersey. Lincoln suspected the real reason was Julia Grant's dislike for Mrs. Lincoln. Mary *was* insanely jealous of women around him. Lincoln would as lief stay home, though his wife deserved the recreation. They'd lost two of their four sons, had watched their beloved Willie die in 1862 in the prison of the White House. But she'd put on her brave face, get gussied up . . . she spent plenty for clothes, that was sure. At Ford's was a benefit for her favorite actress, Laura Keene, who was appearing in an amusing comedy, *Our American Cousin.* A pity his older boy, Robert, was too battle-fatigued to go. The Stantons had also excused themselves, which hardly surprised Lincoln. Stanton had little sense of humor. Lincoln would go, accept it, too. He knew he was tired, worn thin, older than his fifty-six years. His belly bothered him, he slept badly, he stooped and shuffled—hardly the indefatigable frontiersman. Victory was his, but at what cost? To what end? So much to do.

Booth was busy, too. Though he'd booked a box at Grover's Theater the day before, in case the Lincolns and the Grants went there, Ford's would be easier. He knew the Ford family well, received his mail at their office. A stagehand named Edward Spangler had agreed to help. He said the locks on the doors to the Presidential box were broken, which would make it easier. Walking toward Ford's that chilly morning of the fourteenth,

Booth heard people singing "When This Cruel War Is Over" as they waited for the ragtag of General Joseph Eggleston Johnston's army, then at bay in North Carolina, to surrender. So Booth was delighted when he overheard Harry Ford tell the stage carpenter that the Presidential party was coming to his theater. The partition between boxes seven and eight was coming down. Booth was sorry now he had no use for O'Laughlin, who'd shown up drunk at the hotel that morning. Still, things were no longer dull, as he'd said in a letter to his mother the day before.

With characteristic agility, Booth leaped through the day. At Ford's, he inspected the Presidential box. An easy jump of twelve feet from it to the stage, across that and out the back door to the alley, where Spangler would be holding a horse. Then along the escape route, east across the Anacostia River into southern Maryland, down to Surrattsville, across the Potomac into Virginia and on to Richmond. John Wilkes next watched a rehearsal, though he knew the play as well as Laura Keene. During the third act, there was a line—"You sockdologizing old mantrap"—that always brought a big laugh. Only one actor (Harry Hawk that night) would be onstage. So there it was.

Booth now went to a livery stable to arrange a fast mare for the evening. Then back to his hotel to dress all in black and pocket his wallet, an unused diary, a compass, his watch, a gimlet, a small brass derringer and a long knife that, unsheathed, bore the inscription "LIBERTY AND INDEPENDENCE. AMERICA—THE LAND OF THE BRAVE AND THE FREE. SHEFFIELD, ENGLAND."

Booth soon afterward dropped in for a moment at Mrs. Surratt's boardinghouse and, before long, the widow woman set out for Surrattsville. Weichmann agreed to drive her.

The Herndon House, one block from Ford's, was Booth's next call. To the reliable Paine, he gave the job of killing Seward in his bed as he lay recovering from injuries received in a carriage accident. Paine was eager, but he didn't know Seward's home, couldn't learn the lay of Washington. No trouble. Herold would guide Paine. They would strike near 10:15 P.M., so that the Union hydra heads would all roll at once.

On to the Kirkwood House, where Atzerodt should be. But the Prussian was out boozing, so Booth pushed a note under his door. Then, most curiously, he left a card for Vice President Johnson, who stayed at Kirkwood House, reading: "Don't wish to disturb you. Are you at home? J. Wilkes Booth." That gesture has reverberated ever since.

Booth went on to Deery's saloon after picking up his horse at the stable. He drank brandy and water, thoughtfully watched billiards and then hurried downstairs to Grover's Theater's office. There he wrote a letter to the editor of Washington's *National Intelligencer* explaining why he had killed. He signed the letter, it's said, "J. W. Booth—Paine—Atzerodt—Herold," and so he crossed forever his Rubicon.

Next he showed his mare's speed to some stagehands from Ford's and then riding on Pennsylvania Avenue saw the actor John Matthews. Booth knew him well, used him for information, had once even tried to enlist him in his kidnap plots. Now he asked Matthews to deliver the *National Intelligencer* letter the next morning. Matthews agreed. While they chatted, a file of Confederate prisoners was marched past. Booth exclaimed, "Good God, Matthews, I have no country left!" and galloped away. He passed a carriage escorted by outriders. It was General Grant and his wife. They were on their way to the train station, bystanders told Booth. Well . . . only "the ape" was left to him.

Booth seems then to have found Atzerodt. He ordered the drunken immigrant to enter Johnson's room around 10:15 and kill the Vice President. Atzerodt demurred. Too dangerous. Johnson may have been drunk and foolish at the second inauguration, but, as Lincoln said, "Andy ain't no drunkard"—and nobody disputed Johnson's courage. Booth insisted, threatening Atzerodt. Atzerodt at last consented, to placate the enraged star, and Booth left. Atzerodt continued drinking.

At Taltavul's tavern, alongside Ford's, Booth soon was setting them up for Ford's stagehands. He excused himself to go into the empty theater. He went to the pine door leading to boxes seven and eight, those above and directly left of the stage. The broken locks would admit him, but he had to keep others out. He took a board that had supported a music stand. He carved a niche in the plaster wall to jam its end firmly against the door. The fragments he scooped up with one of the five pictures of girlfriends he carried. In the door to box seven he bored a hole with his gimlet. Now back to the hotel. He loaded the single-shot derringer, packed a disguise and two Colt revolvers in his saddlebags. Then to the last meeting with Paine, Herold and Atzerodt. He'd take Lincoln. Paine would enter Seward's house on the pretext of bringing a prescription from Seward's doctor. Atzerodt had his job. When all were finished, they'd rendezvous at the Navy Yard Bridge, go on to the South, maybe even Mexico. He told them of the *Intelligencer* letter. There'd be no turning back.

By 9:30, Booth was in the alley behind Ford's. He called for Spangler to hold his horse, but the stagehand was occupied with the play. Young Joseph Burroughs came to hold the famous actor's mount. Booth entered the theater, nodding left and right, and walked under the stage through a passage to the street. He ordered a whiskey at Taltavul's. At the bar, but unknown to Booth, were Lincoln's valet, Charles Forbes, and his Police Force bodyguard, John F. Parker, clearly not by the body. Some acquaintances needled Booth, telling him of Edwin's latest successes in New York and elsewhere. Wilkes smiled graciously and replied, "When I leave the stage for good, I'll be the most famous man in America."

Outside the tavern, Booth chatted with other admirers, refusing a drink from Captain William Williams of the Washington Cavalry Police. After accepting a chaw of tobacco from the ticket taker, he ascended to the dress circle and watched for his moment. It approached and he moved toward the first door. He was astonished to see no one barring his way. The President was unguarded! As the theater rang to comic lines, Booth entered the vestibule of the Presidential box. He barred the door with his board, then tiptoed to the door of box seven. Through the gimlet hole he saw the President, holding his wife's hand. To the right, on a sofa in box eight, Major Rathbone sat making cow eyes at his fiancée. Onstage, Hawk began his boffo lines in Act Three, Scene Two of Tom Taylor's ever-popular comedy. Booth opened the door. As Hawk spoke and the President smiled, Booth aimed the derringer just behind the left ear. It was about 10:15.

"You sockdologizing old—" and the laughs came, muffling the explosion, the thumped-melon sound of a half-inch lead ball entering Lincoln's skull. The 1,675 spectators flinched as the President's head moved slightly to the right and forward and slumped soundlessly. Booth said, softly, *"Sic semper tyrannis."* Major Rathbone jerked upright, jumped at him, was repulsed by a knife slash to his left arm. Mary Lincoln's face bore the puzzled look of a bludgeoned cow, then crumbled to hysteria. Booth's hand found the railing. He vaulted. Noises now. Screams. There was a tear as his spur caught the Treasury Guard's flag decorating the box. A thud as he hit the stage, the snap of his left shinbone. Hawk stood paralyzed. Booth! Shouts from the audience . . . "What? . . . Stop that man! . . . What? . . . The President? . . . Part of the play? . . ." Some later said they heard Booth cry, "Revenge! I've done it!" Others that he shrieked, "Death to tyrants." Others said that he merely limped away, brandishing the knife. Certainly, once backstage, he pushed away an actor, then a stagehand, hobbled to the rear door, out to his horse. A blow to young Burroughs' head with his knife hilt, a kick. Then the pounding hooves off toward the Navy Yard Bridge leading South. Everywhere, sounds ripping the night:

• At Seward's house, maniacal screams and groans fill the street as the huge Paine runs amuck, slashing down Seward's son, a soldier, a nurse, at last falling on the helpless Secretary himself, cutting again and again down across his face, his neck, until the knife grates against the iron brace supporting Seward's injured neck. Then Paine screaming, "I am mad, I am mad!" knifing a State Department courier, running from the house to find his guide, Herold, gone, spurring for the Navy Yard Bridge to Booth and safety. Paine runs, the rendezvous, everything forgotten, and leaves a badly wounded Seward, who will recover.

• Around Ford's, a fugue: the sobs of Mary; sad, knowing sighs from doctors; belligerent inquiries by the police and Stanton's men, the clank of cavalry sabers and bayonets restraining crowds, soon the grunts of men carrying Lincoln across the street to Petersen's boardinghouse, to be stretched across a too-short walnut spindle bed in a little room off the hall. The deathwatchers listen to the President's hopeless breaths tear the room and soon, the nation. Stanton whispers orders, directs the investigation, rules America from Petersen's gaslit cubbyholes.

• In the streets, men shout, fire guns, mob those who say they're glad the son of a bitch is dead, as the news is spread by jungle drums of rumor ("Confederates, Mosby's raiders, Jubal Early's . . . the last bloody raid . . . Lincoln, Seward, Johnson, Grant, all dead, for God's sake, look out!" —and, listening, we hear in our time Lyndon Johnson's conspiracy fears after Kennedy, hear "They'll get me, too" in his pulse). The uproar reaches Atzerodt, riding blind drunk, heading for the Kirkwood House and his death date with Johnson. The shouts scare him. He abandons his horse. He'll sell his revolver for drink money and try to make for upper Maryland.

• Those listening most closely hear in all this the sounds of more distant thunder, storms gathering over the death of Lincoln's policy of magnanimity to the South. Like echoes of Booth's escape, Lincoln's death brings on night hooves of the KKK and the counterforce of carpetbaggers. In the dying breaths of the sixteenth President, we catch those of the nation's innocence.

Lincoln died at 7:22 A.M. on April 15. Stanton, who had taken control of the Government by virtue of his wartime powers, was supposed to have said, "Now he belongs to the ages," though some eyewitnesses said he merely asked a minister to lead them in prayer. All agreed Stanton did a curious thing when the President breathed his last—took his top hat and ceremoniously settled it upon his head, as though crowning himself. At 10 A.M. Holy Saturday, 1865, Salmon Chase gave the oath of office to Andrew Johnson as seventeenth President of the Republic. Incredibly, in the uproar, the character assassination of the new President began, as men like Senator William Stewart of Nevada said Johnson had been drunk and mud-caked that morning, never mind that he was seen sober and somber at Lincoln's deathbed during the night and comported himself well at his oath-taking. All in all, things were out of joint.

During the frenzied night, the nation had learned the news in stories bold-bordered in black. But a few Americans were not surprised. Astonishingly, a town in Minnesota throbbed with news of Lincoln's death and a small newspaper in New York had published a bulletin that Lincoln had been killed—both *before* Booth acted. In the confusion, these facts were lost, though not forever forgotten. As for the major media, despite a telegraph blackout the Associated Press broke the news about midnight, followed later by every major correspondent. Uncertainty and caution after the first flash prevented mention of Booth as the killer, even though the testimony of dozens of witnesses, theater folk and others, identified him under the wrathful interrogation of the police and Stanton, from his command post in Petersen's rooming house.

Throughout America, weeping women, angry men, rabid mobs poured out to lament and protest the act. Before twenty-four hours had passed, mobs had even set upon former Presidents Franklin Pierce (for being a Democrat, hence "Southern") and Millard Fillmore (for not draping his home in black). Crowds everywhere attacked known rebel sympathizers as the rumor spread of a giant Confederate conspiracy. Sympathy and compassion for defeated "erring sisters" vanished. Demonstrators and even Andrew Johnson shouted for hanging Jeff Davis and all other Confederate leaders (to a sour apple tree, as the song went). People who dared whisper against the martyred President were summarily beaten. Only in the South were there signs of jubilation, as with a Texas paper which wrote that the killing was "ordained by God." More sensibly, the Richmond *Whig* said, "The heaviest blow which has ever fallen upon the people of the South has descended." Overall, in its reflexive combination of grief and violence, the nation did not see its like again until the murder of Martin Luther King, another leader who combined political power (and consequences) with a high and authentic moral tone.

Almost from the derringer's report, Stanton and his deputies—especially La Fayette C. Baker—worked furiously to catch and dispose of the assassins. Stanton had barked orders through his perfumed beard. The telegraph service was to be cut, except the secret War Department line, until they could give the "correct" story to the press, to the ambassadors, to the world. Booth was not to be identified until they were sure. Search his rooms, bring in his friends, prepare posters, offer rewards no witness could refuse. All trains out of Washington were to be searched, all roads were to be sealed (though seemingly not fast enough, since Booth's escape was suspiciously easy). All known Secesh agents to be corralled. Alert eight thousand troops, plus Navy vessels, to interdict travel. Above all, get Booth and his associates, such as that maniac responsible for the attack on Seward. As for rights, they were suspended—habeas corpus, press freedom, whatever. This was war.

Stanton's reign of terror worked—in all the ways that such things do. It worked more than partly because Stanton's War Department had known for several weeks that Booth, the Surratts, Arnold, O'Laughlin, Atzerodt, Herold and, at the end, Paine intended to harm Lincoln. Weichmann had told them. Yet, until April 15, Stanton and Baker did not move against the plotters. When they did, it was quickly. By Monday following Black Easter, Stanton's men and the Metropolitan Police had arrested Arnold, O'Laughlin, Spangler, Mrs. Surratt and Paine and had detained many known Confederate agents, sympathizers, bystanders and assorted "witnesses." To anyone ignorant of Weichmann's information—which he was especially eager to amplify after an interview with the police the morning following the assassination—the catch would seem the result of impressive police work.

Some of the apprehensions, though, seemed either lucky or part of a large scheme. Arnold was picked up in Maryland supposedly as a result of a letter from him to Booth found in Booth's trunk, though papers in the National Archives reveal he was arrested on Saturday, a day before the letter was identified as his. Weichmann again? The letter saved Arnold from the gallows since it begged off from further plots, but to Stanton's delight it implicated the Confederate leaders. Sam had counseled waiting to "see how it [presumably the plot] goes down in R____d."

O'Laughlin was brought in from Maryland with Arnold. He, after all, had been in Washington the day of the killing, had been seen with Booth, had known Weichmann.

Spangler was fingered early as a stooge of Booth's. His arrest was ordered when a huge coil of rope, suitable for delaying pursuing cavalry if strung across a road, was found in his room.

Mrs. Surratt was arrested in the early morning of the eighteenth. The officers wanted her as the mother of John Surratt, known to them as a conspirator, and suspected of being Seward's assailant. John, however, was headed for Canada by then and hadn't been here for two weeks, as his mother told them. No matter, she was charged with conspiracy. After all, her tavern was an infamous Secesh gathering place, and she was in on it according to Weichmann.

Lewis Paine, feebly disguised as a mud-daubed laborer come to fix a sewer at two in the morning, had the bad luck to appear at Mrs. Surratt's when the police were there. His story and appearance (he'd been hiding in woods near Washington; some say he climbed a tree) won him immediate arrest and nearly immediate identification as the mad-dog Seward slasher.

Meanwhile, detectives and military police were after Surratt, Atzerodt, Herold and the "arch-fiend," John Wilkes Booth. Detectives called at the Kirkwood House, and in searching Atzerodt's room found many items connecting Atzerodt with Booth, Herold and Surratt—all quite neatly laid out, as though for the finding. The hounds ran on. Atzerodt? A coward may head for relatives. Booth and Herold? South, obviously. But Surratt? A professional would go to the Confederates in Canada. On Easter the Washington Superintendent of Police, Major A. C. Richards, spirited Weichmann away from his rivals in Stanton's command and pell-melled to Montreal to apprehend Surratt. They missed him. John Surratt was not captured and tried for two years—and then under cloudy circumstances.

Atzerodt they caught on the twentieth asleep in his cousin's farmhouse at Rockville, Maryland, north of Washington. Returned to the capital, he bleated what he knew. Kidnaping, yes. Murder, no. He hadn't struck Johnson, had he? But like the others he was shackled hand and foot and taken on board a monitor anchored near Washington, "for his own protection." The word was spread again of superior police work, but Atzerodt's brother John, a policeman, had provided the lead to his whereabouts.

To the South, things were not so active, though that was the logical escape route. Maryland had never seceded from the Union (Lee's campaigns had intended to rectify that), and it was strongly prorebel, particularly to the southeast of the Yankee capital. Somewhere out there Booth and Herold—reunited on the road to Surrattsville—were at large still, despite rewards that eventually reached $50,000 for Booth and $25,000 for Herold. But arrests were to come. On the eighteenth, the Cavalry caught wind of Dr. Mudd. The doctor told his cousin he'd set Booth's leg early Saturday and sheltered two men briefly. The cousin informed the police. Mudd was soon brought in. Weichmann said Mudd had been in Washington to see Booth twice and had met him frequently near Surrattsville. They had merely discussed land deals, Mudd said. He was shackled hand and foot and, like the others, in due time taken aboard a monitor in the Potomac. By Stanton's order, a hideous canvas hood was placed over the head of each conspirator—except Mrs. Surratt. The hood prevented speech and hearing and was a barbarous exercise in sensory deprivation.

The Cavalry sweeping the Southern route—all lusting after the rewards —also brought in a drunken John Lloyd, who rented Mrs. Surratt's tavern at Surrattsville. Given Weichmann's choice of being hung as a conspirator or feted as a stoolie, Lloyd stammered that he'd seen Booth and Herold on the murder night. They'd stopped to get some carbines secreted there and some whiskey. Booth seemed injured. Lloyd also said that on Mrs. Surratt's visit on the fourteenth she'd told him to get "the shootin' irons" ready, that somebody would be by for them. Thus he incriminated Mrs. Surratt, elating Baker and particularly Stanton—who now busied himself preparing indictments of all the captured conspirators, along with Jefferson Davis and sundry other Confederates he thought deserved punishment. Immaculately scribed in Stanton's precise hand, these indictments (only recently discovered by the Library of Congress) were perhaps beyond the Secretary's province. The duty customarily lay with the Attorney General. But Stanton ignored this legality, among others, in his zeal to legitimize radical Reconstruction and to keep the matter wholly in his grasp.

All this time, Booth and Herold were hiding in a thicket near the Zekiah Swamps, about thirty miles south of Surrattsville. They were concealed by a sympathizer named Captain Samuel Cox and cared for by Thomas Jones, the chief rebel signal officer on that stretch of the underground route. Booth was cold and hunted and his leg pained him. He lay, waiting for a chance to cross the Potomac and get to Richmond. He passed hours writing in his diary, telling how he'd killed Lincoln and yet "I am here in despair . . . doing what Brutus was honored for—what made William Tell a hero; and yet I, for striking down an even greater tyrant than they ever knew, am looked upon as a common cutthroat." Worse, he found no mention in the *National Intelligencer,* which Jones brought him, of his letter (Matthews, afraid, said he had burned it). Instead, there were denunciations, even by the leaders in the South. He recorded that the Government must be suppressing his letter, his side of it. He told Cox they would never take John Wilkes Booth alive and wrote in his diary: "I have too great a soul to die like a criminal."

But he was fleeing like a criminal. On April 20, Booth and Herold tried to cross the Potomac but were scared back by shots from a patrolling gunboat. The next night, in the fog, they made it, rowing blindly. They fetched up at Nanjemoy Creek but were rebuffed by a supposedly pro-rebel Colonel Hughes. They then drifted downstream to find Jones's acquaintances. In fact, everything was downstream from then on.

Ashore, another erstwhile sympathizer, a Dr. Stewart, refused to aid them. Booth sent him $2.50 and a nasty-nice note on a diary page. The night of April 23, the two fugitives slept in a Negro's shack. The next day, they commandeered the man and his team for a journey to the banks of the Rappahannock. There, waiting for a ferry, they fell in with three rebel parolees (or, conceivably, Mosby's raiders detailed by someone to escort them to Richmond). With them, Booth and Herold crossed to Port Royal, sought shelter and were sent to the farm of Richard Garrett, about ten miles north of Bowling Green. Booth was introduced by Captain Willie Jett, his Confederate friend, as Boyd, a wounded ex-soldier seeking lodging. In the ten days since Lincoln's murder, Booth had traveled about eighty miles.

On the twenty-fourth, La Fayette Baker is supposed to have drawn a circle around Bowling Green and announced that despite all the reports of Booth in Canada, Mexico, Texas, they could find the escaped assassin within that ten-mile radius. This divinatory act has never been explained. A Major O'Beirne reported that he had rooted out word of Booth and Herold a day earlier and requested authority to capture them and claim the $75,000 but was refused. Baker first said he "deduced" their location, then that a "Negro informant" told him about the fugitives (this informant's deposition has never been found).

But however it struck the trail, the Cavalry did find Booth and Herold. The horse soldiers went by steamer on April 25 to Port Royal, raised dust galloping past Garrett's and immediately found Jett in Bowling Green. They wanted information about the strangers they'd heard about in Port Royal, and if they didn't get it, Jett would hang at once. They got the information, and before dawn on the twenty-sixth, they were at Garrett's.

Commanding the troopers were former Lieutenant Colonel Everton Conger and Lieutenant Edward Doherty. Second in command and chief detective was Lieutenant Luther B. Baker, cousin of the oracular La Fayette. With them in this detachment of the 16th New York was a religious-nut sergeant named Boston Corbett.

They stood farmer Garrett on a chopping block and told him they'd string him up if he didn't say where the assassins were, but the old man was speechless, and they were making the noose when one of his sons announced that Booth and Herold were sleeping in the tobacco barn. The troopers surrounded the $75,000 on the hoof. Conger, Baker, Doherty shouted for the men to come out, they knew who they were. The trapped men shouted they wanted time. Debate ensued until finally Herold gave up, was yanked from the barn door, handcuffed, and tied to a tree. Davey yelled, "Who is that man in there?" Herold's cry caused bewilderment. Was it Booth (though Herold later said it was) or a trick? The other man pleaded for time, then for the troopers to retreat a bit to give him a fighting chance, finally that they should "prepare a stretcher for me, boys." All very theatrical. But it didn't move Conger and Baker. They'd burn the barn, they called. The Garretts shouted at "Boyd" to surrender. They heard him arranging a barricade. The fire was started. It tore the night. The officers could see the man standing upright, silhouetted, his carbine cradled, pistol in his right hand. His crutch was thrown aside. Then a shot and he fell. It was 3:15 A.M., April 26. He was pulled out and laid on a straw mattress on the Garretts' porch. A mortal gunshot wound behind and below the right ear through the spinal cord, exiting on his left. Baker called the man Booth and the dying man looked up in what seemed surprise, forever adding a measure of confusion to the puzzling case of John Wilkes Booth.

The officers were furious—Booth was to be taken alive—and they raged: Who shot him? Or did he kill himself? Corbett stepped forward to say he did it because God told him to. And so the assassin had his own assassin, Oswald his Ruby. The head-shot man whispered that they should "Tell Mother I died for my country." He weakened in agony and small cries.

Herold and the others watched Booth die around 7 A.M., eleven days to the hour after Lincoln. After collecting his personal effects, they had the body sewn in a horse blanket. It went by wagon and ferry across the Rappahannock and on to find the Cavalry's steamer. Along the way the wagon collapsed, dumping the body into a ditch. The stiffening corpse stayed sometimes unguarded while the officers searched for a new wagon, then for a landing place for the steamer. And Captain Willie Jett escaped during all this, not to be recaptured or to testify until early May. By early morning on the twenty-seventh, the body arrived at Washington. There it and Herold were transferred to the moniter *Montauk.* Herold was ironed and hooded and put into the hold with some of the other conspirators. An autopsy was performed on Booth, for so was the putrefying body identified by a desk clerk, a dentist and a doctor—all familiar with his distinguishing marks. However, close relatives, including his brother Junius, imprisoned as a suspected collaborator, were not summoned to identify the body—an oddity that led later in the century to several mummified "Booths" touring with carnivals.

Then, even more oddly and on Stanton's orders, La Fayette and Luther Baker made a dumb show for the curious crowds of preparing to bury the body at sea. They lowered a shroud, weighted by cannon balls, to a skiff and rowed downriver. Stanton wanted no relic-seeking or Booth-the-hero cult nonsense springing up. When the crowds dispersed, Booth's body was secretly buried in an ammo vault of Washington's Old Penitentiary. His last name was painted on the coffin cover. The result of Stanton's secrecy, in one of history's ironies, was a mortal suspicion about Booth's remains, so similar to our time's "autopsy mysteries" about John Kennedy.

Stanton's behavior further mystified things. Colonel Conger had galloped for Washington and his share of the reward as soon as Booth expired. He told La Fayette Baker the news. Baker was ecstatic. He rushed to tell Stanton. "We have got Booth," he announced. Stanton's reaction? "He put his hands over his eyes and lay for nearly a moment without saying a word. Then he got up and put on his coat very coolly." Yet when Baker next said Booth was dead and gave Stanton his effects, including the diary, the Secretary sprang to work with characteristic energy.

At Stanton's insistence, President Johnson ordered a military tribunal for the conspirators. Nine officers selected by Stanton would deliver the verdict. They included General Lew Wallace (who later wrote an imitation of Christ called *Ben-Hur*). The prosecutors were headed by Judge Advocate General Joseph Holt, who reportedly once said, "Not enough Southern women have been hanged in the war." Immediate protests to a military trial were voiced, notably by Horace Greeley. But Stanton maintained the assassination was an act of war. By the time the trial began, he would have Jeff Davis in jail for it. Besides, a court-martial circumvented normal rules of evidence and other legal niceties. President Johnson did ask the Attorney General for a ruling on the legality of the trial. It said everything was OK. Critics said it was judicial murder.

They had reasons. The trial began May 10, 1865. Throughout, the conspirators and Southern leaders were inadequately represented by lawyers, who offered feeble pleas of insanity for Paine, of stupid complicity for the others. The attorneys were reluctant to defend proved monsters. Herold and Paine were hopelessly guilty. Atzerodt had moved to attack Johnson, leaving incriminating circumstantial evidence. Arnold and O'Laughlin admitted their kidnap roles. Mudd? No proof, other than his acquaintance with Booth and setting the assassin's leg, but that was enough. Spangler had shoved Booth's pursuers back into the theater, had called, "That's not Booth," and besides, had met with the killer, witnesses said. Mrs. Surratt —well, little except her proximity to events, plus Lloyd's and Weichmann's testimony about her bearing suspicious packages to Surrattsville.

The defendants came clanking each day from solitary confinement in hoods and irons to the dingy courtroom, where the hoods were removed, but they remained shackled except for Mrs. Surratt and were forbidden to testify freely, even to face the judges and witnesses. They heard, though, their officer-judges frequently interrupt testimony with outrageous opinions of their guilt. They heard witnesses perjure themselves— notably, a congenital liar called Sanford Conover (real name, Dunham), who claimed he'd observed the Confederate Cabinet plotting the assassination. Conover also instructed other Government witnesses in perjury, including spies, pimps, deserters and gamblers summoned to prove the defendants guilty. The Government introduced patently phony letters (one retrieved from a bottle in the sea, they said) to implicate Booth's band and the Southern leadership in a vast scheme directed from Canada. Holt hammered at the objective, evidence of the killing, pursuit, capture All were found guilty on June 30. On July 6, the individual sentences were delivered.

Jefferson Davis *et al.* were to stay in prison.

Mudd, Arnold and O'Laughlin would spend their lives in jail.

Spangler got six years.

Herold, Paine, Atzerodt and Mrs. Surratt were to hang.

So all was in order, except perhaps the last. Women were revered in Victorian America. The press hadn't liked trying Mrs. Surratt at all, there seemed so little evidence. Now vehement protests burst out. And a deal for the woman was in the works. The tribunal figured they would show that no one gets away with killing a President or thwarting Reconstruction but would forward a petition for mercy to President Johnson.

The President said he never got it. Mrs. Surratt's daughter, Anna, pleading for her mother's life, was rebuffed at the White House the morning of July 7. Unbelievably, the executions were set for that day, one day after sentencing. Andrew Johnson signed the order at 10:30 A.M. The traps fell at 1:26 P.M. Atzerodt whimpered and cried to the end. Herold stood mute. Paine joked with guards, seized a straw hat and put it on. He proclaimed Mrs. Surratt's innocence, then said his last words, "You know best," to his hangman, who'd assured him he'd try to make it painless. (As it was, Paine slowly strangled, his huge neck refusing to break.)

It was over for them, mostly over for the Government.

It could leisurely pursue John Surratt—he'd not been lured by his mother's plight—to England, to the Vatican (where he had enlisted as a papal Zouave guard), to Egypt, and eventually bring him back in 1867 to be tried in another questionable court proceeding and, miraculously, released after a jury failed to reach a verdict.

Mudd, Arnold, O'Laughlin and Spangler, in a final twist by Stanton, were diverted from the prison in Albany, New York, to the pestilential silence of America's own Devil's Island, at Fort Jefferson in the Dry Tortugas. O'Laughlin died there of yellow fever in 1867. Mudd fought it as a physician and won. He, Arnold and Spangler were pardoned in 1869 by Johnson. Booth's body rotted until it was exhumed in 1869, identified again (or not) and reburied in the family plot in Baltimore.

Those are the facts as a consensus of Lincoln scholars see them. But, like Booth's body, the questions will not stay buried.

Here are the most puzzling queries—so reminiscent of the Kennedys, of King—hovering over Lincoln's assassination. They emerge from the myriad accounts of the murder, including the latest additions: Weichmann's memoir, an alleged hypnotic reincarnation of Booth and the discovery of a code charging that Stanton was Lincoln's Judas and Booth his Brutus.

The first question must be: Were Booth's conspirators acting independently of others who might want the Administration beheaded? Any answer lies in Booth's possible motivation. We've seen his egocentricity. "I must have fame," he said as a boy. And he told Captain Jett, before revealing (if it were needed) that he was Booth, "It was done for notoriety." But can this Oswaldian rationale be all? His voice, hence career, was failing in 1865, but a frustrated lust for fame and a failing voice might not have been sufficient impulse for assassination. Freudians speculate that Presidential assassins—and Booth, we recall, *was* our first—may kill to rid the nation of the "bad father" who had promised them much, delivered little and punished severely. It could be that Booth's father, with his fame, with his long absences, was the progenitor of Wilkes's hate (the opposite side of the love denied). Yet how can anyone prove that?

It is simpler, maybe more accurate, to ascribe his acts to Confederate patriotism.

In January, 1865, Booth left a letter with his well-loved sister Asia and her stage-comedian husband, John Sleeper Clarke. It outlined kidnap plots and floridly proclaimed his love for the "old flag," now besmirched under Lincoln. He signed it "A Confederate doing his duty upon his own responsibility." Along with getting Clarke jailed for a while, this letter could be Booth's honest declaration of his motives. Except . . . except that in Booth's trunk the police found a Confederate secret cipher and other documents, including letters, that may well have been in code. Paine, when caught, was carrying a pocket dictionary. He seemed no intellectual, but Noah

Webster was often used as a code book. And throughout the investigation of the conspiracy, letters and pamphlets surfaced that kept mentioning oil, cotton, horses. It's true Booth owned a few unprofitable oil shares, but Union intelligence officers knew these as Confederate underground code words, too, and so they wondered. They mused, too, over Booth's frequent writings to and about his "mother." Even his dying words could have been code.

Then there were Booth's several trips to Canada, where resided a mysterious "Jenny," never explained and so a possible spy contact. There were coincidences, such as when the rebel raiders struck New York just after Booth had visited their chief city of Montreal and while he himself was in New York playing in *Julius Caesar.* In his escape from Washington, Booth had the aid of men who were part of the underground conduit. His most able fellow plotter was John Surratt, a professional spy.

Further, where did Booth get the money to support the conspiracy (a question asked of many American assassins; notably, James Earl Ray)? In late 1864 and early 1865, his performances were few. He had made money before, as much as $20,000 a year, but his expenses were high. He sought to sell his oil shares (oil, again), in June, 1864, but that venture was fruitless. What about the infamous Confederate operatives such as Messrs. Howell and Ficklin, who dealt in "oil" and "cotton" and at least one of whom had visited Mrs. Surratt's? It could have been that Booth was a fully certified spy, working under a perfect cover as a loud-mouthed, hard-drinking, flirtatious tragedian, whose profession gave him free access to theaters and agents both North and South.

But even if Booth was a spy, there is no evidence that he was *directed* to kill Lincoln. In fact, all the physical evidence, however contradictory in other ways, suggests he decided on it independently. And *that* suggests he was either a damned poor spy or none at all. We have our choice of motives: vanity or patriotism or congenital madness (his eccentric father, named after the heroic foe of Rome's Tarquin tyrants, was called Mad Booth—and when Wilkes was accused of Lincoln's assassination, an actor friend said he wasn't surprised: "All the goddamn Booths are crazy"), or as a professional hit man or, most improbably, as an avenger. That last comes from the tale that Lincoln's assassination avenged the hanging of John Yates Beall, a Confederate officer executed for an attack in mufti on a Union prisoner train near Buffalo. The story goes that Booth and Beall were school friends, had reunited in Canada and that when Beall was sentenced, Booth went to Washington to implore Lincoln to spare him. On his knees, he begged Lincoln and won his friend's pardon, or so he thought. When Beall died anyway, Booth resolved to kill Lincoln. Unfortunately, it seems that a scandal magazine invented this motivation.

Similarly, nothing links the assassination directly with the Confederate Government. Though it is a point of law that *not* doing something to prevent the killing can be construed as conspiracy (as with current suspicions in the Kennedy killings), that seems tenuous, since Davis repeatedly repudiated the act, not to mention serving time for it. The Confederates may have known about the attempts (from Surratt, their courier?), even have wished it well, but they may also have wished it would go away, especially since there was a bona fide Confederate plan—remarkably similar to Booth's—to kidnap Lincoln in 1864, with which Booth's stagy enterprise could have interfered. So no one can show that Davis and his Cabinet ordered Lincoln dead. Indeed, they lamented as the full fist of Stantonian Reconstruction fell on the South. They knew the basic rule of assassination between countries has, since the Greeks, been that the weaker does not assassinate the stronger (a point to consider when speculating that Castro ordered JFK eliminated). Reconstruction was an example. The South did not benefit from Lincoln's death.

Who might have benefited, then?

Some believe Lincoln died in a Roman Catholic conspiracy. It's fact that Booth and Arnold were schooled by Catholics (not unusual in Maryland) and that John Surratt, Mrs. Surratt and Mudd were devout Catholics (as was Weichmann, a schoolmate of Surratt's in a Catholic seminary). When Surratt slipped off to Canada, he found refuge with Canadian priests and he later found employment in the Vatican. Also, Mrs. Surratt's confessor in her death cell was ordered by his archbishop never to reveal what she had told him—an extraordinary measure, considering the traditional confidentiality of the confession. Consider that many priests denounced Lincoln's nonsectarian deism and that the Church tolerated the Confederacy. But nowhere in these coincidences is proof of a Catholic plot except in American minds still steeped in Plymouth Colony bigotry. The Roman Catholics could not gain by Lincoln's death.

Equally likely, and more racy, are the accusations that Mary Todd Lincoln connived in the murder of her husband. Mary was vain, extravagant, jealous, bossy and she had one brother, three half-brothers and three brothers-in-law serving the Confederates, one of whom—David Todd—brutalized Yankee prisoners at Richmond. It's true that by 1865 she owed $27,000 in clothing bills, which could make her vulnerable to blackmail. It's true that people who hated her called her "two thirds pro-slavery and the rest Secesh" and whispered that she was a spy for the Rebels. It's rumored that while in the White House, watching a son die and a husband age, she had two love affairs, including one with a gardener. And, most damning, it's true that it was Mary Todd Lincoln who requested that John F. Parker be exempted from the draft and assigned to the White House detail as the President's bodyguard. Parker, who stood cheek to jowl with Booth at Taltavul's saloon the night of April 14, leaving the President unguarded. Strangely, also, he escaped reprimand from Stanton for his negligence; perhaps he redeemed himself with his arrest of a wandering whore the next morning. But even accepting half the rumors about Mary, including an inexplicable fondness for Parker, we cannot maintain with objective evidence that she betrayed Lincoln. On the contrary, there is much to prove she loved him deeply. Until she died, half-mad in Springfield in 1882, she did nothing that supported her accusers' case; in fact, she continually accused Parker of treachery. Nor has any credible evidence since come to light to make her Lincoln's Clytemnestra.

Certainly more plausible is the case against Andrew Johnson. Orchestrated by Stanton and the Radicals, the seditious noise started before the funeral cortege deposited Lincoln's body in Springfield. The abolitionists, at first satisfied with Johnson's anti-South tirades and the Surratt execution, soon saw that this tailor from Tennessee was not going to impose Stanton's military dictatorship, or hang more rebels, but instead would be lenient and implement the ignorant Illinoisan's policies. Soon they claimed that Johnson had benefited *most* from the assassination. Exhibit A was Booth's calling card. It still is. Why had Booth left it? It may have been for Johnson's secretary, whom Booth knew and could use for information. Perhaps he hoped for a pass through the Washington pickets (but why, if he were a spy?—it's said he had a forgery in Grant's name). Was Booth renewing an old acquaintanceship made in Nashville, where rumor once had Booth and Johnson keeping sisters as mistresses (if so, why)? Could Booth have wanted to implicate Johnson and thus cripple the new Presidency (but why, if Atzerodt was to kill Johnson)? Was the card a lure to get him out where he could be killed? It could even be that Atzerodt was an unwitting decoy (assigned by whom?) who would simultaniously throw off pursuers and implicate Johnson. We have no answers.

In any event, Stanton's party assailed the new President. It is said his drunkenness at the second inauguration was to steel himself for the murder or kidnaping he expected that day. It claimed that Booth's card was a signal of intent, that Johnson's brief appearance at Lincoln's deathbed convicted him of heartlessness, that his alleged drunkenness the next morning, his appearance, suggested he had palavered that night with the killers. Harnessed to Johnson's avowed Presidential ambitions, this was powerful, circumstantial stuff. Stories were offered that Johnson was not in his room on the fourteenth (because, presumably, he had a hand in killing Lincoln). That Stanton had confided after the shooting that he thought Johnson was party to it. That Mrs. Surratt had perished to protect Johnson, who'd ignored her petition for mercy. When Johnson escaped conviction after impeachment, every abolitionist weapon had been used against him. But there was not then, nor is there now, proof that the seventeenth President plotted to kill the sixteenth. Rather, Johnson tried to continue Lincoln's policies and even kept Stanton until 1867, when he finally fired his dour Secretary and bitter enemy.

In Lincoln's time, these theories—Booth as rebel spy, a Catholic conspiracy, Mary did it and Johnson did it—enlisted great support. They flourished in the climate of uncertainty and in the mad distress generated by a fratricidal war. Today, we have similar weather, compounded of assassination, Vietnam and Watergate, in which, because so many things have happened, we assume anything could be, however cloudy. Yet history may tell us, as it has told Lincoln scholars, that such contemporary theories are quaint paranoias, nurtured in vapors soon to dissipate. In Lincoln's case, there is just one stubborn, weighty storm front; it hovers around Edwin Stanton and calls him a murderer.

The circumstantial evidence suggesting that Stanton betrayed Lincoln ranges from absurd to credible. The recent hypnotic reincarnation of Booth exemplifies the silly anti-Stanton stuff. Out of the mouth of a farm boy named Wesley (a sort of bucolic Bridey Murphy) comes Booth to say Stanton was a secret member of the Knights of the Golden Circle—that rococo bunch of Secesh gallants who took their name from a circle centered in Havana, which Caribbean port was to anchor a vast slave empire including the American South, Central America and, presumably, the Sargasso Sea. As such, Stanton directed the Circle's plot against Lincoln —even aranging for a stand-in for Booth at Garrett's farm and the subsequent successful escape of the actor to England, where he lived for years before dying, lonely, in Calais, France. Wesley doesn't vouchsafe precisely how all this was accomplished, nor does he seem to realize that such murder-and-escape stories are mythic and go back at least to Cain. Nevertheless, the case against Stanton is reasonable.

First, he was an unlovable man, whose behavior as Buchanan's Attorney General and Lincoln's War Secretary caused Gideon Welles (Secretary of the Navy) to record: "He has cunning and skill, dissembles his feelings . . . is a hypocrite." Welles did not add, though he might have, that Stanton also was peculiar in some ways. He once dug up the body of a favorite servant girl to look on her again. He exhumed his daughter's body and kept it, suitably contained in metal, in his room for a year, the better to mourn. When his wife died, he dressed her for burial in clothes like those she'd been married in. He slept with her nightgown and cap beside him. Coupled with boundless ambition, such necrophilia could produce a dangerous Secretary of War.

Certainly, there is little doubt that Stanton wanted to succeed Lincoln either electorally or as the South's military dictator. He had three major obstacles: the war, Lincoln and Johnson. The war he prolonged, then won. His accusers say he felt threatened, though, by Lincoln's growing popularity, and so he decided to strike by assassination—if not directly, then by *allowing* it to happen. God knew, he had warned Lincoln often enough. *Cui bono?* the accusers ask. Well, the Government's most powerful officers were Lincoln, Johnson, Seward, Stanton. The first three were targets and Stanton's rivals for power, and although Stanton's defenders strain to establish that desperadoes went to the Secretary's door that night, the evidence is otherwise. Only Stanton and a servant proclaimed that shadowy figures lurked on the steps, seemed to be pulling at the Secretary's broken doorbell—a mechanical failure that saved Stanton, it was said. But the men who brought word of Booth's shot to Stanton's house said the doorbell worked just fine. Why would Stanton want to establish that he, too, was a target? Why did the conspirators miss him, while getting to Lincoln and Seward?

Perhaps they thought Stanton was too well protected. But they could have seen otherwise. If, indeed, O'Laughlin had, as the Government said, scouted Grant on the thirteenth (and found him well protected), someone could also have found that Stanton was unprotected. He was conscious of security, certainly. He did tell Grant not to go to *Our American Cousin*, and the Grants promptly left town "to see their children," one of whom was in Washington. He told Lincoln that Major Eckert could not accompany the President as bodyguard. The questions come: Could Stanton have been protecting men he wanted to live and was he safe himself because he was a plotter? Did Grant leave town because Stanton knew something was up for Lincoln?

Stanton *did* know it, too. Weichmann's report, received at least a month before the assassination, specified that men gathering at Mrs. Surratt's were plotting against Lincoln. All such threats were reported to the War Department and presumably then to Stanton. Did he regard that one as routine because there had been so many? If so, why had Mrs. Surratt's—

according to War Department records—been under surveillance for a month before the killing? Was the failure to act the mistake of a clumsy bureaucracy or part of a plan?

If planned, Stanton's April 14 refusal of Eckert as Lincoln's bodyguard makes sense. Stanton told the President the redoubtable major had urgent business. That night, Stanton ate supper, visited the bedfast Seward and went home. Eckert just went home. They may merely have been avoiding a tedious evening, yet the suspicion grows. Feeding it are the many statements from other officials, such as Provost Marshals David Dana and Ward Lamon, that they believed someone high up knew of the coming assassination attempt. Yet that, too, may well be hindsight—particularly if Booth's diary is to be believed and he didn't decide to kill Lincoln until the twelfth or so (more perplexing, the diary entries were made *after* the killing, while Booth was fleeing). And the fact remains—Lincoln was unguarded except by the dandy Major Rathbone. His bodyguard was drinking. His valet, Charles Forbes, may have been in the box rather than in the bar with Parker—authorities disagree—but if so, he was scarcely suited for dealing with homicidal, gymnastic actors.

Return, then, to the diary. That should establish whether Booth acted alone. The trouble is, it was delivered to Stanton alone, by La Fayette Baker, right after it was taken from Booth's body. Only one journalist in 1865 even mentioned its existence. It was not offered in evidence at the tribunal's show trial! It just vanished from the War Department files and didn't reappear until John Surratt's trial in 1867, at the insistence of his attorneys. It was discovered then that eighteen pages were missing, cut out of the section covering the days immediately preceding the assassination. Booth's diary was like Nixon's tapes.

Consider, also, the peculiarities of Booth's escape. Why was the most logical escape route left unguarded and open, while the Northern roads were quickly blocked? Did Stanton want Booth to escape? Had he provided the conspirators with the password to get over the Navy Yard Bridge? The Southern route *was* open and the pursuit down it was handicapped by conflicting orders from the War Department (Major O'Beirne's detachment was within a few miles of Booth on the twenty-third, when it was recalled). However, it's equally true that Atzerodt went North and made it through the check points.

Anyway, why would Stanton have wanted Booth to escape? So his men could catch him, after being tipped off? How did the Cavalry find Jett so quickly? Was Baker's "deduction" about Garrett's flimflam? Stanton did bless Boston Corbett as a "patriot" and let him go, despite orders that

Booth was to be taken alive and that anyone who shot the actor would be severely punished. But maybe Stanton's deep religiosity welled up for Corbett. Maybe Stanton's cool reaction to Booth's death was not relief but pain. Perhaps, as many think, Booth made good his pledge not to be taken alive. The position of his death wound, the supposedly small caliber of the slug, indicated a pistol—not Corbett's carbine—and so Wilkes may have made his own exit while Corbett grabbed for glory.

Did the disrupted telegraphy service on the fourteenth bear on Stanton's implied complicity? His accusers say it was his intention to create the impression of a large-scale Confederate operation, thus to arouse panic in which he could usurp power. Perhaps he didn't want rumors to spread before fact did. If so, the rebutters ask, how come some Northern communities broke the news of Lincoln's assassination the afternoon of the fourteenth, *before* it happened? Unless mental telepathy was at work, someone else was. Did Stanton's people err and let slip what was coming? Did the reports come from the Confederate underground? The Golden Circle? The local priest? We don't know, and never will, it seems.

Even Booth's body assails Stanton. To this day, legends persist that it was not Booth shot in the barn, not his body Stanton buried. Wesley, the hypnotized farm hand, says Wilkes rests in Calais. Some think Booth's body was lost on the way to Washington. In 1870, a man calling himself John St. Helen claimed to be Booth (he accused Andy Johnson), and in 1903, when a man called David E. George died in Enid, Oklahoma, it was said that St. Helen and George were the same man and both were Booth. The body was embalmed and shown for decades at carnivals. Several Confederate soldiers said Booth had escaped, contacted them and died in Texas, California, Mexico, Virginia . . . and so on. Distant relatives and self-styled "grandchildren" have asserted Booth survived. O'Beirne reportedly said he knew that three men were in the barn and one had gotten away. Hadn't "Booth" looked surprised when his name was called? Hadn't Herold said at first it wasn't Booth with him? Again, these are usual hallucinations after soul-rattling killings.

The trouble is such questions ignore ones closer to Stanton. For example, why didn't Wilkes's brother Junius Brutus, Jr. identify the body, since he was so handy to the monitor, being in the Old Capitol Prison under suspicion? Why was Booth identified by comparative strangers? Why did Dr. May, who did the autopsy of Booth, first say it looked nothing like him, then identify him by a scar on his neck? Why, then, did the Surgeon General obliterate the scar by removing some of Booth's vertebrae (in still another eerie resemblance, critics of the Warren Report say the Kennedy autopsy reports are irregular, contradictory, even falsified)? What happened to the lady admirer who is said to have bribed her way onto the monitor and snipped a lock of Booth's hair, only to discover the hair was auburn while Booth's was raven black? Why was there controversy over his identity in 1869, when the body was exhumed and shown to the *family?* Well, legends die hard, and John Wilkes Booth is one of them. Inquiries over his death were complicated by Stanton's desire for secrecy, by the surreptitious burial to prevent hero worship—an act that in itself is part of a cover-up, Stanton's adversaries insist.

With Booth and his testimony secretly interred, the matter of truth was left to people like Weichmann. His memoir—written in the 1890s and drawing heavily on contemporary histories—insists on the guilt of Surratt, Mrs. Surratt, Booth and all the rest. As for Stanton, he calls him "the man of iron and blood" (appropriate in those Bismarckian days), remarks on his kind heart and nobility. Of his posttrial experience, Weichmann writes: "When the ordeal was over, Edwin M. Stanton, who had sternly called me to account, became my friend and protector, and was only too glad to accord me the justice which I had won by my conduct." One is tempted to ask, What conduct? except as an informer who knew Booth and his anti-Lincoln crowd and who reported them before Stanton's boss was killed. What other secrets might Weichmann have? And if the Government's case rested on stooges, isn't it odd that Stanton did not summon as witnesses or defendants the several other people who assisted Booth: Matthews, Chester, Jones, Cox, odd people like an Anna Ward, whom Weichmann reported as very suspicious in her dealings with Booth? Why not question Booth's mistresses, correspondents, business associates?

Possibly Stanton was acting legally (though he violated judicial procedures with his investigation and trial), punishing only those he could prove were involved. His police brought in buggyloads of suspected conspirators, but they were released with the Nixonian fiat that further investigation "was not compatible with the public interest." That only led skeptics to more questions.

Was there another conspirator shadowing Grant? Booth couldn't shoot both Grant and Lincoln with a single-shot derringer (a recent speculation, however, has him carrying two derringers—one of which he lost in the Presidential box, where it was later found and concealed for years). In fact, had Grant and his military escort attended the theater, Booth would have had a hard time getting to the President.

Why had Stanton not followed up his department's immediate leads— its foreknowledge of the Surratts, the report of Booth and Herold's flight

South? Surrattsville was South. But they didn't make arrests there until Monday.

Why was there no sustained pursuit of John Surratt? Stanton knew where he was, could have had him arrested in Liverpool just after his escape from Canada. Yet Stanton revoked the reward for him. Was the Secretary trying to cool the situation or was he afraid? It turned out that Surratt said nothing about Lincoln's assassination when finally tried. Why?

Could other witnesses establish a tie between Stanton and Booth? They could have met at the Second Inaugural ball, since Booth was there with his Senator's daughter and Stanton had been invited.

Why was Edwin's photo, not Wilkes's, shown to witnesses? Whatever the reason, it confused eyewitness identifications of Booth, inducing even more skepticism about eyewitness testimony, if that were possible. Why did witnesses Rathbone and Harris change their testimony between April 15 and May 10 to exclude a statement that someone had called at the Presidential box less than an hour before the killing with a message for the President? If this was so, why wasn't Parker's absence noted then? Or was the message a signal to Parker that someone waited outside?

Why did the depositions of key witnesses, such as La Fayette Baker's, disappear? Why did Stanton's prosecutors feel compelled to manufacture evidence to convict the captured conspirators?

All interesting questions, but probably unanswerable. Even if Stanton did conceal the truth, those who survived could have uncovered it later. None did. Unless we can accept as true a recent flare from the banked fires of this mystery.

In 1957, a Mr. Ray Neff discovered what seems to be a code inserted by La Fayette C. Baker in a bound volume of *Colburn's United Service Magazine* for late 1864. In this British military journal, Neff supposedly deciphered a message dated February 5, 1868, saying that Stanton was Lincoln's Judas and that he, Baker, was in danger from Judas' agents. It went on to say Booth committed the deed as Brutus, with Judas' aid. A second message was also deciphered that said that "Ecrt [Eckert] had made all the contacts, the deed to be done on the 14th. I did not know the identity of the assassin, but I knew most all else when I approached E.S. about it." The remainder laid the murder on Stanton, the motivation being Lincoln's decision of April 13 to allow the Virginia legislature to be reseated so as to decide on again joining the Union. The plot, according to this code, involved more than fifty people, including businessmen who wished to profit from the South's dismemberment, Army and Navy officers, a governor and "at least 11 Members of Congress."

This cipher has never been discredited. It *was* a common Civil War code. Its messages jibe with Booth's initial claim of the size of the plot (even with Wesley's hypnotic remouthing of them). The motive is plausible. Booth's politics were well known. He could have been used by *sub rosa* conspirators capitalizing on his sense of "honor." Baker's signature following the magazine ciphers is certified genuine. Such a plot would explain the cover-up and the subsequent attempts on Baker's life—which culminated in 1868 with death from what resembled arsenic poisoning. But it would not explain how such a far-flung conspiracy failed exposure in the years following.

Indeed, in all the years, we are left with the questions. Some silly, some pertinent, all unsettling. As of today, we must be content with what we know and not trust too much what we suspect. Yes, Lincoln may have been Stanton's pigeon, or some other group's, or it could have been as the Government said—Booth and his unmerry men. All we know with certainty is that in Booth's character, in the questionable aspects of the assassination, we find the lineaments of all our political killings since. To understand that, we must leave these characters as fate did—mute and historical.

Weichmann stood on his testimony until his death in 1902, though he suffered nervousness and harassment until the end.

John Surratt, after his trial, worked as an auditor in Baltimore. He revealed nothing new about the assassination up to his death in 1916 of natural causes.

Edwin M. Stanton died in 1869, his personal ambitions unfulfilled. His abolitionism won, however. Its morality triumphed, though it spawned strong reactions that have swum upstream to us. The cause of his death was debated. Some vowed he slit his throat, others that he passed naturally.

John Lloyd died an alcoholic, saying he'd testified against the conspirators on pain of death.

Dr. Mudd lived honorably until 1882. The fight to clear his name goes on today.

Edward Spangler, sick with TB from the Dry Tortugas, was sheltered by Mudd until his death in 1875.

Sam Arnold died in 1906. Mudd, Arnold said before dying, told him he had no connection with Booth's conspiracy.

William Seward lived until 1872 as a grand old statesman.

Jefferson Davis was released from prison in 1868, went off to Europe, returned to the United States and died in 1889.

The men who turned Anna Surratt away from Andrew Johnson's door both committed suicide soon after the executions.

Major Rathbone married Miss Harris, moved to Germany, became mad and murdered his wife. He died in a lunatic asylum.

Willie Jett became a traveling salesman. He died of syphilis.

Boston Corbett, the religious fanatic who had castrated himself the better to resist sin, wandered awhile, became a doorman for the Kansas legislature and one day fired two pistols into the crowded chamber. He was put into an asylum, escaped and vanished—some say to peddle patent medicine and survive into our century.

Thomas Eckert became an industrial magnate in the telegraph business and later a judge in Texas. He died in 1910.

Edwin Booth paid Garrett for his burned-down barn and continued as America's greatest actor. He and all his family suffered ignominy because of John Wilkes, whom Edwin called "a rattle-pated fellow." Edwin died in 1893, ending the era of the Booths.

Abraham Lincoln was buried in Springfield after the greatest mourning our nation had seen. His body was the object of another planned kidnaping in 1876—to be held for ransom—but the plot was discovered and the perpetrators imprisoned. The $75 coffin was buried under steel and concrete in 1901. That year it was opened for the last time. Lincoln seemed to have changed very little in appearance.

What had changed was America. We had murdered our first President. As the *Illinois State Register* said on April 15, "The effect of this terrible blow cannot now be estimated." It was easy enough to yoke the South in recompense for Booth's act. It was less easy to regain our innocence. In the years that followed, we found it was lost forever in the mystery of ourselves. We can say that our first assassination was the hardest. After Lincoln, we knew how.

II

AFTER LINCOLN, THE DELUGE

"Assassination has never changed the history
of the world."

—DISRAELI, May 10, 1865,
on Lincoln's death

As though jolted loose by the wheels of Lincoln's funeral train, the demons of assassination politics scourged America and the world following 1865. Booth's death-kiss proved aphrodisiacal. In the forty-nine years from Lincoln's death until 1914, when the murder of Archduke Franz Ferdinand at Sarajevo unleashed the hounds of the Great War, one head of state or major minister fell nearly every eighteen months.

Lincoln's funeral cortege itself, wailing at each whistle stop, crossroad and town, proved the efficacy of assassination. The cars snaked through the North and around the South's hopes for a merciful reconciliation. Crowds cried vengance on the rebels. The dead President's lenient attitude toward the defeated states perished under the hooves of carpetbaggers and their enemies, the Klansmen. The world saw that assassination worked, even if Disraeli did not, and even if the effects were ultimately incalculable. Assassination was affirmed an instrument of change, not a casual killing. Lincoln's death, together with an emergent Continental anarchism, seemed to open a golden age of assassination. Certainly, this was so in America.

Andrew Johnson watched, quaking in Lincoln's boots, as thirteen officeholders were shot at during his inherited term. Twelve were killed, most of them Republicans, changing things down South. Compared with that, Johnson's impeachment proceedings were safe, however much people whispered he'd benefited from just such a murder.

During Ulysses S. Grant's tenure, from 1869 to 1877, there were twenty attacks on public servants. Everything from sheriffs to collectors to governors was in season. Eleven were slain.

Assassins were busy elsewhere, too. The world's stage resembled *Hamlet*'s body-strewn last scene: in 1870, a prime minister of Spain; and through the years, the President of Ecuador and dozens of lesser functionaries of Latin America, the Balkans and Europe were shot, stabbed and bombed, until, in 1877, the killers seemed to pause for breath.

In America, this hiatus was the term of Rutherford B. Hayes, a span as uneventful as its President is unremembered. If, as is thought, assassinations protest ineffective government, then Hayes's Administration was the best of the nineteenth century. But then came 1881.

The Czar of all the Russias received the first message that assassins were alive again. On March 13, 1881—nine days after James Garfield was inaugurated as our twentieth President—Alexander II was shattered by a bomb lobbed his way by radicals. American newspapers reacted with outrage (Lincoln was still on their minds) and blasted the totalitarian rule that could cause such crimes, such nihilists. For his part, Alexander II cried, "To the palace to die," and he did.

The next pertinent comment on assassination came four months later, on July 2, 1881, from James Garfield. Shot twice from behind with a .44 British bulldog revolver, the new Chief Executive cried, "My God, what is this?"

It was, of course, assassination again come to an American President. It proved that Lincoln's murder was not an aberration but a persistent illness roaming the body politic—and that its causes and effects were as varied as its executors. Charles Guiteau, the addled man collared immediately for shooting Garfield, seemed to be many things, though they were summed up in the phrase that won the immortality Guiteau did not. He was ordained our archetypal "disappointed office seeker."

Garfield was a winner. Guiteau was a loser. The score was kept by each against what the land of opportunity had promised and what to each had been delivered. For both men there was the incongruity of their reward with what might have been expected. For the victim, America had fulfilled his dream. For his killer, the dream left an ashy morning mouth, a hangover that has sickened American assassins down to the present.

James Abram Garfield was a Republican, like his predecessors Grant and Hayes. Like them, he was a Civil War veteran (what *man* wasn't, after all?). He was self-made, working his way up from canal laborer to college president, to general, to Congressman—and finally to President. Not without a struggle, to be sure. The meaning of the dream, of the bootstrap ethic, was struggle.

With Chester A. Arthur as the Vice Presidential nominee, Garfield was elected in November, 1880, over the Democratic war hero Winfield S. Hancock, who was forgotten before the campaign banners were down. His plurality was fewer than ten thousand votes. Still, the nation embraced this new leader. He seemed thoughtful and certainly struck a fine figure with his imposing beard, his vigorous youth (he was only forty-eight) and his workingman's physique. Boys were told that someday they, too, might rise so far, so fast.

Charles Julius Guiteau had, unfortunately, always believed that. He was thirty-nine when he shot Garfield, a 5'5", 120-pound man who had started along almost every route America's success map offered—and never arrived. Business, religion, politics—he tried them all, and in the end they brought him that July to the Baltimore and Potomac railway depot with his eight-dollar revolver.

Guiteau had been a sickly, nervous child, who became the youngest when the next two children died in infancy. His mother suffered *post partum* psychosis with Guiteau's birth. She died when he was seven, dealing the boy an emotional blow hard to endure. For Guiteau, however, a domineering patriarch was real and near. His father was a zealous Huguenot-descended tyrant who beat his family religiously while alternately preaching the virtues of the Oneida Community's "Bible communism" (free love, fear of God, hard work) and Reformation Protestantism (just fear of God and hard work). The elder Guiteau saw the world as a struggle between good and evil. Charles would be good, or else.

Not surprisingly, Guiteau grew up with a mania for self-improvement. Such activities could dampen the evil lurking in him and simultaneously lead him to the success America expected (other assassins—notably James Earl Ray—tried wholeheartedly before their killings to be "better" or "somebody"). Thus Guiteau's several careers all aimed at making it, as Garfield had.

By 1860 he was at the Oneida Community in New York State, a convert to founder John Humphrey Noyes's beliefs. This delighted his father, with whom Guiteau had quarreled over Noyes's doctrines (Charles was then practicing body-building). But Guiteau found the community's mutual-criticism sessions embarrassing and, even in a place where Puritan sexual morality was anathema, he did not do well with women. His work in the animal-trap factory bored him, accented his own trapped feeling. Finally, he retrieved what remained of a bequest of his grandfather's from the communal purse and went to New York with an ambition to form a theocratic daily newspaper. He said he was "in the employ of Jesus Christ and Company, the very ablest and strongest firm in the universe." Probably the notion of the Savior as the chairman of the board had never been better expressed, but the paper didn't get started. It seemed no one wanted to invest in Jesus' medium. So it was back to Oneida for a while, full of humility, and then back out again, full of anger.

Guiteau next went to Chicago, found work as a law clerk and, with the ease customary then, was admitted to the Illinois bar in 1868. In 1869, he married a YMCA librarian named Annie Bunn. It was an unhappy union. When he was not practicing his speeches and assaying his schemes for success with Annie, he was beating her. "I am your master," he'd holler. His law practice consisted of bill collecting, for which he was marvelously endowed with glibness, persistence, callousness and his own nature as a deadbeat. He and Annie lived by moving into apartments and boarding-houses, then leaving before the bill was presented.

Yet a leonine ambition somehow survived this weaselly existence. Guiteau sought its accomplishment in 1872 during Horace Greeley's Presidential campaign. He became a familiar figure at Democratic headquarters in New York. Although people avoided this nervous, volatile man who was constantly composing campaign speeches no one would deliver, Guiteau became convinced that if Greeley was elected, he would be made minister to Chile. His wife later recalled that that was all he talked about. He made diplomatic addresses to her, or to a mirror, and bought, on credit, proper clothes. When Greeley lost, Guiteau was morose for months. He did manage in 1874 to sleep with a prostitute, who testified to the fact so as to facilitate his divorce on the grounds of adultery. He continued to collect bills, most often keeping the whole amount repossessed as his "commission." When he was exposed as the most notorious shyster in town by James Gordon Bennett's *Herald,* he initiated a suit against the New York publisher for $100,000 in libel damages. But he decamped for Chicago when another man brought charges against him.

In 1880, Guiteau became a politician—a Republican, obviously (Greeley, the Democrat, had failed him). In Boston, he composed a campaign speech for Grant, the Stalwart Republicans' choice. (The party of Lincoln was divided between the Stalwart, or conservative, wing and the Half-Breed, or liberal, faction.) What better aid could a formidable orator offer? But when Garfield, the compromise candidate, won the nomination, Guiteau switched both location and loyalty. He went to New York, there to shuffle about in shabby dress among the ward heelers at the Republican head-quarters. He beseeched known and unknown politicos to let him take the stump. He had a new speech, appropriately strident and anti-South, called

"Garfield *vs.* Hancock," which, if delivered, would assure the Democrats' defeat. Their proposals to give Treasury money to the South for rebuilding, to forgive war debts, would be annihilated. Guiteau could guarantee Garfield's election.

He had the speech printed. In New York, he passed out copies to prominent Republicans. Some offhandedly said they thought it interesting. Guiteau was elated. Once, he tried to speak his piece at a Negro rally on Twenty-fifth Street, but the half-dozen people who listened tired of his manic disjointedness at about the same time he became too rattled to continue.

Nevertheless, when Garfield won, Guiteau was sure "Garfield *vs.* Hancock" had tipped the election. Now he would go to Washington and collect his reward, preferably an ambassadorship, preferably to Vienna. "We have cleaned them out," he wrote to Garfield, whom he'd never met.

With ten dollars—an insurance commission—in hand, Guiteau went to Washington on March 5, 1881, to press his application in person. He had badgered Garfield by mail since October, telling him, among other lies, that he'd soon marry a wealthy woman (he'd seen her at church in New York) who would perfectly adorn the Ambassador's residence in Vienna. He had also trapped General Grant at the GOP office in New York, asking that the former President sign a letter recommending him for the envoy's post. When all failed, Guiteau went to Washington. His days there count down from a *Death of a Salesman* to the death of a President.

March 10: In Garfield's office, Guiteau presses on the President a copy of his speech inscribed "Charles Julius Guiteau" and "Paris consulship." Guiteau later said, "That is the only interview I ever had with General Garfield on the subject."

' *March 11:* He sends Secretary of State James Blaine the speech, with a note saying: "It was *this* idea that elected General Garfield"—in the name of his Christianity and gentlemanly mien, Guiteau asks for the consulship.

March 25: He writes to Blaine again, asking for the consulship as "a personal tribute" and complimenting Garfield's choice of Blaine "for his premier."

March 26: He writes to Garfield, saying Blaine approves of him for the Paris job, and reminds the President of the favor due him.

April 2–4: Playing what he thinks is politics ("You tickle me and I tickle you," he later said), he first offers to help make Blaine President in 1884, then writes to Garfield that he'll help the incumbent defeat Blaine.

And so it went. Guiteau's already worn wardrobe deteriorated with his spirits, as his dream, *the dream*, receded in the succession of snubs. His mind, never stable, sought refuge in invention. To salvage what he could of respectability, Guiteau used the President and Blaine as references and stayed in fashionable boardinghouses. Each day, until irate secretaries banished him, he'd appear at the White House, purloin stationery and send a note to the President, asking once more for the consulship. Then it was off to the State Department, or Congress, to importune whomever he'd encounter. A contemporary observer said "his own egotism" sustained him. In mid-May, the inevitable occurred: Guiteau's frustration, his ambition, his mental instability coalesced with a political crisis that provided him with both his scapegoat-target and the motivation for murder. Two New York Senators, both Stalwarts, resigned to protest Garfield's appointment of a Half-Breed as customs collector in New York. Guiteau's sense of patronage was outraged. He clipped a Brooklyn *Eagle* editorial deploring Garfield's act as one sure to destroy the Republican Party.

On May 18, he was later to testify, he went to his rooming house "greatly depressed in mind and spirit from the political situation, and I should say it was about half past eight, before I had gone to sleep, when an impression came over my mind like a flash that if the President was out of the way, this whole thing would be solved and everything would go well. That is the first impression I had with reference to removing the President."

Thus was born in trance—as with Theodore Roosevelt's attacker thirty years later—the idea of killing a President. Of course, for Guiteau, it was to be a "removal," a gesture to save the Republicans, hence the Republic. He would be rewarded, he thought. The more he thought about it, in fact, the more he was convinced he had been inspired to this removal, that it was a "divine pressure" commanded by God and certainly not the Devil's work. Riding this conviction, he slid down the days until July 2.

May 23: Guiteau wrote to Garfield that "Mr. Blaine is a wicked man, and you ought to demand his *immediate* resignation; otherwise, you and the Republican Party will come to grief."

June 6: He entered John O'Meara's gunshop to examine the largest pistol on display, the five-shot, .44-caliber British bulldog with a white-bone handle. "That will kill a horse," the amiable shopkeeper told Guiteau, who knew nothing of guns.

June 8: Borrowing $15 from a cousin, Guiteau bought the bulldog, a box of cartridges and, oddly, a woman's penknife—all for ten dollars. He took the fancy-handled gun because, he said later, it would look better in a museum. O'Meara showed him how to load and pointed out a good place to learn marksmanship, in a wood by the Potomac, not far from the White

House. Guiteau would practice nearly every day, then repair to Lafayette Square, across from the Executive Mansion, where he relaxed.

June 12: Guiteau—like other American assassins—stalked his victim. He thought of shooting the President that Sunday in church but feared he might hit someone else. The temptation was strong, though, to kill in a sacred place.

June 16: With the compulsion to explain that has marked several of our assassins—clearest in the diaries of Booth and Sirhan—Guiteau composed an "Address to the American People," saying Garfield had wrecked the Republican Party "and for this he dies." There emerged from the cocoon of his obsession the usual justification for political murder: "This is not a murder. It is a political necessity . . . [it will] save the republic."

June 18: Guiteau had read that Garfield would go to Long Branch, New Jersey, with his sick wife. He resolved to shoot the President at the depot then, but softened when he saw the frail Mrs. Garfield on her husband's arm and, besides, it was a "hot, sultry day." This peculiar susceptibility to emotional and climatic changes has marked other assassins, as we'll see in the cases of John Schrank, who attacked Theodore Roosevelt, and Giuseppe Zangara, who fired his pistol in the direction of Franklin Roosevelt. Such deflections, unhappily, are only temporary for the dedicated assassin.

June 25: Fixed in his goal, Guiteau visited the District of Columbia Jail to see for himself his future accommodations. He concluded that it was a "very excellent jail."

July 1: Evening in Lafayette Square. Guiteau watched Garfield leave the White House, cross Pennsylvania Avenue and stroll to Blaine's house nearby. Following, Guiteau stopped in an alley. Soon the Secretary of State and the President appeared, on their way back to the White House. Their amiability proved that the Half-Breeds were winning, just as Guiteau had said. Guiteau trailed Garfield and Blaine to the White House, watched their backs but did not attack. Again, he said it was too hot and sultry.

But the morning of July 2 was just right.

Guiteau left the fashionable Riggs House at 5 A.M., ambled to Lafayette Square, where he read a newspaper. At seven, he returned to the hotel for a good breakfast. In his room, he wrote a few letters, wrapped a package containing his autobiographical writings and put his revolver in his right hip pocket. He wore a clean white shirt, a black vest, coat, trousers and a hat. A bit before nine, he left the Riggs House, ducking a bill for the last time. A horsecar took him to the depot. There he arranged for a taxi to whisk him away from any lynch mob that might form after the shooting. It would take him to the Congressional Cemetery, an appropriate place close to the jail, whence he would run to turn himself in. Then he had his shoes shined. He had twenty cents left, not enough to pay the taxi driver two dollars for his escape, but for Guiteau that was a small matter. He left his package with a newsstand vendor, went to the rest room to verify that the revolver was in working order and waited for Garfield.

The President arrived about 9:20. Unguarded, he and Blaine strode through the ladies' waiting room. Guiteau stood behind a bench. When the two were almost across the room, Guiteau drew the bulldog, walked up behind the men and shot Garfield in the back, low and on the right. He fired again and the bullet grazed the collapsing President's arm. Guiteau ran for his taxi, but a policeman stopped him near the exit. "I wish to go to jail," he told the officer. "Arthur is President and I am a Stalwart." In his left hand, he held a note for General William Sherman. It explained how he had shot the President several times to make his death as easy as possible and asked for troops to protect the jail from violence.

On the depot floor, Dr. Smith Townsend, the District of Columbia health officer, examined Garfield's wound. He told the President it wasn't serious. Garfield replied, "I thank you, Doctor, but I am a dead man." The blood spread over the gray traveling suit as the President was put onto a mattress, carried to a police ambulance and taken to a second-floor bedroom in the White House. The Cabinet rallied to his bedside. Lincoln's son, Robert Todd Lincoln, was Secretary of War. It had been sixteen years since four conspirators had been hanged for the murder of his father. At the White House, Lincoln said, "How many hours of sorrow I have passed in this town."

Immediately after the shooting, while the nation waited to learn whether or not Garfield would recover and so whether or not Guiteau would hang, the rumors of conspiracy spread. People remembered the Lincoln affair and shuddered. James Brooks, chief of the Secret Service, vowed to run down every lead. Word came in that behind the shooting were socialists, or still-smoldering Southerners, or disgruntled business leaders, or Continental nihilists. Henry Ward Beecher, like the Warren commissioners of our own time, called it the "act of an isolated lunatic." And Brooks could find no evidence of a conspiracy. He had only Guiteau, safe in the District of Columbia Jail (though, as with Booth's conspirators, rumor had him in irons on a monitor in the Potomac—an ironic myth nourished by Garfield's being attended by Joseph K. Barnes, Army Surgeon General, who'd treated Lincoln after Booth's shot).

Guiteau relished his notoriety. He prepared statements for newsmen; thus he helped create our first media assassination. He was quoted widely, most often saying that he had acted to save us all, at the behest of the Deity. Unmoved, the press vilified him while building Garfield to heights of human perfection unscaled even by the martyred Lincoln. The President's long illness gave writers ample time to canonize the stricken general.

In early September, the President, weak and in great pain, was conveyed in an excruciating rail journey to the New Jersey seashore, where he hoped he would feel better. Nothing helped. Though he rallied periodically, Garfield was doomed by the bulldog's bullet, which had smashed ribs and vertebrae before nicking a large artery and stopping behind the pancreas. An aneurysm formed on the artery, halting the bleeding. It kept him alive until it burst on September 19, when he died after an eleven-week struggle against chills, fever, vomiting, increasing weakness and his own mystification. "He must have been crazy," Garfield had said of Guiteau.

With Garfield's death, the nation went mad with mourning and with anger. It now seems familiar to us—the princely funeral, the family grief, the national keening, the eulogies, the selling of a martyred President. There were also the cheap rumors, the denigrating folk songs, the phrenology pamphlets showing Guiteau's criminal, un-American mind.

He was brought to trial two months later, in November, 1881. The issue was simple: Was he sane and so culpable? The decision was to mark our treatment of assassins for generations, but it and the effects of our second Presidential killing are quickly told.

Guiteau's behavior was manic. In the courtroom he cavorted like the Chicago Seven. He mocked his well-meaning lawyers (including his brother-in-law) and heaped abuse ("old hog . . . fraud") on the prosecution. He told Judge Walter Cox he stood in court as "an agent of the Deity." Judge Cox was lenient, perhaps because, in another irony, he had in 1865 defended Michael O'Laughlin and Samuel Arnold on charges in the Lincoln assassination, had then seen authorities ride roughshod over the rights of the accused. This consideration was lost on Guiteau, who claimed not only divine justification—"the actual interjection of some foreign substance into my brain"—but also secular approval. He displayed letters from admirers (James Earl Ray would get hundreds after Martin Luther King, Jr.'s death) and announced that the Stalwarts would spring him so that he might stand for President when he was acquitted. His defense sought, naturally, to show him mad (just as Richard Lawrence, who attacked

Andrew Jackson in 1835, had been declared insane and so was spared death). But the prosecution stood by England's common law, the M'Naghten Rule, which stated that a person who knew the nature and consequences of his act, and knew it was forbidden by law, was sane and subject to trial. An alienist affirmed that Guiteau did know these things. Guiteau's former wife said he was sane, although how she arrived at that opinion is unknown.

The defense labored to show that Guiteau was chronically aberrant. His sister recounted how he had threatened her with an ax. A letter from his late father was introduced, which opined that Charles was "a fit subject for a lunatic asylum." Witnesses told of his odd behavior at Oneida and elsewhere. But it was useless. The nation was aroused. Two attempts were made on Guiteau's life after he was imprisoned (one by a disgusted guard) as the rage reflex of Booth's alleged slayer, Boston Corbett, and much later Jack Ruby took effect (it didn't help Guiteau when a New York landlord swore the bill collector once vowed he'd have fame, if need be the way John Wilkes Booth had won it).

The prosecution told the jury Guiteau was feigning madness just as he did in business—that he was an "artful simulator." As with Lincoln, the Government seemed to *need* someone guilty and executed. As with Lincoln, it worked to assure that verdict. Despite having the acknowledged killer in jail, the state's lawyers coached witnesses on their testimony and bribed some experts to testify that Guiteau was, within the M'Naghten Rule, sane. They suppressed or destroyed letters and documents that might show that he was crazy.

On January 21, 1882, the jury heard the last plea for Guiteau. He made it himself: "To hang a man in my mental condition on July second, when I fired on the President, would be a lasting disgrace to the American people." He wept and postured. Four days later, after the prosecution's summation, the jury retired for one hour and five minutes before coming in with the guilty verdict. All appeals were denied. Guiteau was sane and must pay with his life. The new President, Chester Arthur, refused clemency. Guiteau was hanged at 12:40 P.M. on June 30, 1882, before a crowd of 250, some of whom had paid $300 for the privilege. When the trap dropped, he was singing a childish poem he'd composed that morning, which ended, "Glory Hallelujah, I am going to the Lordy!" At the autopsy, the physicians were especially interested in his brain. Close examination revealed abnormalities indicative of syphilis or malaria.

Today, few know the name Charles Julius Guiteau, which would probably have surprised him. No more, however, than the establishment in 1883 of the Civil Service Commission and the merit system, which eliminated the craven office-seeking that apparently at last had maddened him. After Garfield, too, some citizens agitated for stricter control of guns, although Guiteau was hardly a gun nut and had bought his revolver legally. The legal profession awakened to the possibilities of "moral insanity" (i.e., severe antisocial or regicidal tendencies without overt delusions or extreme aberrant behavior) and so moved toward new defenses for assassins. Doctors called as expert witnesses paid closer attention to hereditary madness, recalling that Guiteau had had one uncle, two aunts and two first cousins who were certified crazy. And there were the usual calls for more protection for our Presidents. As events proved, it was needed.

In the twenty years, two months and four days between Garfield's last walk and William McKinley's reception at the Pan-American Exposition in Buffalo, New York, the Western world changed rapidly. A middle class burgeoned, while a working class demanded its fair share. Industry ruled, but Marx was in reaction.

The fluxing economic and psychological and political realities loosed strikes, riots and assassinations. A chief cause was economic unrest and its concomitant, the nihilistic notion that if industry's captains and Government's ministers could not assist the mass of men to better lives, then we'd be better off without them. As early as Garfield's assassination, Ulysses Grant proposed a remedy for the fear that stalked America and the world between 1881 and 1901: "If this is the outgrowth of nihilism, I am in favor of crushing it out immediately by the prompt execution of the would-be assassins and their followers."

Leon Czolgosz, the self-styled anarchist who killed McKinley, would suffer just that. But the act of this stooped factory worker was a natural outgrowth of his times, which seemed to many to need violent remedy.

Like John Wilkes Booth and Charles Julius Guiteau, the men who attacked McKinley and Theodore Roosevelt thought they were saving the Republic's best traditions. For Czolgosz in 1901, the popular McKinley symbolized "prosperity when there was no prosperity for the poor man." For John Schrank, the attempt in 1912 to kill Roosevelt—he failed but wounded him—was a fulfillment of a prophetic dream in which the dead McKinley had ordered him to kill Roosevelt.

Czolgosz' melancholy adventure began in Detroit in 1873, the year of the nineteenth century's Great Depression. Ironically, after conceiving Leon in Poland, his parents had emigrated in search of prosperity only to arrive in a country seriously disturbed by unemployment and consequent efforts by workers to unionize. In Detroit, his father worked for the city sewer system and his mother did laundry. Times were hard everywhere. Violence ignited as the International Workers of the World (or "Wobblies"), the Knights of Labor and numerous nihilist and anarchist movements led strikes against railroads, mine operators, steel-makers. They won some, but the unions mostly lost as the strikes were broken by militia, police, scabs and Pinkertons, frequently in bloody battles. Yet the unions persisted. On May 1, 1886, a national demonstration for the eight-hour work day was called, and almost 300,000 workers complied. Two days later in Chicago—then a center of agitation for the "short" day—a bomb was thrown at police from a crowd of workers assembled in Haymarket Square to listen to anarchist speakers and to protest police brutality (the police had the day before fired into workers striking the McCormick Harvester Plant). Seventy police were wounded (seven died) and the enraged cops charged the crowd, shooting as they came. After the dead and wounded had been gathered up, eight anarchists were arrested and tried for murder. They were found guilty, though no proof connected the defendants with the bomb. Four were hanged, one committed suicide in prison and three got life. The incident focused national attention on the anarchists and generated public mistrust of them, labor unions and worker violence. Unions were blackened, to the employers' delight, and the anarchists reacted with more strident rhetoric.

Leon Czolgosz heard it all, and was especially prone to listen. For one reason, the year before the Haymarket riot, when he was twelve, Czolgosz' mother had died soon after the birth of her eighth child. It seemed tumult, violence, dispossession totally enveloped him. The family then lived in northern Michigan, in a Polish settlement, where Leon learned to speak Polish and finished five and a half years of schooling. He was the studious one of the family. He read and grew up shy, quiet and solitary. Occasional displays of anger broke his calm. When he was sixteen, the family moved to Natrona, a Polish town close to Pittsburgh. Leon went to work in a bottle factory for seventy-five cents a day. The next stop was Cleveland, where he found a job in a wire mill for ten dollars a week. He worked there until he was twenty-five, the dreary tenor of his existence leavened mightily by a strike in 1893, which set him thinking and reading about capitalism, anarchism and the validity of the Roman Catholic faith in which he'd been raised. After the strike was settled, he returned to work as Fred C. Nieman (literally, Fred No-man), ostensibly using an alias because he feared official retaliation for his participation in the strike. He continued reading and joined a socialist discussion group.

The discussions, his taste for sociological and utopian writing and his later flirtation with real anarchists were all the intellectual life Czolgosz ever had. His work was menial. He and his family, although industrious and ambitious, hadn't yet made it as the dream had forecast. Not that they were without everything. They'd all chipped in to buy fifty-five acres twelve miles from Cleveland, and Leon liked it on the farm, walking in the woods, doing chores. But he still worked in the mill, and in Cleveland his life was as straight, hard and uniform as the wire he made. He hung around saloons, drank an occasional whiskey, smoked, played a desultory hand of cards. In 1895, when he was twenty-two, his father facilitated these activities by buying a saloon. The socialists arranged to meet upstairs and Leon often sat in with them. But still, life just went on.

Then, in 1898, he had a nervous breakdown. A healthy, normal factory worker vanished, and in his place stood a pale, agitated potential killer. He quit his job in August, 1898, and took to spending days at the farm, reading an anarchist newspaper published in Chicago. He went in to Cleveland occasionally to see a doctor and he took medicine, but it didn't help. The assassination of King Humbert I of Italy in July, 1900, raised his interest, and he clipped a newspaper account of the act. Media contagion seemed to set in—a phenomenon more marked in our time—and he took the clipping to bed with him for weeks.

The summer of 1900 was far more active for McKinley. He'd been renominated in June, the sign that his Administration had done well by the Republican Party and America. With Roosevelt as his Vice President, he could well expect to defeat, as he had in 1896, William Jennings Bryan (and his free-silver, anti-imperialist running mate, Adlai E. Stevenson). President McKinley looked back with pleasure on his life. He was descended from Scotch-Irish and English who'd come to America in the early eighteenth century (no recent immigrant, he). His grandfather James had been manager of a charcoal furnace in Ohio, and William had reaped the benefits, the dream's rewards. They were so like Garfield's. A term of college, then heroism for the Union in the Civil War, then a law practice, election to Congress and a long, powerful career there helping the policies of his friends Grant, Hayes and Garfield.

McKinley annexed the Hawaiian Islands in 1898 and, with the sinking of the *Maine* in Havana harbor as a motive, whipped Spain the same year, thereby winning the Philippine Islands. Trade interests also demanded a canal across the Isthmus of Panama, and that was high on the President's roster of priorities. While Czolgosz was musing over King Humbert, McKinley was putting down the stubborn Philippine insurrection, not to mention dispatching American warships to China to protect our interests during the Boxer Rebellion. His heroic Vice President mightily approved of these expansionist policies and was even more eager than McKinley to lower tariffs a bit and move into the world's markets. Together, they were a formidable team. They marched to victory in November, 1900, and on to a gala inauguration on March 4, 1901. McKinley was at his peak, bluff and hearty, immensely popular and assured of bill-passing influence in Congress through his friendship with Mark Hanna and assorted "fixers." The nation appeared tranquil, almost freed of the acrimonious sectionalism that was the residue of the Civil War. His party was unified, unlike Garfield's. His only sorrow was his invalid and dotty wife, Ida. A pity, since he was only fifty-eight.

Czolgosz was twenty-eight. He carried 140 pounds on a 5'7" frame and now bore a placid, nearly bovine expression on his round face. After a long period of listlessness during the election furor, he went to the family farm and asked for the money he'd put in it (rather like Guiteau at Oneida). The family promised it, perhaps partly because Leon hinted that he might soon be dead. On May 5, 1901, he attended a lecture in Cleveland by "Red Emma" Goldman, the thirty-one-year-old Russian anarchist who then went about preaching the virtues of no government. Soon afterward, Czolgosz contacted an anarchist club in Cleveland, introducing himself as Fred Nieman and inquired whether its members might be "plotting something like Bresci [King Humbert's assassin]." The implied terrorism seems to have put them off (five days before Czolgosz shot McKinley, an anarchist paper ran a warning that a spy, noticed in Chicago and Cleveland, might be trying to infiltrate them—the description matched that of Czolgosz).

Leon did go to Chicago, early in July, traveling on his farm money. He called on Goldman, who hurried away to catch a train for her home in Rochester, New York. Not many days later, Leon turned up in West Seneca, a town near Buffalo (and not far from Rochester). Why he went there, no one knows. He later told police it was to find work, which was both uncharacteristic of his recent behavior and puzzling. Was there more work near Buffalo than in Chicago or Cleveland? Perhaps he was fascinated by the aura of the Pan-American Exposition, a show of dazzling technological progress (including the X ray) that had opened May 1. Whatever, he stayed in West Seneca, passing time, until August 29, when he left, exchanging a broken revolver for part of his bill, and took a boat from Buffalo across Lake Erie to Cleveland. He stayed only a day, then returned to Buffalo. On August 31, he rented a room above a saloon, registering as

John Doe. By then he knew what was to come.

September 5: McKinley spoke before fifty thousand persons, telling them he now favored reciprocal trade and lower tariffs. Everyone cheered. Czolgosz watched and was disgusted with the panoply, the honors accorded the President. "It wasn't right," he later said. But that didn't confirm him in murder. He had decided some time before, and he'd bought, on September 2, for $4.50, a .32-caliber Iver Johnson revolver, decorated with an owl's head on the grip and in good condition. Hardly a devastating weapon, but then Leon was new to this.

September 6: The public reception opened at 4 P.M. McKinley had returned from a visit to Niagara Falls, as had Czolgosz. After a tour of the fair grounds, the President would shake hands for ten minutes, an obligatory gesture for the leader of a democracy (much like the behavior of Gerald Ford, which twice endangered him). McKinley was guarded by soldiers, police detectives and the Secret Service—about fifty in all—as the line advanced. It was a hot day and no one paid attention to the small man, neat in his gray suit—a workingman come to see his President—who shuffled in line, his right hand swathed in a handkerchief. After all, many were mopping their brows. When he reached the President, a Secret Service man shoved him gently ahead. He extended his left hand, the President his right. Czolgosz slapped McKinley's hand aside and fired the Iver Johnson twice through the handkerchief, setting it afire. The first slug ricocheted off the President's breastbone (later, like the "magic bullet" of the JFK murder, it fell out of McKinley's clothes). The second burrowed through his walruslike girth, traversed the stomach, the pancreas and a kidney and came to rest near McKinley's back muscle wall.

So it was done. Vengeful guards jumped Czolgosz and nearly killed him. "Don't let them hurt him," McKinley called.

"I done my duty," Leon muttered.

McKinley was taken to the home of John Milburn—president of the exposition—after emergency surgery in the fair's hospital. Doctors were hopeful, so much that they refused the aid of the newfangled X ray Thomas Edison sent them. But John Hay—who had been Lincoln's secretary, a friend of Garfield and now McKinley's Secretary of State—shook his head and said the President would die. McKinley agreed. Though he rallied at first like Garfield, gangrenous blood poisoning consumed him bit by bit. He told his doctors, "It is useless, gentlemen. I think we ought to have prayer." He sighed, "His will, not ours, be done," mumbled the last verse of "Nearer, My God, to Thee," and died about 2:15 A.M. on September 14.

His funeral, like those of our other slain Presidents, was grand. "Nearer, My God, to Thee" became more popular. The national mourning was loud and prolonged. Mrs. McKinley understood "her dearest's" death but not much else, and she retired to their home at Canton, Ohio, uncertain of what had happened.

The most immediate effects were the swearing in of Roosevelt as President and the trial of Czolgosz. There wasn't much to the latter. For one thing, Leon kept uttering outrageous anarchist things: "I don't believe one man should have so much service. . . . I thought it would be a good thing for the country to kill the President," and so on. For another, he refused the aid of his lawyers, who weren't anxious to assist him, anyway. The trial lasted eight hours and twenty-six minutes. The jury was out thirty-four minutes before it declared Czolgosz guilty. He had been, the jury thought, just as a panel of five experts had said, "the product of anarchy, sane and responsible." Czolgosz was electrocuted at 7:12 A.M. on October 29, 1901 —fifty-three days after shooting McKinley. As they strapped him into the chair, he said, "I killed the President because he was the enemy of the good people—the good working people. I am not sorry for my crime." The autopsy revealed no cerebral abnormalities. In a remarkable display of haste and hatred, sulphuric acid was poured into the coffin.

Acid could not eradicate certain effects and questions, however.

First, as we might expect, the good working people weren't helped by Leon's act. If anything, some were put out of work. There was a minor Wall Street panic and an immense antianarchist wave. Employers fired and mobs attacked known anarchists. Goldman and others were arrested, abused and threatened before proving they were innocent of McKinley's death. Paterson, New Jersey (where Giuseppe Zangara was to live), was targeted for sacking, since it was a notorious anarchist stronghold, full of working stiffs and other low types—but authorities intervened.

Second, the familiar conspiracy talk began. Why had Leon gone to West Seneca? What was he doing there with the broken revolver he'd given the hotelkeeper? Was he an agent of some splinter group of nihilists? But no proof ever came that he had acted in concert with others.

Third, questions again arose about what constituted sanity in a murderer. After Czolgosz' execution, several psychiatrists considered his case. They concluded that he had become schizophrenic during his breakdown and gradually built delusions—chiefly, that he *was* an anarchist and that it was his *duty* (as he'd said) to kill the President. Why else all the senselessly brave talk from a man who knew he was doomed? As with Guiteau, some jurists wanted thenceforth to be more careful in defining madness in the accused.

Fourth, laws were enacted to the detriment of Czolgosz' kind. New statutes banned the immigration of known anarchists and nihilists. They were called human sewage. More to the point, the Secretary of the Treasury directed the Secret Service to provide full-time and complete protection for the President. It had taken Lincoln, Garfield and McKinley, but now professional security men would guard the Chief Executive.

Lastly, the policies of McKinley were not changed. Roosevelt made that clear, saying, "It shall be my aim to continue, absolutely unbroken, the policy of President McKinley for the peace, the prosperity and the honor of our beloved country." Unlike McKinley, Teddy did avoid serious assassination attempts during his tenure from 1901 to 1909, no doubt due largely to Secret Service protection. John Schrank waited until 1912 to take a shot at him, when he ran as the third-party, third-term Bull Moose incarnate. He was unguarded then.

Schrank fit the mold of our previous assassins. He was smallish (5′4″, 145 pounds), young (36), neat, male, opinionated, missing parents (father dead, mother remarried), a loner and possessed of self-esteem just this side of megalomania. Further, like Booth, Guiteau and Czolgosz, he was less than three generations from Europe (Schrank was born in Bavaria, in fact) and was correspondingly devoted to the principles he felt were embodied in the Constitution of his adopted land. Assuredly, they did not include a third-term "king" (from 1865, we hear Booth's fears of "Emperor Abe"). Yes, Schrank was typical.

Except that he'd had these two visions.

The first, he later reported, was the day after McKinley died. There he was, John Nepomuk Schrank, in a room gazing at a coffin surrounded by flowers (so far, the same dream Lincoln had had), when a figure reared from the casket and pointed toward a man in a monk's habit. The pointer was McKinley, Schrank saw, and the monk, unlikely as it seems, was Roosevelt. The dead McKinley then intoned, "This is my murderer. Avenge my death."

The second came eleven years later, on September 14, 1912. Schrank never explained the interval, any more than he did his lapse in heeding McKinley's command. Anyway, this time Schrank was in a room on Canal Street in New York (the hotel was called the White House). He was writing a lugubrious, self-admonishing poem called "Be a Man" (it *was* the time of Kipling), when a voice said, "Let not a murderer take the Presidential chair. Avenge my death." A tap on the shoulder and Schrank turned to look into the pale face of McKinley. Understandably, he left a week later to obey the dead President.

Between visions, unlike Guiteau and Czolgosz, Schrank seemed to glimpse, nearly to grasp, America's possibilities. He was the immigrant (arriving in America in 1889) who had it made. True, he was parentless. But he was raised and cared for by his aunt and uncle. His uncle opened a Bavarian saloon in New York, paid Tammany to keep it open and, in time —maybe seeing that his dreamy nephew needed a patron—signed it over to John. Schrank thus was made an entrepreneur. He had a wedge into American success, yet he never drove it home. Instead, he drank beer, talked, lamented his one love affair (in 1904, his girlfriend died when the *General Slocum* burned in the East River). He read widely, too, especially the writings of political terrorists and patriots. He didn't care for Marx's socialism, but George Washington, Lajos Kossuth, Thaddeus Kosciusko, Jean Jacques Rousseau were favorites. He also wrote poetry and kept a journal full of the great thoughts that came to him.

Two years after taking over the saloon, John sold it and moved into a tenement his uncle had purchased. Commerce was too stifling for him, he felt. Now he could take long walks, read more, write—occasionally tend bar to make a bit of money. He never argued politics. His uncle had taught him that that was death for saloonkeepers.

In 1912, Schrank was living in New York's White House Hotel on the $800 per year generated by what was then his tenement building. His aunt and uncle had left it to him and it was valued at $25,000. Along with his bartending, the bequest meant he could muse for the rest of his life, since he was very thrifty. It seems never to have occurred to him—as it had to Guiteau—that he could make more money, could take advantage of the markets, the free-enterprise prosperity that McKinley, Roosevelt and William Taft had sparked. He would rather compose his essay, "The Four Pillars of the Republic." He specified them as (1) a two-term limit for Presidents, (2) enforcing the Monroe Doctrine, (3) eschewing wars of conquest and (4) ensuring that only Protestants could be President (he feared Roman domination). He placed the greatest weight on the first pillar, saying that foreign-born citizens like himself could scarcely "respect our institutions" when somebody like Roosevelt wanted a third term.

After the second vision—in September, 1912—Schrank decided he would kill Roosevelt. He would do it while Teddy campaigned. He borrowed $350 and bought a steamship ticket that would take him South along the Atlantic Coast, probably to New Orleans. For no good reason, that seemed a good place to shoot a Bull Moose. Before leaving, Schrank wrote on the back of a water-and-light bill, "Down with Theodore Roosevelt. We want no king. . . . We will not yield to Rome." Then he bought a .38-caliber Colt and a box of cartridges. Total cost: $14.55. The gunshop owner told him that unless he had a permit, pursuant to the Sullivan Law, the revolver would have to be made inoperative. Schrank pleaded that he was leaving New York, showing his steamship ticket. The owner yielded (which raises a question about the effectiveness of gun-control legislation), and Schrank, whose total firearm experience consisted of once having fired a pistol on the Fourth of July, walked away armed.

Then, like many assassins, Schrank stalked his man. Debarking at Charleston, he trailed the whistle-stopping Teddy to Birmingham, through Georgia, to Chattanooga, where he saw Roosevelt for the first time (and, presumably, connected his abstract idea with a personal animus). But there were no good opportunities to shoot. Then Roosevelt went home for a rest, leaving Schrank to swelter in the Midwest's Indian summer and await the candidate's next swing through the Republican heartland. Schrank moved slowly from Nashville to Evansville, and on to Louisville and Indianapolis, until he read that Roosevelt would leave Oyster Bay, New York, on October 7 for another Midwestern tour. Schrank and Roosevelt arrived in Chicago the same day, October 12.

Again, the Bavarian saw his target but did not shoot; he later said it was because he didn't want to dirty the "decent, respectable reputation" of Chicago (a nicety lost on its citizens, who even then lived between machine politics and organized crime). It seems that Schrank had no such friendly feeling for Milwaukee. He went there on Sunday, October 13, and awaited Roosevelt, whose itinerary called for a speech there the next day. Schrank spent Sunday in Milwaukee, drinking beer near the Hotel Gilpatrick, whose Progressive owner had inveigled Roosevelt into attending a small supper there the next evening before the speech. Schrank seems to have learned that, drunk on and, quite uncharacteristically, tipped the musicians for playing "The Stars and Stripes Forever."

The next evening, Schrank stood in front of the Gilpatrick, immaculate in suit, batwing collar and fedora. He waited, standing about six feet from the open car parked in front. At eight o'clock, Roosevelt came out, entered the car, stood and waved to the cheering crowd (greeting them as Franklin Roosevelt was to do in Miami, twenty-one years thence, just before the shooting started). Schrank's right hand thrust forward between two onlookers, the Colt went off and Teddy staggered backward against the seat.

The bullet tore into his right chest, below and to the right of the nipple, then angled upward for about four inches, fracturing a rib. No doubt it would have gone through the lung, perhaps out his back or deflected into some other organ. But Roosevelt had folded his fifty-page speech in half and put it in his breast pocket, along with his metal spectacle case. The bullet lost much force penetrating the hundred pages and the case. Otherwise, he later said, he would have been killed.

After the one shot, Schrank was tackled by Roosevelt's stenographer. Police dragged him away as Teddy ordered his driver on to the auditorium. He was satisfied that he wasn't seriously hurt. As he shouted to the audience of nine thousand hysterical followers, "It takes more than that to kill a Bull Moose!" He spoke for fifty minutes before seeking treatment for shock and loss of blood. He recovered quickly at Mercy Hospital in Chicago and went home on October 21. Although he was, again, a national hero, he lost the election to Woodrow Wilson. Schrank's bullet remained inside him the rest of his life.

Schrank outlived Roosevelt by twenty-four years (and said he was "sorry to learn" of Teddy's death). His act was not subject to the rumors and speculations usually surrounding assassinations and their attempts. The dreams had done it, that was all, the dreams and a pistol. Schrank was never tried on the charge of armed assault with intent to kill. A sanity commission of five alienists examined him. It concluded he was "suffering from insane delusions, grandiose in character . . . he is insane at the present time." One alienist went on to say, "I think his disease is original paranoia, that is chronic and in my opinion is incurable."

At the court's order, Schrank—called "Uncle John" by his fellow patients—spent the rest of his life comfortably enough in mental hospitals. Perhaps directly due to them, he was luckier than Guiteau and Czolgosz.

Schrank lived to see an assassination—that of Archduke Franz Ferdinand at Sarajevo in 1914—trigger World War I. He lived to see the war threaten the end of Western civilization as it had been known. He heard the sounds of the jazz age through the radio and the machine-gun rattle of Prohibition violence. He read—for he still kept up—about the Syndicate and Al Capone, and about the troubles in Chicago, that nice town, and about the killing of Chicago's Mayor Anton Cermak during an assassination attempt on FDR. He heard about Huey Long's great fall down in the bayous. He even saw the beginning of World War II, that final assault on the traditions of the West. He protested none of it, until 1940, when he announced that Franklin Delano Roosevelt should not seek a third term and that if Uncle John could, he'd save the nation again from a Roosevelt dictatorship. He didn't add that he wished Giuseppe Zangara had been a better shot.

Actually, Zangara did pretty well—and there is considerable speculation that he accomplished just what he, or someone, wanted: to kill Cermak and not Roosevelt. It was February 15, 1933. In two weeks, the United States, to which Zangara had immigrated ten years before, would inaugurate Roosevelt as its thirty-second President. Most hoped this polio-lamed aristocrat would somehow bring the country out of the Depression, bring back the joys and jobs of the jazz age. Zangara really didn't care. He was glad he had no work. He'd worked too long. Now he was in Miami's Bayfront Park with an eight-dollar, 32-caliber revolver in his pocket, a five-foot, 105-pound man dwarfed in the crowd waiting for Roosevelt.

The President-elect was coming ashore that evening from Vincent Astor's yacht. He'd been fishing for twelve days. Despite routine warnings about possible danger, Roosevelt had decided to say a few words in Miami. He loved the American people, he said, and he needed all the support he could muster. So an informal speech was announced and the people gathered in the park, near a bandstand built to resemble a Shriner's vision of Oriental splendor (it had, in fact, been constructed for their convention). Roosevelt would speak from his car, which could be parked on the curved driveway fronting the bedomed pavilion. Behind him, on the stage, would be the dignitaries—Miami officials, FDR's advisers and Cermak, who had come to Miami to plead for Federal patronage and funds from the new Administration and to repair the political damage Cermak had suffered by his tardy endorsement of FDR (though, to be sure, when the crunch had come, Tony got out the Chicago Democrats in gratifying numbers; now there was the matter of judgeships and the like).

It was nearly 9:30 when Roosevelt's light-blue Buick touring car curled around the driveway and past Zangara, whose size prevented him from getting up front. These big Americans pressed forward and Zangara couldn't see over them or get up near the driveway. He shoved against them. One Iowan told him, "It isn't proper for you to go and stand out and push yourself in front of someone else." Propriety was far from Zangara's mind. The whole situation reminded him of 1923, when he'd had a vague notion of killing King Victor Emmanuel III in his native Italy but was prevented from doing so by the crush of the crowd. He scuttled forward as best he could.

Roosevelt spoke briefly, delivering 132 words calculated to show that he was a regular guy, a sportsman who could put in a day's work or go fishing as well as the next, even if he *was* handicapped. He sat on the top of the rear seat in bright light, waving, chatting, smiling for the newsreel cameras. A perfect target, if anybody wanted a shot at him. In a minute or so, he was finished. He slid into the rear seat and waved Cermak down from the bandstand for a greeting. Miami officials started forward with a fake telegram of welcome, suitably large. The crowd moiled, the human walls split.

Then there was little Zangara, up on a chair about twenty-five feet from Roosevelt's car, teetering as he pulled the stiff trigger of his revolver as fast as he could. Five shots (like firecrackers, FDR later said) and five people went down. Three bystanders collapsed with head wounds, a woman twisted, shot in the belly, and Cermak folded over, a bullet smashing under his right armpit and into his lung. He fell back off the running board to Roosevelt's left.

Immediately, confusion and jerky movement. Zangara was overwhelmed by police and bystanders, his clothes were torn from him, his defiant shouts in broken English lost as he was thrown onto the rack of a limousine, sat upon by three cops and carried off to the lockup. Cermak called, "The President, get him away!" Roosevelt ordered his car to stop —his driver had started to move away from the danger—and that Cermak be put in with him. The President-elect cradled the wounded mayor. As he later said, "I held him all the way to the hospital and his pulse constantly improved. . . . I remember I said, 'Tony, keep quiet—don't move—it won't hurt you if you keep quiet and remain perfectly still.' "

It was good advice but bootless. Cermak, like Garfield and McKinley, seemed to get better at first, but in three weeks he was dead from "complications" caused by the bullet, his doctors said, though the official cause of death was ulcerative colitis. The other shooting victims pulled through. Amid hosannas for his salvation, Roosevelt went on to his inauguration, to the New Deal, to World War II and election to four terms. Zangara—first given eighty years for the assaults before the mayor died—was electrocuted for the murder of Cermak. He welcomed death, since it ended the stomach-ache he said over and over made all rulers unbearable to him. Zangara's death did not, however, end two things: the irony that he had killed the successful immigrant personified and the rumor that he had been after Cermak all the time, that the mayor had not accidentally perished in a fusillade of gunfire aimed at Roosevelt.

This rumor is so persistent, as are so many alternate theories of our assassinations, that we must scan the lives of Zangara and Cermak, the loser and the winner immigrants, if we are to fathom why anybody would contend, despite Zangara's vehement denials, that little Giuseppe was after big Tony. Start with the killer. What sort of man was Zangara?

Overall, he was poor, sick and angry. He was born in September, 1900, in Ferruzzano, Calabria, a harsh part of Italy's boot toe. Giuseppe's mother died when he was two. His father, as gruff and dictatorial as Guiteau's, took him out of school and put him to work at the age of eight. Zangara said he was sure this hard early work had given him the terrible pains he suffered all his life and that the rulers were at fault for making people labor so hard. He knew, too, that he hated the rich, because their children passed him on their way to school while he had to work on the streets.

There's no doubt that Zangara was a sickly child (his autopsy showed no stomach disorders, but he did have a damaged gall bladder that could have pained him), and he grew to be a short, lightweight man, with black, bushy hair above a lupine face marked by sad brown eyes. Perhaps to escape from home, Zangara joined the Italian Army as a teenager and served five years. After his arrest, he said it was when he was a soldier in 1923 that he'd felt like killing King Victor Emmanuel III. (No proof exists of this—it might have been a fantasy, but if he had succeeded, Zangara's stomach troubles would have been cured a decade sooner.)

As it was, he immigrated to the United States, arriving on September 2, 1923. He found his way to Paterson, New Jersey—still an anarchist center—where his uncle lived. He found work as a bricklayer, his uncle's trade, and joined the AFL's Bricklayers, Masons and Plasterers Union. He made good money, about twelve dollars a day, and saved most of it. People remembered him as quiet, a loner, equally inept with women and the English language, in every way unremarkable except for his continual bellyaching (which an appendectomy didn't help) and his occasional outbursts against kings, Presidents and all authorities. He even slandered Calvin Coolidge, who certainly never tried to attract such attention. His uncle said all he did was eat (soft food) and sleep (he once rented two rooms, one to keep space between him and his neighbors). Zangara didn't drink much, because it hurt his stomach.

Giuseppe lived that way until 1929's great crash. That year, he became both a naturalized and a foot-loose citizen, as though inspired to explore this country before everyone went broke. He visited Miami, because he thought the sun would help his stomach. He returned to odd jobs in New Jersey, but he wasn't the same. In 1931, he left Hackensack to spend time in Los Angeles, bounced back to New Jersey, then in 1932 moved to Miami permanently. (These peregrinations remind one of another convicted assassin, James Earl Ray, as a general malaise seems to fix on a man.) In a time when jobs were hard to keep, Zangara had willfully become an idler after laboring all those years. While the Presidential campaign, the Depression debates roared about him, he fished, bet the dogs, made trips to Palm Beach, Key West and Panama. He paid close attention to Roosevelt's victory over Hoover, not that he cared. He hated, he swore, all Presidents equally. He said he would have killed President Hoover if he hadn't read that February about Roosevelt's coming to Miami. He reasoned that Hoover was way up in Washington, where it was cold, bad for his belly, whereas Roosevelt would be right at hand, where it was warm. "I see Mr. Hoover first I kill him first," he stated at his trial. "Make no difference. Presidents just the same bunch—all same." Presumably with that in mind, Zangara went to the Davis Pawnshop in downtown Miami and bought his pistol, a nickel-plated United States Revolver Company product. It looked like Czolgosz' weapon. When questioned later, the pawnbroker said it wasn't against the law to sell the gun, and it wasn't. "He got the money," Zangara reflected. Anyway, revolver in pocket, Zangara headed for Bayfront Park and his encounter with his opposite, Tony Cermak.

"Ten Percent" Tony his enemies called him. They said he skimmed that much in kickbacks and assorted favors during his years of power. That sort of stuff, power plays, got him killed, they said. Amateur crooks don't push the Mob around and get away with it, they said, not in Chicago. Zangara did the job on the great reformer, that was all.

Not so, Cermak's friends said. The mayor had been the best thing that ever happened to Chicago. If only he'd lived to finish cleaning up the town; if only that demented man hadn't shot at Roosevelt . . . Tony was almost saintly, the epitome of the good, self-made man, his admirers said.

Both sides could make a case.

Like Zangara, Cermak was foreign-born. He was born near Prague of Bohemian parents, and during his long ascent, he was known as a bohunk whose power base lay in Chicago's West Side Slavic neighborhoods (he was later interred in the Bohemian National Cemetery in a mausoleum that would not have been out of place at Forest Lawn). Cermak's father, a coal miner, brought the family to America, to Braidwood, Illinois, in 1874, the year after Anton's birth. Braidwood then was a mining town and, like Zangara, Cermak grew up knowing only work. He had perhaps three years of elementary school. After that, it was the mines and long hours of filthy, dangerous, dark work. Once he drove mules for about $1.50 a day, a better job than working in the mines. Cermak learned to distrust his big-business employers and to drink a lot. He was often jailed for fighting.

He also became a "labor agitator," helping organize workers in the steel mills of Gary and in the mines around Braidwood. Periodically, he moved with his family to Chicago as the Cermaks tried to break out of their working-class world. They failed until Tony gave up proletarian ways and became a capitalist ("Capitalism kill me!" Zangara had cried before he sat in the electric chair).

When he was nineteen—in 1892—Cermak started his own hauling business in Chicago's Bohemian sections. He carted wood, coal, whatever, and he prospered with hard work, unfailing geniality and loads of political hack work in the wards from which the Carter H. Harrison faction drew its strength (though Harrison was assassinated in 1893, his followers retained power for another twenty-five years). By 1902 Cermak was an Illinois state representative and by 1907 secretary of the United Societies for Local Self-Government, a saloon lobby organized by ethnics to combat the growing sentiment for Prohibition. By 1909 he represented Lawndale, as Democratic leader in the house. Tony was known as a man who took care of his family and his friends. They took care to ensure that he was always his ward's committeeman, an irreducible position of clout in machine politics.

In 1912, Cermak was elected bailiff of the Municipal Court of Chicago, and from that incontestably powerful post, he attacked the first "big fix" administration of the notorious Republican Mayor William Hale "Big Bill" Thompson. Big Bill, whose two terms established the mayor's office as the primal source of corruption in Chicago, didn't take this bohunk's criticism kindly. When Cermak ran for sheriff in 1918, he lost, despite riding popular sentiment in attacking Prohibition and the hated Germans, our blood enemies of the war. It was back to the city council to take over the seat of his friend Otto Kerner, whose son in the sixties would become governor of Illinois and later spend some time in jail.

After that, it was upward for Cermak. In 1922, he was elected president of the Cook County Board of Commissioners—a position that gave him both considerable patronage power and influence with candidates for city, county, state and Congressional elections. In 1928, Cermak was boomed for governor, but he was outmaneuvered for the nomination by Irish politician George Brennan. That same year, he ran for the U.S. Senate and was defeated. Stung, he turned on his chief rivals among fellow Democrats and ethnics, the Irish, and wrung the party leadership from them. With help, he intended reforming the Democratic Party and winning the city from Big Bill, who was by then serving his second term. To do that, Cermak needed political support, police support and the tacit approval of organized crime's shadow government. (Everyone knew that the police and the gangs were linked other than as cops and robbers. For example, Johnny Torrio—before Al ousted him—and Capone each pocketed about $100,000 a *week* during the twenties, an operation impossible without police connivance. You couldn't otherwise miss all the thousands of immigrant families cooking alcohol, the whores and the numbers, any more than the six hundred-plus unsolved murders.)

In short, to run—or to reform—Chicago, Cermak had to have the mayor's patronage power. The mayor could dictate who became policemen, commissioners, judges, and so control the various factions. Cermak turned to an old friend, Moe Rosenberg, for help in remolding the Democratic Party to a machine tough enough to defeat Thompson. Moe and his protégé Jake Arvey (later a power in Richard Daley's Chicago) had benefited from Cermak's influence. Moe and Jake (then an alderman) and Tony worked to reforge a puissant party so that all the spoils would be theirs. Once Cermak had that, he could turn it whatever way he willed.

In 1931, Cermak was elected mayor over Big Bill, and across the nation the press rejoiced at the defeat of Thompsonism. Cermak's chief backers, public and private, were Rosenberg, Arvey, Patrick Nash and Melvin A. Traylor, president of the First National Bank of Chicago. The group represented business, government and respectable society. Rosenberg later testified that they'd wanted "to put Cermak in the mayor's chair, which we did." Thompson's charges that Moe and Tony were in collusion in a gigantic receivership business garnering huge fees for foreclosures didn't sway Chicago voters nearly as much as did the Democratic precinct captains. Registering every body in a graveyard and every wino didn't hurt, either. Cermak had made it. With his reorganized party behind him, he possessed the greatest power ever held by a Chicago mayor. Using it, he laid what some think were the foundations for his murder by Zangara, who, the speculation goes, was a dupe and a hit man for organized crime.

The theory goes that because of the alliance needed to put him in the mayor's office, Cermak had close connections—closer even than Big Bill's —with the rackets. When Capone was sentenced to eleven years for income-tax evasion in 1931, Cermak saw his opportunity to bring organized crime under the mayor's control—whether for good or for ill depends on how one views Cermak's character. Either way, Capone's incarceration left a vacuum that could be filled by the mayor.

Coincidentally came the 1932 national elections. During the Democratic Convention, Cermak held out for the renomination of Alfred E. Smith. Opposing FDR, he kept the bulk of Illinois's votes committed to Traylor, his banker friend. When Roosevelt won the nomination, Cermak relented and delivered Chicago's votes. But he still felt uneasy about the vital Federal patronage. He needed sympathetic judges, for instance, to put away unfriendly crooks. Moreover, there was the Chicago World's Fair coming up. For that, the city's image, his image, should be burnished as bright as a clean cop's badge.

Out of these needs—to direct the Mob and to clean up the city—came the events that fed the legend of tiny Giuseppe Zangara as a contract killer.

First, organized criminals became uneasy about Cermak now that he was mayor. They'd seen that he was tough with political opponents. Like Huey Long, and our own time's Richard Nixon, Cermak in office was suspected, in a contemporary writer's words, of using "surreptitious means such as wire taps, mail drops, surveillance and stool pigeons to ferret out information concerning the weaknesses and foibles of administrative and political friends, taking great pains to learn the identities of his enemies." If Tony would do that, wouldn't he move on some mobsters? He was, the talk went, acting as his own police commissioner, dealing closer with the underworld than any mayor ever had.

December 19, 1932—six weeks after the elections—brought the catalyst, so the story goes.

That day, members of Cermak's special police unit raided the Capone headquarters at 221 North LaSalle Street, hard by City Hall. With Detective Sergeants Harry Lang and Harry Miller in the van, the cops charged in to find several men, among them Frank Nitti, who said he was there to put a bet on a horse. Nitti, the renowned "enforcer," was fresh from Leavenworth on a tax rap, returned to operate as Capone's regent now while Al was away.

Truly, what happened next wasn't altogether clear until the trial of Sergeant Lang, which came after Cermak was dead, and even then the images wavered darkly in the mirrored accounts.

A detective named Chris Callahan swore he searched Nitti, found him unarmed and was holding his wrists for the cuffs when Frank asked, "What's this about?" Then, Callahan said, Sergeant Lang leveled his gun —Callahan jumped aside—and shot Nitti three times in the neck and back. Lang next shot himself in the finger. Nitti was sent to the hospital to die and the police announced that he'd been shot resisting arrest, as Lang's wound proved.

Unfortunately for that story, the durable Nitti recovered, to be tried for shooting Lang (but really as much as anything for importing a gunman—

Louis "Little New York" Campagna—to kill Cermak). That was the reason for the raid, Lang testified, to arrest Campagna. Lang's story didn't wash. Nitti was acquitted, largely because Lang's self-inflicted wound suggested perjury. Next, the sergeant himself was arrested and indicted for perjury and shooting the gangster.

But well before Cermak's death and Lang's arraignment, rumors and events wriggled in the strange illumination of the underworld. A story mushroomed that Cermak's favorite gangster leader, Ted Newberry, had offered Lang $15,000 to kill Nitti and run the "greaseballs," as Newberry reportedly called the mafiosi, out of town. Whether that was true or not, the January 7, 1933, issue of the Chicago *American* reported:

Ted Newberry, gentleman turned gangster, died like a gangster today. His body was found early today, shot through the head and one hand almost severed by shotgun slugs, in a ditch alongside a gravel road near Bailey Town, Porter County, Indiana.

Newberry's body was identified by a diamond-set buckle given to him by Capone.

After the shooting of Nitti and Newberry's last ride, Mayor Cermak, a widower since 1928, moved from his suite at the Congress Hotel to a bungalow at the top of the Morrison Hotel. Access was by private elevator only. A Hearst newspaperman named John Dienhart, cloying in his admiration of Cermak, reported after the mayor's death that he'd visited the mayor and been told Cermak moved after he saw greaseballs hanging around the hotel. The story is questionable, but it is certain the mayor ordered a bulletproof vest early in 1933, and that after the shooting of Nitti his force of bodyguards was increased from three to five.

More evidence that Cermak thought he was endangered came out at Lang's trial. His partner, Miller, amplified the Campagna tale. The mayor had ordered the raid, Miller said, telling the police they'd find Nitti and Campagna at the headquarters, that Cermak thought Campagna was in town to kill him because he planned to shut down gangsterism for the duration of the World's Fair. The gossip mills ground on, though no one would print much about the affair, not with Cermak a national martyr and all. Complex rumors agitated the city. Had Miller confirmed Nitti's belief that Newberry had paid Lang, one of the mayor's own bodyguards, to kill their mutual enemy? Had Tony set up Nitti? Had the Mob decided it had been betrayed by Cermak, who seemed now to want to take over its affairs, and so had wasted Newberry? Was that, too, the reason for Cermak's death, not the gnomish Italian's stomach-ache?

The jury convicted Sergeant Lang, who said he'd "blow the lid off" Chicago politics and "wreck the Democratic Party" if he went to jail. Almost immediately, the judge granted him a new trial. He never was retried, but the police force dismissed him as "unfit." All very interesting.

But what part in this *Untouchables* script could Zangara play? Is it possible that irritated mafiosi had assigned him to kill Cermak? If so, why?

The only credible motives for Capone men's hiring Zangara would appear to be: Cermak was crowding them or Cermak was a genuine reformer. A police captain's recollection could apply to either. Cermak had told him, the officer said, "I need your help in shoving them out of town before the fair begins." Would that set off the Mob? If it did, is there any evidence that it would use Zangara and a .32 revolver from twenty-five feet amid a crowd and atop a chair?

Not likely. Indeed, almost nothing substantial supports the theory that Zangara killed Cermak at organized crime's behest. It is equally true that legitimate if peripheral questions fueled the suspicions and that America's propensity for sentimentalism perhaps forever confounded the case of Anton Cermak, Franklin Roosevelt and Giuseppe Zangara.

The assassin himself repeatedly said Roosevelt was his target, not the immigrant success Tony Cermak. The day he was executed, when he had nothing to lose, no retribution from alleged employers to fear, Zangara said of Cermak: "I wasn't shooting at him, but I'm not sorry I hit him."

Again and again, Zangara declared his intentions. The day he was brought to face his new sentence on the charge of murder, the defiant Zangara shouted to the court, "I'd kill any king or President," and that he didn't know of Cermak until after he was arrested. "But I want to kill Roosevelt!" he shouted. "I'm no scared about anything, because I'm sure I'm right!" On hearing sentence pronounced, he screamed at the judge, "You crook man, too." On this occasion, as from the beginning, the judge and lawyers and newsmen were astonished by Zangara's courage, his obstinate insistence that capitalism and his stomach, those alone, had brought on his attack. It seemed unbelievable (more recent assassinations evoke even higher-voltage skepticism).

Quite properly, Zangara had the last word on his beliefs. When he came to be executed, Giuseppe stated his expectations. Some were in his autobiography, which he handed to a death-room official. "There is no God," he said. "It's all below. . . . See, I no scared of electric chair." And Giuseppe marched over and sat in it. He glared around, the brown eyes full of contempt and behind them, the welcome for his release from pain. "Lousy capitalists," he cried again. "No pictures." That, at least, he had enjoyed. The notoriety, like Guiteau. Zangara had read all the newspaper stories, all the rumors and conjectures. Perhaps that made up for the long life of labor, of inferiority, of baffled dreams. "Goodbye. *Addio* to all the world," he said. Czolgosz would have cheered. "Go ahead. Push the button."

They did, in the execution cell of the Florida state prison at Raiford on March 20, 1933, at 9:15 A.M.—thirty-three days after the attack in Bayfront Park. Again, physicians examined the assassin's brain. They found Zangara's normal, if small. The fact may have comforted the sanity commission, whose report to Zangara's judges stated that while he had a "psychopathic personality," the verdict on his sanity rested with the court.

Zangara's body was unclaimed. He was buried in an unmarked grave in the prison graveyard. Presumably, he lies there still, along with the rumors that he was a hit man, or a terrorist, or anything except a maddened little man striking absurdly and at random against a world he could not abide. An assassin's death, of course, most often ends nothing. In Zangara's case, the effects—small and large—linger to this day. In the small category, a Mrs. Lillian Cross believed she had saved FDR's life by deflecting Giuseppe's arm, although the police said no one grabbed him until all five shots had been fired (to newsmen, Zangara said Mrs. Cross was right, but in private he said no, the police were).

A minor point, as well, is that although all accounts report five shots, if you count the bullet wounds in the five people, there may have been six —a fact first reported here with the hope that no "second gun" theorists will emerge with a grand conspiracy theory rather than accept the physical fact that bullets ricochet off things like cars, concrete and bones with a capriciousness matched only by eyewitness accounts.

In larger realms, it was revealed after the funeral hysterics and the first one hundred days of the New Deal that, in addition to patronage, Cermak discussed with Democratic National Chairman Jim Farley the income-tax-evasion charges the mayor heard he might face. Naturally, the largest legacies were political. Some Democratic politicians, for example, wondered at the rightness of the Twentieth Amendment, ratified shortly before Zangara's attack. It specified that if the President-elect died, the Presidency fell to the Vice President-elect (Roosevelt's Vice President was the undistinguished John Nance Garner from Texas, which may have been why the judge, in sentencing Zangara to death, said he did so because Roosevelt's death would have precipitated a catastrophe similar to that spawned by Sarajevo). There were, as usual, political murmurings about the Secret Service's thoroughness, since, as usual, the Secret Service announced two days after the incident that one "demented" man was responsible for it. Yet these political consequences were small compared with others.

In Congress, two laws were proposed. One would have authorized "investigation" of all those suspected of advocating the assassination of public officials (certainly, the Paterson-style anarchists, but also everybody else). The second—the Dies Law—would deport aliens or anyone who advocated overthrowing the Government. Though not passed as formulated, these proposals, born of Zangara, forecast the House Un-American Activities Committee and eventually the Red scare and McCarthyism.

Fittingly, perhaps, the grandest effect descended on the city of Chicago. With the death of Cermak, West Side bohunk power was broken. The pieces fell to Nash, Democratic county chairman and one of Cermak's faithful mayoral backers. Under Nash's prodding, the Democratic-controlled Illinois legislature passed an extraordinary bill authorizing the Chicago City Council, dominated by Nash-Cermak aldermen, to choose the new mayor (previously, a special election would have provided Cermak's successor). Nash selected an Irishman, Edward Kelly, for mayor. Thus was created the Kelly-Nash machine. It still reigns in Chicago. Almost Biblically, after Kelly came Martin Kennelly, and Kennelly begat Hizzoner himself, Richard Daley, and Daley begat John Kennedy, and . . . so the Irish won, after all, partly through the chance convergence of a Bohemian and an Italian immigrant. Perhaps that is a lesson of democracy. That and maybe, too, the demonstration, beginning with Guiteau and ending with Zangara, that Civil Service Commissions do not stop the business of patronage, any more than does punishment deter the murderous bent of those citizens, twisted or straight, who would protest, seek fame or allay their discomforts through assassination. Down in Louisiana was a mighty Senator who'd learn that next.

III

END OF THE KINGFISH

The spirit of violence is un-American.

—FRANKLIN D. ROOSEVELT, on hearing
of the shooting of Huey Long

*What did he want to shoot me for? . . . I
don't know him.*

—HUEY PIERCE LONG,
September 8, 1935

Moments before Giuseppe Zangara was electrocuted on March 20, 1933, for the seemingly capricious assassination of Anton Cermak, the diminutive anarchist shouted at his executioners, "All capitalists lousy bunch of crooks."

Of course, Zangara made clear before his death, the chief capitalist crook was Franklin Roosevelt, the crippled aristocrat he'd tried to kill but who'd escaped him to be inaugurated President just sixteen days before.

Less clear was how deep Zangara's cry lay in the Mesabi range of ironies underpinning American assassinations. Even Giuseppe might have been surprised to learn that his sentiments echoed those of the next prominent American politician to be assassinated—a man who ultimately posed as great a threat to Roosevelt as did the immigrant's five wild bullets.

The man was Huey Pierce Long, the "Kingfish." In March, 1933, he represented the sovereign state of Louisiana as its junior (soon to be senior) Senator, a title that belied his absolute power in that state and the growing national entrancement with his neopopulist demagoguery. Long's Zangaraesque remark came about March 3, a day before FDR's inauguration. The Kingfish burst into a Washington hotel room occupied by some of the incoming President's brain-trust advisers. He had come from a bitter Congressional dispute over a bank-reorganization bill (a bill too conservative for Long), grabbed an apple from a table, took a bite and, ramming his be-appled hand against an adviser's chest, announced, "I don't like you and your goddamned banker friends." Then the Kingfish and his bodyguards strode out, leaving a shaken advisory panel, including one Senator hiding in the bathroom.

Obviously, a battle had been joined. Long's contempt for the class represented by the new President, for the traditional power structure of the United States, for the delicate balancing of a Government's obligation to provide for its citizens—especially now, in Depression times—against its constitutional mandate to protect them from itself, threw down a challenge not ended until the Kingfish was himself the victim of an assassin. Only then, in September, 1935, was Long's threat to succeed Roosevelt stopped. Only then was his fearful, fascinating demonstration that unlimited power governed efficiently—and pleased the poor masses—removed from the national stage.

And only then did another irony become as clear as Zangara's death-room scream: we saw Long's killer had reversed the order set by the killings of Garfield and McKinley, even of the attempt on FDR. We could understand the frustration of the have-nots, those deprived of their share of the dream America offered. But this assassin—Dr. Carl Austin Weiss—was a member of an upper-middle-class establishment as foreign to Long's hard-bitten beginnings as were Roosevelt's to Zangara's.

Long and Weiss came together in the thirty-three-story marble Capitol of Louisiana, built by Huey Long as a monument to the progress of what indubitably was *his* state, out of lives so different they should, perhaps, each have had identifications (Hillbilly/Cityboy—Baptist/Catholic—Politician/Physician—Dictator/Fascist-fearer) stitched on their jackets. The aftermath of their encounter would for each man's survivors, and for historians, be vastly varied.

Huey Long was in the Capitol the night of September 8, 1935, doing what he was born to do—run things. "I was born into politics," he had once told the U.S. Senate, "a wedded man with a storm for a bride." Right now, it was Louisiana, but soon he thought it might be America. Long entered the corridor, where Dr. Weiss waited, from the House of Representatives chamber, an art-deco room forming the east wing of the Capitol. He'd been in the House prodding his compliant legislators to support the forty-two bills he was backing at this, the fourth special session of 1935.

Though he was a United States Senator who, technically, had no business on the floor of Louisiana's legislature, everyone acknowledged that Long ran things in the state's House and Senate. It was, people snickered, the "Longislature," and it was through its special sessions that he administered the state. He'd order a titular governor, his old friend and crony

Oscar Kelly Allen, to call a special session. Allen did as he was told (Long once reminded the aptly initialed O. K., "I made you and I kin break you"), and into Baton Rouge would come the legislators, only too glad during the Depression of the ten dollars per day, plus mileage, and the benevolent attention of the Kingfish. Once there, they'd be shown the bills Long's aides had prepared beforehand. Then they'd meet in solemn session to consider what Long wanted. Their deliberative method, once used only for emergencies but now the common legislative procedure, was simple and effective. The House met the first night. One member introduced all the bills, asking that the rules be suspended so that every proposed law could be referred to one committee. The speaker of the House, selected in accordance with Long's wishes, agreeably gaveled each bill to the Long-dominated Ways and Means Committee.

The night of September 8, the speaker was Allen J. Ellender, who would be elected United States Senator in 1936, taking Huey's seat, and who, in the fallout from the Kingfish's death, would proclaim, "If dictatorship in Louisiana, such as was charged to Huey Long, will give to the people of our nation what it gave to the people of my native state, then I am for such a dictatorship." Long agreed, incidentally, with Ellander on dictatorship. A few weeks before he'd told the Senate, "A man's not a dictator when he is given a commission from the people and carries it out." The people's commission obviously now was in order.

Last night the bills had been sent into Ways and Means, after a cursory reading that was fully reported in the Baton Rouge newspaper that had thumped this morning on Dr. Carl Austin Weiss's porch. Today they had been reported out, duly approved. Tonight they'd be read again. Tomorrow, the ninth, they would be read the third time, passed and sent to the Senate for that august body's scrutiny, which usually took about four hours. By midnight of the fourth day, Louisianians would have the new laws by which they would live for generations. Governor Allen would sign them without question (indeed, a story went that O.K. once signed a leaf that had blown through an open window onto his desk).

This special session featured some "must" bills. House Bill Number One was a gerrymander designed to deprive Benjamin Pavy of Opelousas of re-election. Pavy and his district attorney had for too many years opposed Long in their St. Landry and Evangeline parishes, and Huey was sick of it. It was rumored Huey might even "tar-brush" Pavy, saying the old jurist had Negro blood in him. Coming out of the House into that corridor which ran the width of the Capitol, past the governor's office and on to the Senate chamber, the Kingfish had no idea that the small man in the white linen suit halfway along was Judge Pavy's son-in-law. All he knew was that anywhere there was opposition, no matter how slight, he'd scotch it. He'd once put it this way: "Once disappointed over a political undertaking, I could never cast it from my mind."

Another bill proved that. For over a year the Senator had been directing a drive to humble completely and finally his last potent political rivals, those in New Orleans, the cussed city where what remained of anti-Long power lay. He'd just about done it. He'd brought the city to heel financially, for instance, and this bill was allied with that. It specified that the state pay the salaries of the city attorney of New Orleans and his assistants, a clever and foolproof way of insuring control over the offices, over that incestuous group of Frenchified snobs who'd never done a damn thing for the poor folks in all those years *they'd* controlled the state.

Two other bills suggested Huey Long's larger visions of September, 1935. One would move Louisiana's primaries up from September, 1936, to the preceding January. Since the Democratic primary *was* the election, a pro forma victory in January would assure Long an office, simultaneously freeing him to campaign for another job during the rest of 1936—like maybe the one in the Oval Office. The second measure was also simple enough on its face, but behind it were serpentine ambitions and fears. It provided for a mandatory fine and a jail sentence for any person exercising any power that violated Louisiana's rights as reserved to the states under the Tenth Amendment to the Constitution (which states: "The powers not delegated to the United States by the Constitution, nor prohibited by it to the States, are reserved to the States respectively, or to the people"). With considerable justification, Huey said his law merely defended the sanctity of states' rights. But he and his knew it was also intended to prevent Federal patronage from going to his political enemies, those Rooseveltites who were trying to weaken his hold on the people. Huey was giving them hell. Naturally, folks in "Loozyana" as Long called it, whooped it up when Huey hided those New Dealers in Washington. They'd had *their* New Deal since 1928 when Long was elected Governor. They applauded when Huey called James Farley "the Nabob of New York," and dubbed Harold Ickes "the chinch bug of Chicago." Ickes had replied that Huey had "halitosis of the intellect," but that hadn't stopped Huey Long. He'd told Ickes to go "slam-bang to hell." Folks remembered, too, that in March, a week before Zangara's execution, Huey had said, "Hoover is a hoot owl and Roosevelt is a scrootch owl. A hoot owl bangs into the nest and knocks the hen clean off and catches her while she's falling. But a scrootch owl slips into the roost and scrootches up to the hen and talks softly to her. And the hen just falls in love with him, and the next thing you know there ain't no hen." Yessir, this law would keep them out of Louisiana affairs, unless it was declared unconstitutional, and that would take a while. For the present it was as Huey had once said: "I am the Constitution just now."

Altogether then, the bills on the agenda summed up Long's concerns under one rubric: power. The Senator intended to keep his, to consolidate it locally and state-wide and to achieve it nationally. As a master politician, the Kingfish understood Roosevelt's plight. Long's "Share Our Wealth" proposals and societies, which urged redistribution of the nation's money, were more alluring to many of the Depression-weary than the more conservative New Deal programs. His irreverence, his country-preacher oratory may have been derided in the Senate cloakroom, but they stirred the poor, and there were lots of them just then. More critically, Long could point to genuine accomplishments in Louisiana, and he often did. Roosevelt would have to move leftward, toward him, he figured, in the coming 1936 election campaign, but it might not be enough. Huey just might be able to defeat Roosevelt. Already several big corporations, sick of the price-setting National Recovery Act and other New Deal measures, had secretly pledged campaign funds to Huey. But defeating FDR this time was unlikely. More probably, Long could with a third party siphon off enough liberal and disgruntled voters to throw the election to a Republican, who wouldn't know how to run things, either. Then Huey, for sure, could beat the ineffective GOP in 1940, since the country would be crying for a strong, radical candidate. Thus reasoned Huey and his followers (while, in Washington, Farley was telling FDR what he already knew—that Long couldn't be disregarded nationally, that he might have the "balance of power," that Huey "might spell disaster," since a secret poll showed that he could get three or four million votes at that time). Against that potential political energy, the machinations of Ickes, even the income-tax investigations of Long's closest aides by Henry Morgenthau's Treasury agents, the same ones who'd put Capone away, might well be powerless (Long himself, that morning of September 8, had wrestled with his overdue tax return—he was sure it would be audited). It seemed on that warm Sunday evening as if nothing could impede the Kingfish, at least in Louisiana. Nothing except the slight figure of Weiss in the corridor.

Huey stalked out of the House in his curious heel-pounding gait, as if he were hopping rails. His phalanx of bodyguards got in one another's way, too, since Huey rushed here and there, cajoling, ordering, securing votes, altogether the successful salesman of salvation out on his rounds, while his protectors, sometimes as many as twenty-five during special sessions, lurched to and fro in his wake. These guards—two, particularly, Murphy Roden and Elliott Coleman—had reason to be vigilant. In their heads, doubtless in Long's, too, were the premonitions that had surrounded the Kingfish ever since he'd come to power in 1928, a fear of assassination ever more persistent as rumors and actualities of plots reached the Senator (who was, his brother Earl said, a terrible coward). Just the day before— Huey's men were later to claim—a telephoned warning had come. Thus the clearing of the House galleries, the extra state police on guard, the additional members of the State Bureau of Criminal Investigation and Identification (which was, everyone knew, Huey's secret police—"Cossacks," as his intimidated enemies called them, or "Huey's skull crackers," as his brother Julius named them). No public official in America, not even "Prince Franklin," was better protected. "Sure, I carry a gun," Huey said once, joking. "Sometimes I carry four. Can't tell when somebody's going to shoot the king."

Again, Long was right. Coming west down the corridor from the House, passing some of the thirty kinds of marble he'd specified for the Capitol, he headed for an appointment with the doctor. He'd left Ellender, the other legislators and favor seekers in the house, and now he was windmilling his way to the governor's office, eighty feet away down the corridor connecting House and Senate. His bodyguards were beside and behind him as he rushed past the private elevator that ran to his twenty-fourth-floor suite, to barge through the double doors of the governor's office. His main corps of bodyguards—Roden, Coleman, Joe Messina, Paul Voitier, Louis Heard—halted to wait outside, along with a Longite state supreme court justice who wanted the Kingfish's counsel on political matters. The group stood in the center of the corridor, on a circular design facing the governor's doors, where the corridor widened slightly for aesthetic effect and where recessed marble pillars broke the wall's straight line and flanked a bust of Robert de La Salle, the explorer who had named the state in honor of his patron, King Louis XIV. In a few seconds, Huey bustled out of the governor's anteroom, calling over his shoulder to "get the boys out early in the morning" for the vote, his eyes "popping like saucers." He moved toward his guards and friends, and from beside one of the pillars Weiss came forward, a small figure in white, his eyes circled by dark-rimmed glasses and in his hand (almost everyone agreed later) a small black automatic. Then:

The doctor glides through the guards up to Long, he may say something, his hand raises, Huey blinks, the bodyguards swivel white-eyed to Weiss, the supreme court justice moves his hand, which holds a panama hat, in a fending gesture, and there is a shot, then (some say) another, then a bloody spot on the Senator's shirt six inches above and to the right of his belt buckle, and Long's eyes roll, he emits a scalding groan and runs, "like a wild deer," away from the doctor and the sound of a scuffle, away west toward the Senate. Hardly anyone sees him go, so much is happening.

Roden is down, the doctor on top of him, as Roden strains for Weiss's gun. Coleman, a few yards away, aims and shoots; the bullet grazes Roden, who's scrambling to his feet. Another shot from Coleman. Weiss, now crouched, shudders, begins his slow-motion fall; the little automatic skitters across the circular design. Now guns are in every guard's hand. Roden and others fire blindly and repeatedly, emptying their pistols into Weiss. The body jerks, palpitates, as bullets ricochet in the corridor, which is filled now with screams, with people ducking, flattening against walls, with state patrolmen galloping to the scene with submachine guns, with newspaper reporters hurrying to find out what's happening. Is it the firecrackers that often mark Louisiana legislative sessions? Or what? After maybe thirty seconds, the shooting ceases. Weiss's body, wounded sixty times, at last is left alone to pump blood onto the marble floor.

In April of that year, one of the few surviving anti-Long legislators, Mason Spencer, had addressed the legislature on a special-session bill that gave the state sole control of all local elections. Spencer had said, "When this ugly thing is boiled down in its own juices, it disfranchises the white people of Louisiana. I am not gifted with second sight, nor did I see a spot of blood on the moon last night, but I can see blood on the polished marble of this Capitol; for if you ride this thing through, you will travel with the white horse of death." It had seemed another bootless threat then, or perhaps a rodomontade in the Southern tradition, but now the marble floor was bloody and we were again forced to ask: What is it this time? What moves one of us to assassination? Is this a representative act attributable to an intolerable political situation, or what? To ask, too, just who is Dr. Carl Austin Weiss, and what were his motives, and have we been told the truth about the assassination of Huey Long? Was Weiss crazy and acting alone or the cool agent of a plot? If a plot, whose and why? Many asked whether Weiss, in fact, did mortally wound Long, or whether the Kingfish died because in the panic a stray shot from a bodyguard gaffed him. Who *was* Huey Long, for that matter, that he should be so endangered? Savior or home-grown Hitler?

The questions ricochet farther than the shots in the corridor, where, for now, the frame is frozen in the climactic scene of *All the King's Men* (the adulatory book written afterward by Robert Penn Warren, a young English instructor at nearby Louisiana State University, or "my university," as Long called it). Weiss lies dead as bystanders mutter, bodyguards curse and identification is made. Long, in flight down a stairway, is found and taken to the hospital for treatment. Oddly, he has a cut lip, which will raise many more questions. There will be an operation under less than ideal circumstances and a deathwatch reminiscent of those for McKinley and Cermak, and then Long will die, saying, "God, don't let me die. I have so much to do," and be buried in front of his Capitol ("Huey's silo," brother Earl called it) with unprecedented pomp. Political legacies will be won, lost, saved and squandered in interesting ways that take us to today, as Long's son Russell serves in the U.S. Senate. People, various as politics itself, will use Long's death and Weiss's to their own ends. Hundreds of thousands of campaign dollars will disappear. The political factionalism that may, finally, have caused Long's death will worsen in Louisiana. Nationally, with a populist threat removed, Roosevelt will win three more terms, an ambition that Long's posthumous book, *My First Days in the White House*, implies was an honor in store for the Kingfish. And the questions will have partial answers, at least. They begin now, with the figures tableaued in the corridor, in the lives of Long and Weiss, where lie the first clues to the meaning of their deaths.

Huey Long was older than Carl Weiss by twelve years. He was born August 30, 1893, in the hard-shell Baptist, red-clay, red-necked parish of Winn in north-central Louisiana—as far emotionally as geographically from the lusty, luxuriant Creole culture of New Orleans. One commentator said of Winn parish, "Its harvests were scrawny. What cattle it had were scrawnier; its people were scrawniest." Far, indeed, from New Orleans, and muddy with envy the whole way. Winn imbued Huey with its flavor. The parish hadn't entirely embraced the Southern cause in the Civil War. Many of its subsistence-level farmers, the fabled yeoman agrarians, figured they were slaves, too, and so wouldn't fight to keep slavery as an institution. The attitude persisted. Huey Long, Sr. once asked his son Huey, the seventh of his nine surviving children, "Didn't Abe Lincoln free the niggers and not give the planters a dime? Why shouldn't the white slaves be freed?" During Huey's childhood, one of his homeland's political heroes was the Populist William Jennings Bryan ("The Great Commoner," who ran against the soon-to-be-assassinated President McKinley and who in one of his campaign speeches created the phrase Long adopted for his populism—"Every man a king, but no man wears a crown"). Not surprisingly, Winn parish went socialist in 1908 after Eugene Debs spoke there.

Though he liked, as much as any politician, to boast that he was born in a log cabin, Huey's birthplace was actually a comfortable six-room farmhouse, albeit built of logs. In fact, the Longs after 1900 were relatively prosperous people for a time, despite the Populist leanings of Huey Long, Sr. The father of the future Kingfish farmed 320 acres, sold some other land to the railroad, some more to home builders serving the growing town of Winnfield, and by 1907 had one of the most impressive homes around Winnfield, the parish seat where Huey was raised. Old Hu also valued education and eventually all his children got some college. The household demanded twice-a-week church attendance, complete with evangelical preaching, and the Longs encouraged reading. Huey learned the Bible nearly by heart (a passage in Leviticus became his favorite—it stressed sharing wealth) and read Hugo and Shakespeare—a bonus of working for a book salesman as a teenager (later he'd be fond of Plutarch's *Forty-Six Immortals* and other histories of great men who shaped events). Unfortunately for Huey's ambitions for college, the extra money for that ran out before it got to him, and he went to work early. He retained an admiration for the trappings of higher education, though. When he had the power, he quadrupled the size of Louisiana State University, built athletic facilities, financed trips for students to see the LSU football games (he helped organize the Sugar Bowl), composed fight songs, and sometimes high-stepped at the head of the marching band with the indulgence of his hand-picked bandmaster, Castro Carazo, who'd been plucked from leading the orchestra at New Orleans' Roosevelt Hotel, where Long loved to dance. Long also endowed scholarships with the help of LSU's president, J. M. "Jingle Money" Smith, whom Huey had selected and who later went to prison for using university money to speculate in wheat. The Kingfish's last public address, three days before Weiss met him, announced one thousand "practically free" college educations for Louisianians. He didn't need to add that the recipients might look to their political allegiances—most folks knew Long used everything politically, carrot-and-sticking his way onward and upward.

At first, however, it didn't seem as if Long were going far, unless it was far from home, from which he ran away when he was ten. He may have been fleeing the tedious farm work. But he returned to live up to his ginger-colored hair and bumptious manner with a rowdy boyhood that included auctioneering (he hated farm sales, he claimed later, because they usually meant a man had lost everything), working as a printer's devil, book peddling and an occasional fistfight (Earl Long recalled he'd once pitched in to help Huey, only to have Huey run off, leaving Earl to carry on alone). He was known by neighbors such as O. K. Allen as quick-witted, slick (abiding only by those rules he liked) and fast-talking. Really, he was most interested in talking with people, selling them an idea or a program. While in high school, he once, on a bet, sold an elderly Negro a nonexistent secondhand coffin, so the old man would be prepared for death. Naturally, he was a debater in school. He autographed his textbooks "Hon. Huey P. Long," plainly marking his goal, and also ran the mile, a combination ideal for politics. His last year, he won a debating scholarship to LSU, but there just wasn't enough money. Long did the next best thing: became a traveling salesman. That was in 1910.

Carl Austin Weiss was five that year. He lived in New Orleans, though he'd been born in Baton Rouge on December 18, 1905. Carl's father was a physician, doing some postdoctoral work at Tulane and practicing as an eye, ear, nose and throat man. While Long was on the road as a drummer, the elder Weiss (Dr. Carl Adam Weiss) moved back to Baton Rouge and began a large, prestigious practice (Long once stormed in with a speck in his eye that Weiss removed—it was the only time Huey and the accused assassin's father met). Little Carl was the opposite of Long. He was small-framed, dark, long-nosed and wore glasses. He was raised as a devout Catholic, the religion of southern Louisiana (a state that, in its religious and ethical divisions, resembles the two Irelands). Carl was introverted as a child, a lover of books and music and a fine student—as obedient and kind as a Boy Scout should be. He possessed a biting temper, but unleashed it only occasionally. For the rest, as a teacher phrased it, "It was as if he had discovered a secret zone of calm in which he moved serenely." Or, as others had it, Carl was a serious, self-controlled boy, high-strung and under tension of his own making. Perhaps that's why he turned to mechanics in his youth. Figuring out how things worked separated him from people and lent him tranquil objectivity. He built a radio. He learned about electricity. He was fascinated by guns, was first in his neighborhood to get a .22 rifle and later had pistols. He didn't hunt much, not like his father. He preferred disassembling the guns, putting them back together or shooting at targets. Weiss graduated at fifteen as valedictorian from a Catholic high school and entered LSU in 1921.

That was a good year for Long. He was twenty-eight, a lawyer, an elected state official on the Railroad Commission (the future Public Service Commission), a cantankerous foe of large corporations who was reaping political benefits from that liberal stance. Not bad, really, looking back, and the best was yet to come. He'd thrown himself into salesmanship, and he saw that it paid. He'd peddled Cottolene, for example, a cooking oil. Stomping through the red-dirt country, raising its dust on the unpaved roads (he'd see to *that* when he was governor), he sold Cottolene with precept and persuasion. "Stop usin' that hog lard," he'd command the country women and quote a Biblical injunction against Israelites' eating swine. 'Course, they weren't Jewish, but Huey learned early it wasn't always how logical you said it, it was how well. And they'd buy. If they were a little sticky, he would bustle into the kitchen and mess up supper for them. He stayed with farmers overnight, always paid them a dollar, later wrote them about crops, weather, politics (he admired the style of Theodore Bilbo, the rising Mississippi demagogue). They remembered him. Cottolene really greased Huey's way. He met his future wife through it, at a cake-baking contest in Shreveport (where he also tried to finish high school). And he got fired from it for breaking expense-account rules.

No matter. Long could sell anything. He sold produce for a spell in Oklahoma, attended its university's law school for two semesters. Then in Texas, Arkansas, Tennessee, he peddled starch (and got fired), then patent medicine. He got married in 1913 to Rose McConnell, the cake contest winner. By 1914, however, Long was finished with the drummer's trade. At his brother Julius' urging, he'd be a lawyer. At his own, a politician. Huey and his bride went to New Orleans. In eight frantic months, his prodigious memory stored enough law to pass a special exam of the state examining committee and he was admitted to the bar of Louisiana. He was a shrewd lawyer, as his later career showed (Chief Justice William Howard Taft called him one of the most able men ever to argue a case before the U.S. Supreme Court). And he could use the law to his advantage, as he did during World War I, claiming that as a notary public he was a state official and, hence, exempt from service. Besides, he said, "I ain't mad at anybody over there."

Long went to Winnfield to practice. He had all the business he could handle. He eventually prospered, got good fees, bought land and securities. Oil was big then, flowing out of the poor countryside to redeem the "flop hats' " blasted lives. Huey and O. K. Allen and partners established oil companies, sold thousands of dollars of stock, only to have the Standard Oil Company break them by refusing to buy their low-grade oil, instead offering only to pipe it at unacceptable rates. Huey wouldn't forget that. He and Rockefeller's gigantic subsidiary would remain blood enemies. Six months before he was assassinated, he would charge that the company had hired men to try to kill him. For now, he knew the only way to defeat the huge companies and the New Orleans oligarchs was electorally. Searching the state statutes, he found that the Railroad Commission had no age requirement for office. He ran hard. He toured every hamlet and county seat. Like Bilbo, he dressed in white-linen suits, adopting the dress but not the manner of those he attacked. He recited the Bible, told stories, swapped gossip, woke folks up at night to give them his spiel. They liked this spindly red-haired fellow with the cleft chin and pouchy cheeks, liked the rubbery good nature of his face that vanished when he was riled against the robber barons. Then he'd skin 'em proper, arms windmilling, the country oratory spilling out.

Long was elected in 1918 by 635 votes. Not overwhelming, but enough. He moved to Shreveport, devoted more time to politics. As a Public Service Commissioner, he declared a tax war on big corporations. He blocked railroad mergers, opposed telephone rate increases and got refunds for the companies' customers, lowered fares on intrastate railroads. He convinced the commission to levy a 3 percent severance tax on Standard Oil. In 1920, Long backed John Parker, a "gentleman liberal," for governor, but when the dignified gentleman wouldn't go all out after Standard, Huey slandered him, saying, among other things, that a polecat couldn't stay in the same room with him. Convicted of slander and fined one dollar, Huey refused to pay, so the friendly judge passed the hat in the courtroom.

In 1921, when Weiss entered LSU, Long became chairman of the Public Service Commission. One of his first acts was to have Standard Oil's pipes declared a public carrier, like a bus line, and hence subject to regulation. Now anybody's oil could be carried through them. For the next few years, Long built his political constituency (and a big house) and gathered money for a try at the governorship—some said "extorted" from "interests" like those he attacked; to wit, the Southwestern Gas and Electric Company. But then, such was politics.

In 1924, Long stumped the state in the Democratic primary against a Southern French Catholic, who was the lieutenant governor, and a Baton Rouge Protestant, who managed the state penitentiary. Long campaigned for free textbooks for all schoolchildren, free bridges and good roads to let people move about. He called for a renewed tax war on Standard Oil, the "octopus" that epitomized Louisiana's victimization by the New Orleans "ring" faction, the big corporations, the fat cats and the plantation barons. To them, Long seemed no threat, since he was always out there somewhere in the scrub country, a long way from Antoine's. The Old Regulars' ring dictated Louisiana politics, and against it, Huey's appeals looked impotent. Furthermore, Long appeared to waffle on the issue of the Ku

Klux Klan, then busily murdering blacks. The Catholic candidate opposed the hooded bigots, as did the penal officer, at least nominally. But Long, a native of the northern Klan country and beneficiary of funds from known Kluxers, was suspected of being a closet Klansman (much as Harry Truman later was accused), especially since he denounced the law banning masks at all but Mardi Gras events. He retorted that the law extended the government's power too much.

In any event, Huey missed the runoff by ten thousand votes because he had no support in the southern parishes. Yet his day would come. "Someday our people will call the roll again," he prophesied.

Weiss graduated from Tulane Medical College in 1927, the year before Long's people elected him governor. He had switched in 1925 from engineering to medicine. That pleased his father, as did his emergence from introversion. Young Carl made friends, played in a band (he shared a love of music with Long) and was well liked. The year Long was elected governor, Weiss was learning his specialty—ear, nose and throat—during a residency in New Orleans. Late that year, in 1928, the young doctor was on his way to Vienna and Paris for postdoctoral work. He liked Vienna, despite the Fascist rallies, the more because he spoke German, learned from his grandfather. When his studies there were over, Weiss traveled in Germany and Italy. He heard about Hitler's threat, saw Mussolini's transformation of the cradle of the Renaissance into the armory of the Mediterranean. Of Mussolini, Weiss said: "This little Caesar will get his due someday."

In April, 1929, Carl was to be in Paris, taking up a prestigious appointment at the American Hospital. Just then, his new governor was escaping an impeachment conviction by the Louisiana Senate—barely escaping, at that, via a canny blend of intimidation and polite bribery. But Carl didn't get to Paris until June, and by then Long was winging free, transforming the political and physical landscape of Louisiana—the first by distributing spoils, the second by building the roads, bridges and schools he'd promised.

Sometime that year, Weiss visited Belgium's Fabrique Nationale d'Armes de Guerre. He bought an automatic pistol, a .32-caliber built on Browning patents, and added it to his collection. In 1930, he returned home for a visit. The family brought him up to date on things in Louisiana. His brother recalled that he didn't express any strong political philosophy, "just right and wrong. And that was it." That summer, Carl was in New York, to begin yet another residency, this one at the famed Bellevue Hospital. In New Orleans, a colorful governor, soon to be Senator, was telling some rambunctious advisers, "Shut up, you sons of bitches, shut up! This is the Kingfish talking!" Even the sober Weiss might have laughed at that. After all, almost everybody listened to *Amos 'n' Andy,* and while Carl was known as a perfectionist, insisting that everything be done right, he wasn't humorless. He'd opine on Long, too, but he wasn't fanatical about the Kingfish of the lodge. Rather, medicine obsessed him. When he returned to Baton Rouge in 1932, his colleagues thought him destined for greatness. And, in truth, everything inclined favorably. His practice started well. In November, 1932, he met Louise Yvonne Pavy, daughter of a judge in St. Landry parish, then studying for a master's degree in French at LSU. Carl was surprised to learn she'd been in Paris when he had, on a fellowship at the Sorbonne. She'd dated interns from the same hospital. They had so much in common—education, religion, politics—and she was beautiful. They were married December 27, 1933, in Opelousas, her home town, at the local Catholic church. Their son, Carl Austin Weiss, Jr., was born June 7, 1935, three months before the death of Long.

Long had achieved quite a bit, too. From his election as governor in 1928, Huey's put-on bumpkinisms, his courtship of what H. L. Mencken called the booboisie, won him the right to speak for the "forgotten man." Huey made good his promises, too, in the most conspicuous ways possible. By 1935 his administration and his-via-Allen's had increased the miles of concrete road tenfold, of asphalt fivefold, of gravel twofold, and built forty major bridges. Long's suppliers were paid two dollars a ton for gravel when the going rate was 67 cents, but as Huey said, "We got the roads in Louisiana, haven't we? In some states they only have the graft." It was also true that roads stopped at the borders of parishes unfriendly to him. The Long administration gave free textbooks to all the state's schoolchildren (winning a Supreme Court verdict that this did not violate the separation of church and state), and in time it eliminated the poll tax, gave tax exemptions to poor households, passed in the depths of the Depression a debt-moratorium act and levied taxes on large incomes, on corporations, on utilities, on the once-sacred totems of the establishment (Huey did, though, faithfully support the Democratic Party until 1934, even delivering Louisiana to Al Smith in 1928).

Before all that could be accomplished, however, Long's policies had led to impeachment proceedings in 1929 when an alliance of political enemies mounted its most effective challenge to his transformation of Louisiana into his personal fiefdom via patronage, "specially negotiated" contracts, and state boards and commissions of this and that which by 1935 controlled nearly every state job, even schoolteachers (like Weiss's sister-in-law, who was fired in 1935). Frightened by what seemed a fascistic power lust, the Old Regulars and others brought impeachment charges, including attempted murder (supposedly asking a former bodyguard to kill a political foe), bribery, misappropriation of funds, intimidation of officials and the press, cavorting with the Sodom and Gomorrah ilk of New Orleans (specifically, a topless dancer) and general conduct unbecoming a governor. The charges, along with a malfunctioning electronic vote register that adjourned the session, ignited a riot in the Louisiana House, complete with ripped clothes, brass knuckles, knocked heads and legislators rushing the podium to say, Hell, yes, let's stay and impeach the bastard. They did, on nineteen counts (an index of the bitterness engendered: Earl Long bit an opponent on the ear in a related slander of his brother). But Long forestalled conviction by persuading fifteen Senators to sign the infamous round robin—a document that said they thought the charges voted by the House were illegal and they would not vote to convict. The charges were abandoned. The robineers soon were highly rewarded. Huey dealt in lawmakers "like you'd buy a sack of potatoes." He maintained he had been a victim of the old politics, that he had to "fight fire with fire . . . I may not live long enough to do everything I want to do." Affirming this in a eulogy delivered in the Senate after Huey's death, Louisiana's surviving Senator, John Overton, a Long creation, opined that Long's politics were from the start necessitated by the unscrupulous nature of his opponents. That may have been true, as suggested by a meeting of anti-Long men called to order with "This meeting is called for the purpose of discussing ways and means of killing Huey Long." What is certain is that Long, once free of impeachment, never let the opposition up again (in later years, he carried a "son-of-a-bitch" book, like Nixon's "enemies list").

In 1930, while Weiss traveled in Europe, Long decided he wanted to be a U.S. Senator. Maybe more, in time, since that February he told the visiting Calvin Coolidge that he'd had to tear down the old mansion on becoming governor, it was such a wreck, and he sure hoped he wouldn't have to do that to the White House. He guessed Senator would do for a start. With his oratory and invective ("Old Feather Duster" Ransdell, he called the incumbent) and swelling support for his soak-the-rich policies, that was easy. Long then decided he wouldn't take his Senator's oath until he could leave Louisiana in good, safe hands; namely, O. K. Allen's. So, for two years, he didn't venture out of the state. When the lieutenant governor, a former Long ally now defected, tried to take over, claiming Huey was no longer governor, the Kingfish sent militia to the Capitol and prevented the accession. He appointed the president pro tem of the Louisiana

Senate as his lieutenant governor and waited until 1932 to be sworn in and serve in Washington, after Allen's election was assured by the Long organization. No trouble that, since the machine was well financed. Huey had about 10 percent of all his state employees' salaries deducted for his war chest and put in the fabled "deduct" safe-deposit box, later to be a mysterious element after his murder. They also subscribed to his newspaper, the *Louisiana Progress* (later, in line with Long's ambitions, the *American Progress*), formed in 1930 to combat the increasingly critical urban press. Huey's business friends advertised so loyally that its pages carried more ads than the *Saturday Evening Post.* Huey didn't disguise his contempt for the Louisiana and national publications that, looking to Europe, wondered if the Bayou State might not be growing its own fascist hybrid. He once tried to impose a "two cents a lie" tax on their advertising revenues, but the bill was declared unconstitutional. The Kingfish snorted, "When I lie from the stump, I lie big, because no matter what the newspapers say, 90 percent of the people will believe *me.*"

True, and in 1932, Long's wishes elected Overton as Louisiana's other Senator (Senator-making was in Long's line—his speeches elected Arkansas's Hattie Caraway). The Long opposition cried foul, saying Overton's election was fraudulent. For instance, anti-Long members of the Louisiana congressional delegation pointed out, in St. Bernard parish, where there were only 2,500 white people over twenty years old (Negroes were still disenfranchised, not yet freed by Long's removal of the poll tax), some 3,189 votes were cast and Overton got 3,176. The Senate in February, 1933, ordered a subcommittee investigation in New Orleans. The Senate's agents broadened the probe to include Long. Huey and his organization's treasurer, Seymour Weiss (no kin to Carl), retaliated by treating the investigation as a circus so as to defeat the obvious FDR-inspired attack on Long. The hilarity broke down when the committee's investigators declared that Weiss and the Kingfish had gotten illegal money from Wall Street interests for stock purchases, and when brothers Earl and Julius testified that Huey had gotten campaign-box cash from "the interests" in "rolls so big they made his pockets bulge out and spoiled the fit" (of his pajamas, that is—Huey loved conducting business in his bedroom and once insulted a junketing German consul by receiving him in green pajamas, red-and-blue robe and blue slippers, looking "like an explosion in a paint factory").

The family rift seemed not to bother Huey, who was curiously distant from human affairs such as his marriage and children. Too much the politician, one supposes, although he did say in sorrow of Earl, "I cannot attack my own blood." The breach was not entirely walled until Huey lay on his deathbed, although Earl later served two full terms as governor at the behest of Longites, and though Senator Russell Long, the Kingfish's largest fry, remembers his father fondly. In the end, Huey's rhetoric of outraged innocence—"Only stupid politicians take bribes"—(and one of his famous circulars calling the hearings a kangaroo court) prevailed. The crooked-election charges were shelved and Overton sat beside Long in the Senate. But the feud with FDR, whom Long had supported vociferously in the 1932 election by campaigning in several states, was full-blown now—despite Huey's periodic visits with Roosevelt and subsequent declarations that "Frank is all wool and a yard wide." The President, unflattered, wrote to a friend that these Depression times were not normal, the people were "jumpy and ready to run after strange gods."

In August, 1933, the strange god named Long suffered an incident that tilted his halo, and on his birthday eve, too. At the Sands Point Bath Club on Long Island, the Kingfish, after considerable imbibing and ingesting, emerged from the men's room with a blackened, cut eye. Asked what had happened, Huey said a bunch of "J. P. Morgan's gang" had mugged him, presumably because he offended Wall Street interests. Immediately, other stories bloomed. One had it that Long had stood behind a man at the trough and tried to urinate between his legs, and had got slugged for it. That seemed unlikely, even for Huey. A lady companion said she thought he'd just let it swing too much and splattered the shoes of a fellow diner. Hence, the black eye. Whatever, the press had fun. One national magazine collected funds to award a medal to the man, whoever he was, who'd assaulted Long. But Huey didn't mind such publicity. Folks believed him, and two months later, his autobiography, as dictated to the editor of the *Progress,* came out, wrapped in a gold cover featuring a picture of the new $5,000,000 Capitol and the Kingfish himself, published by the National Book Company—a Long enterprise formed for the purpose. Friends and foes alike knew the book tokened an advance of his political front. The next events hastened it and strengthened the hatred, the grudging respect, the love of Huey Long.

Early in 1934, Long unveiled on a national radio broadcast his "Share Our Wealth" program, a neopopulist proposal that couldn't help but appeal to the depressed masses and embarrass FDR to boot. Essentially, it was an expansion of a bill he'd sponsored two years earlier in the Senate that had called for limiting per-family fortunes to $5,000,000. The bill had been defeated, but the Kingfish hadn't quit. He'd cherished the idea of sharing wealth since his young days in Winnfield, when a state senator had told him 72 percent of the nation's wealth was held by 2 percent of its people. Huey used that fact in figuring in 1935 that there ought to be enough for everyone to have a guaranteed $5,000 homestead (i.e., "enough for a home, an automobile, a radio and the ordinary conveniences"), plus a guaranteed annual income of $2,000–$3,000, an adequate old-age pension, college educations for qualified children and generous bonuses for veterans. The money would come from levies limiting any one family's earnings to $1,000,000 per year and from capital taxes on fortunes larger than $5,000,000.

Understandably, the mass response was favorable. Especially so since part of Long's plan was the formation of local "Share Our Wealth" societies, which amounted to pro-Long political clubs. Their organizer (who, by Huey's death, claimed seven million members) was the Reverend Gerald L. K. Smith, a revivalist preacher whose oratory surpassed even Long's in impressing boobs (at least so wrote Mencken) and who loved Long, money and power, in interchangeable order. Smith, bereft of his leader after 1935, became vehemently anti-Semitic and pro-Fascist before World War II cooled that ardor—in peacetime, he founded the Christ of the Ozarks tourist area in Eureka Springs, Arkansas, where before his recent death he presided over a sixty-five-foot statue of Christ, with follow-you eyes, along with other inspirational doodads.

The clubs, the proposal itself, worried Farley and other New Dealers. Critics assailed the economics of the Kingfish's proposal. One calculated that, what with the decline in riches caused by the Depression, Huey would have to confiscate all property, all assets liquid and otherwise, over $50,000 in order to provide the $5,000 homestead to the number of families with less than that. Such carping prevailed little, though. While the New Orleans faction worried over Long's pressure on it, and while liberals wondered how to get rid of Huey, the Kingfish's appeal grew. His enemies muttered that they had to make a move soon.

The year before his death brought Long myriad threats, aggravating his "deadly fear of assassination," as one man called it. He surrounded himself with personal bodyguards, state police, agents of his Bureau of Criminal Investigation and Identification, even the militia on occasions when violence seemed particularly likely. Soon there were more of those. Long's opponents managed to win two elections for Congress. In one, rebellious officials armed themselves and manned the parish bridges to prevent militiamen from going in with ballots marked only with the name of Long's candidate. Hodding Carter, later to win a Pulitzer Prize as the radically moderate editor of the Greenville, Mississippi, *Delta Democrat-*

Times, then was editing the Hammond, Louisiana, paper. Carter wrote: "If ever there was a need for shotgun government, that time is now." Such was the mood as Long's opponents, themselves often intimidated and harassed, huddled to discuss the Kingfish.

Another armed confrontation took place in New Orleans. Longites had at last subdued the city's anti-Huey mayor, "Turkeyhead" Walmsley, and now had New Orleans by its purse strings. Special legislative sessions put the city's employees under state "civil service" control. Other bills impounded the Federal funds—FDR's patronage—intended for Long's political opposition and to keep the city afloat. Those opponents, heartened by the Congressional victories, had in April challenged Huey in the state legislature. These bills routed them, and now Long's men, with militia in reserve, were in New Orleans to enforce the state's new laws. Walmsley's "special deputies" confronted them and a shooting war seemed inevitable. But Huey urged negotiations, reminding the New Orleans Old Regulars they were sure losers. The opposition capitulated and all Louisiana was Long's at the end of that year.

Late in December, 1934, while Weiss was performing tonsillectomies, Long's legislature operated on Standard Oil. At Long and Allen's request, a bill was passed taxing Standard five cents per barrel on refined oil. It was whispered that might be negotiated if Standard refined more Louisiana oil, say 80 percent—a compromise potentially profitable to Longites both politically and economically. While Standard pondered that, events took over. The oil firm fired nine hundred men (before the effective date of another new law that stipulated mandatory pensions) and distressed Huey. Next, a group of Standard employees and other anti-Long gentlemen met in Baton Rouge to protest the new tax. They formed the Square Deal Association, a frankly paramilitary group dedicated to overthrowing Long. As president they chose Ernest Bourgeois, whose name fit—he was a young electrical engineer and strikebreaker for Standard Oil. Assisting Bourgeois was James Mehaffey, an itinerant rabble rouser, who shouted, "You ought to hang every legislator, commencing with your governor." True to that sentiment, the Square Dealers armed themselves and demanded that Governor Allen call a special session to repeal the "demagogue-dictator" laws. Anti-Long forces throughout the state quickly formed Square Deal groups (eventually seventy thousand strong), but Huey said, "They're too lazy to march." The Senator-Governor protected himself, though. New Long appointees authorized by the legislature seized control of the hostile Baton Rouge constabulary and arrested a Square Dealer named Sidney Songy. The story went out that Songy would be forced to reveal who was behind the association.

Panicked, the Square Dealers mobilized three hundred men and seized the courthouse. That turned out to be what Long wanted. He had Allen declare martial law, then announced he'd release Songy. The blue-shirted guerrillas parleyed, then decamped. Then the Kingfish loosed a surprise: Songy was a spy for him. The next day, a hearing was convened and Songy testified he'd heard the Square Dealers plot Huey's assassination. They'd stop his car on the highway to New Orleans on the night of January 24 and —as Huey told the press—"force me in the ditch and then 14 or 16 were going to come along in another car and kill me." When this news went out, the Baton Rouge Square Dealers, as Long had expected, decided on defiance. They assembled at the airport for a showdown. It ended ignominiously. Faced by lines of National Guardsmen, the Square Dealers surrendered their arms. Bourgeois scrambled over a fence in flight, dropping his shotgun and inflicting on one of his troops the only wound of The Battle of the Airport.

Now Baton Rouge, long critical of the Kingfish, was Huey's. Governor Allen stationed machine guns, mortars and troops on the Capitol lawn while another hearing, based on Songy's information, was held. The Kingfish acted as ringmaster. A former East Baton Rouge deputy sheriff named "Red" Davis confessed that Fred Parker, another deputy ousted by Long's men, had offered him $10,000 to kill the Kingfish at the time of the New Orleans trouble. Davis said he'd stalked Huey but, because of Huey's guard, finally quit. Parker had replaced him with Songy, of all people. For his part, Parker refused to testify, as did a Square Dealer named O'Rourke, who was rumored to be in the employ of Standard Oil (coincidentally, both Parker and O'Rourke afterward got jobs with one of the Federal programs in Louisiana). Long crowed over the disclosures, knowing Standard would soon bow to the governor's right to tax it. He pressed no further and the hearings were ended.

Doubtless, the Kingfish by then was fatalistic. He told a fellow Senator: "If there were just a few people plotting it, I think I might live through it, but those people are determined to kill me and I'm not going to live through it." This pessimism, whether genuine or theatrical, didn't stem Long's assaults on FDR. Huey had his strategy: Secure Louisiana through his legislature, make it the utopian example of what he could do, then press on to the Presidency. That early part of 1935, Long was Roosevelt's scourge. He'd pre-empted him with Share Our Wealth. The Kingfish helped defeat the Administration's attempt to ratify American adherence to the World Court. He knew most patriots didn't like that. In February, the backwoods lawyer engineered the defeat of Roosevelt's work-relief bill because it contained no minimum-wage provision. In Roosevelt's office, the President was saying they'd have to steal Huey's thunder, and "Don't put anybody in and don't help anybody that is working for Huey Long or his crowd; that is a hundred percent." Huey just went on, though, riding high. In March and April, he said he'd leave the party if Roosevelt were nominated and, yes, he might be a candidate unless the other parties came round to his thinking. Roosevelt counterattacked on June 19, with a tax proposal less stringent than Share Our Wealth but probably more acceptable in its higher individual and corporate tax rates. Huey said FDR was a "scuttler."

But that was nothing compared with August 9, 1935, when the Senate of the United States heard Long accuse the President of passive complicity in a plot to murder the Senator from Louisiana. That day, the Kingfish waved what he said was the Dictograph transcript of "an anti-Long conference held by the anti-Long representatives from Louisiana in Congress. . . . Here is what happened among the Congressmen representing Roosevelt." Long then read the quotes. A Square Dealer: "I am out to murder, bulldoze, steal or anything to win this election." An unidentified voice: "There'll be income-tax indictments and there will be some more convictions. . . . O. K. Allen will be the next." Another unidentified voice: "I would draw in a lottery to go out and kill Long. It would take only one man, one gun and one bullet." Another unidentified voice: "I haven't the slightest doubt but that Roosevelt would pardon anyone who killed Long." And so on, through what Huey called the "murder conference," attended, he pointed out, by O'Rourke and several thugs. He concluded by saying, "Louisiana will not have a government imposed on it that represents murder, blackmail, oppression or destitution," and that wild tales of the New Deal's inner councils' plotting to have him murdered were now "fully verified."

Huey stalked out, and into his dust the facts vanished. Surely, there had been an anti-Long meeting in New Orleans' DeSoto Hotel for two days in late July. It was also true that Herbert Christenberry, the brother of Huey's trusted secretary, Earle Christenberry (then the world's fastest typist—a man who'd worshiped the Kingfish for years and kept track of the deduct box for him), had arranged a comic eavesdropping device: a microphone stuck on the end of a pole and poked up to the window of a conference room. Herbert inscribed in shorthand what he heard, transcribed it for Seymour Weiss, who sent it to Huey in Washington, where it was waved at Senators like that day's Gospel. Never mind the illegality of the means; it's probably true that intemperate statements such as those Huey quoted were made. Violent talk was common enough in Louisiana just then. But there is no proof that such talk had a corollary in action (one adversary said Huey had just "got hold of some bad whiskey" to imagine the danger), and the quotes were out of context, excerpted from meetings held in that room over two days. To be sure, in the vindictive hysteria following Huey's death, Earle said he'd heard the Dictograph and told Huey it mentioned a man named Wise. Couldn't that just possibly be the good doctor, the "one man and one bullet"? Unfortunately for the theory, Weiss was in Opelousas and Baton Rouge during the DeSoto conference. Yet Huey's charges in the Senate raised questions never completely put down.

Was all this part of the Kingfish's desire for publicity? Of his animosity toward FDR? Of his fear? Or were these genuine plots? Was the formation on August 1, 1935, of another paramilitary organization called, truly, the Minute Men an authentic threat? They did circulate a "Declaration of Independence" for a Louisiana freed of Long's tyranny and boasted they'd take Baton Rouge—if necessary killing Long. Were they for real? Neither the state nor Long found out, since Weiss moved, it seems, before the Square Dealers or the DeSotoers or the Minute Men. Moved within a month and for reasons not then known, only felt in the marrow of political creatures who sensed the unexpected infection and feared it.

Congress adjourned on August 26 in 1935. Long left Washington for a few days' birthday roistering in New York. He took with him his Presidential ambitions, incarnate in the deduct box, now stuffed with alms for his 1936 campaigns and with affidavits detailing the New Deal's attempts to stifle him. In New York, he approved *My First Days in the White House,* his campaign book, which would, he thought, with Share Our Wealth, seize more ragged sleeves of the dispossessed and tug them into his camp. *My First Days* describes in first-person breathlessness the Long Administration's infancy, itself a parody of FDR's "first hundred days." Seemingly, few could take the book as a serious declaration except the Kingfish, who in planning it said if he were elected President, he'd get rid of the two-term tradition and defy "any son of a bitch to get me out."

In Oklahoma City on Labor Day, Long's speech exhumed from his Winnfield youth an old joke meant to bury Roosevelt and Hoover. They had proved themselves, he shouted, like the peddler of two patent medicines called High Popalorum and Low Popahiram, made from the bark of the same tree. "But for one the peddler peeled the bark off from the top down and for the other he peeled it off from the bottom up. . . . Roosevelt and his crowd are skinning us from the ear down and Hoover and the Republicans are doing the job from the ankle up." The call to a third party echoed over the red clay and the squeak of the oil pumps. In a few days, the Kingfish was in Baton Rouge for the climactic special session, safe there in his marble tower.

Weiss spent the last days of his short life in romantic-novel happiness. He ordered furniture for his home, inquired about a new furnace, planned for his future. He practiced medical arts and went home to play with his infant son, to marvel at him and at his wife. The Sunday of the special session he went to church, and he and Yvonne and the baby dined with his parents. Then they all went to their summer cottage on the Amite River, to swim and loll away the hot September afternoon. Carl had often practiced shooting there, but this day they only swam and jollied the child and talked of this and that until about dark, when they drove back to Baton Rouge. In the cooling evening, Carl and Yvonne ate sandwiches and prepared the baby for bed, and about eight o'clock Weiss called his anesthetist to make sure he knew an operation scheduled for the next morning had been switched from Our Lady of the Lake Sanitarium, across the pond from the Capitol, to Baton Rouge General. Then he showered, dressed in his white-linen suit and kissed Yvonne goodbye. He said he had a call to make, "arrangements for an operation tomorrow." He kissed her and left forever, backing his Buick out of their drive and into a different world. The car was found in the Capitol's parking lot. Weiss carried a gun, as many Louisianans did, in its glove compartment, wrapped in a flannel sock. The sock and his medical bag, disarranged, were found in the car later that night. Sometime around nine o'clock, Weiss climbed the Capitol's steps, found his corridor and waited for the sound of a Kingfish approaching.

The story of Huey Long's end abounds with ironies and mysteries. Start with the events in the hospital, with the first irony that Long may not have been doomed to die there in Our Lady of the Lake Sanitarium. Shot but once, it seems he could have survived, but the state's best surgeons summoned from New Orleans were delayed by a highway accident caused by road construction, the jewel of Huey's crown. The surgeon who did operate, Dr. Arthur Vidrine, was Huey's appointee, head of the huge Charity Hospital in New Orleans and dean of a project dear to Long—the LSU medical school built to rival Tulane's. A competent surgeon, Dr. Vidrine went in from the front, cleaned up the soilage where the bullet had torn through the intestines to exit at Long's back and sewed the Senator up. But in the excitement someone forgot to check the victim's urine for blood (a mistake the careful Weiss would not have made), and within thirty hours

Long was dead of internal bleeding from the kidney vessels nicked by the bullet.

Consider how in the hospital the swarming after Huey's power began. His estranged brothers rallied to him (Earl was to be designated the state's next lieutenant governor). And Seymour Weiss, the indicted income-tax evader, asked the dying Long where the deduct box was, knowing Huey had taken it from Washington when Congress adjourned. "Later, Seymour, later" was the reply, but there was no more time. The box never reappeared; its hundreds of thousands of dollars and affidavits were gone as finally, as completely, as the charisma of the Kingfish. True, the Longs' familial power reasserted itself, in Governor Earl and Senator Russell, in 1948, and, naturally, Longites won Louisiana in 1936 riding the revulsion for the disloyal opposition, the "Assassination Party," accused during the campaign by Earle Christenberry of sending Weiss to kill Huey. (Even so, "reform" candidates won in 1940 and 1944, and no Louisianian as potent as the Kingfish has surfaced since his death.) Yet now the succession of power and the money were forgotten in the thrashing, grasping and dying of Long.

Much was forgotten for the moment. Like Huey's odd cut on his lip— which an intern had noticed, which a nurse swore Long had referred to in saying "That's where he hit me." Later it would be offered by the Weiss family and others as evidence that "he" was Carl, that Carl—his temper loosed by the gerrymander against Judge Pavy, by the rumor that Huey would accuse the Pavys of having Negro blood, by his detestation for fascism—had gone to the Capitol to confront Huey, had stepped out and spoken to him, had hit the Kingfish, and then the guns of the bodyguards were out, those hand cannons cutting down Carl and, by accident, shooting Long, while Carl's little self-protection pistol fell from his pocket. So the cut was forgotten, not to be remembered until eight days later, when Long's bodyguards testified with remarkable unanimity about the scuffle with Weiss. Roden had wrestled him, Coleman had struck at the doctor. Huey could have been cut accidentally then, they said, or he could have bumped into something in his flight; and as for any of them shooting Huey, the doctors and the coroner's jury said the Senator's wound was small, hardly noticeable. A .32 would do that, not a .45. And what was Weiss doing with his pistol in his pocket if he was there only to have this conversation nobody remembered with Long? How, Longites asked, could Weiss's brother in future years fantasize that a guilty bodyguard went afterward to fetch the pistol from the doctor's car, messing up the doctor's bag in the process (how even would that guard know Weiss's car—Huey didn't know Weiss when told who had shot him—unless the guard was in on it? Unlikely, since those men had been with Huey for years), and then plant it by Weiss's body, that little "toy automatic," as someone remembered it, which held seven rounds and had one jammed in the ejector and five in the magazine (so maybe there were two shots, one that nicked Roden's wrist watch, just as he said—so what?) and was similar to the pistol Weiss had that week showed a Mr. Fitzgerald and said didn't work right. After all, how plausible was this business stemming from the little cut and Weiss's pistol?

Further into the Kingfish's deathwatch, his assassin was forgotten. Even as Carl's father, his widow, her father the judge, assured the press and the world that this action of Carl's was inexplicable, certainly not a plot—he was not a joiner and certainly he was not a martyr—even as they spoke, the wires of congratulations (like those our assassins always get) came in and the newspaper editorials called Carl not crazy but a savior. Thus flowed, in the reciprocal of Long hatred, the praise for the young doctor's act, and it continued to come as his perforated body was prepared for burial. Forever after that interment in hallowed ground, his family said Carl had not gone to the Capitol to kill Long; that, though they'd tsk-tsked over it at Sunday's supper, he had not been upset over Judge Pavy's fate —in fact, the family welcomed the judge's coming leisure. They certainly weren't afraid of Huey's tarbrushing, not one of the most distinguished and oldest families in Louisiana. No, it could only have been the impulse of idealism, a hatred and fear of oppression, of Long's fascism. Carl had that. Perhaps only that would have taken him to sure death, away from the wife, the child, the profession, the joy of existence.

So that, too, was forgotten, as Long's family and closest friends leaned forward to hear him near the end hallucinate about the poor, the Gallused backwoods folk he'd help, the things he'd do, his campaign, his LSU, until finally, they swore, he said, "God, don't let me die, I have so much to do," and soon thereafter died.

Long, the commoner from Winnfield, lay in state in his Capitol for one full day, dressed in a tuxedo and surrounded by $25,000 worth of flowers. When Long was interred in a bronze, double-walled $5,000 coffin in front of the Capitol, the roads around Baton Rouge were clogged with cars, wagons, buses, 100,000 people in all. Reverend Smith delivered the eulogy. Carazo's band played "Every Man a King" in a minor key, and to the throb of his own dirge, Huey's body was lowered into a massive concrete vault (Mencken unkindly predicted that Louisianians would dynamite Huey's crypt and erect an equestrian statue of Dr. Weiss over the site—they didn't, preferring one of the Kingfish). The music died and it was done.

The surviving echoing throbs we've come to expect—the alarums of plots.

Seymour Weiss said he, too, was sure he'd read the name Wise off the DeSoto Hotel Dictograph record to Huey over the telephone, so Huey's killer was there (Weiss refused to let anyone see the record).

An erstwhile leader of the Minute Men said that was wrong, that there had been another meeting at the DeSoto, a secret meeting attended by five men, who drew straws to see who would kill Long. "We would all have killed him," this bravo supposedly said. "Weiss drew the short straw. He wanted it. He hated Huey because of the nigger business [hypothetically, the racial slur on the Pavys]." This man has never offered proof of his story nor its extension—that if Weiss failed, the rest would kill Long in northern Louisiana with machine guns.

Another tale, sworn to by one man, had it that bitter hangers-on of the Baton Rouge Square Dealers were to meet the week of September 8 to cast lots and decide who was to kill the Kingfish. This man was at the home of a friend when he heard a radio announcement of the shooting in the Capitol. "That wasn't planned," he told Long's biographer. "The meeting was to have been tomorrow."

Soon, too, arrived the predictable rumors that Roosevelt had had it done. The accusations by Earle Christenberry that rival Democrats had orchestrated the short-straw drawing (a tale madly embroidered by Songy, who claimed two men—other plotters—had taken a shot at him the day after Huey was shot). And, last, some Louisiana newspapers reported that Weiss was, indeed, violent on the subject of Long and could with equanimity leave his happy hearthside, drive to the Capitol and shoot Long, knowing he was committing suicide in so doing. "I'm going to kill Huey Long," these sources quote Weiss as having said, and it seems he did —and that someone would have eventually had he not.

But these facts and fictions cushion the basic question, Why? There is no indisputable answer. Only that meeting in the corridor is unquestionable. The doctor in white, the Senator in silk, and each driven—perhaps urged by Cajun voodoo, by bayou vapors—to this clash of ideas or politics or prejudices or visions, so opposed that their confluence could only end in death.

The bequests were many. Ellender and the Longs, the collapse of "Share Our Wealth," the "Louisiana scandals" of 1939, when the Longite tax defenses finally crumbled, populism and fascism in the steady third-party thumpings of Strom Thurmond in 1948 and of George Wallace in

1968—even this, which assesses Long and his assassin, is itself a bequest wrapped in enigmas, in ironies lined up for a final bow:

• Such as Huey Long, he who, though he skimmed and deducted, took legal fees from a state he governed and made thousands from state oil leases through a corporation nicely named Win or Lose; who, though he vandalized civil liberties and raped constitutional processes and burglarized common decency, left Louisiana better in ways than he found it. The backwoods Galluses, rednecks, flop-hats had their day—some vow Huey is still alive somewhere and they run prayers of gratitude to him in newspaper "Personals"—and although we may ask if they'd like another Kingfish, in Long's time their answer was clear. They agreed with Huey, who once said, "Just say I'm *sui generis,*" and we may ponder the portent of their love for such as Long.

• Such as the mystery of Carl Weiss; was he plotter or patriot, or both? Or merely a killer-gardener hewing down something outsized that had grown to shade his inherited garden?

• Such as the relief of Franklin D. Roosevelt (who once called Long one of the two most dangerous men in America—the other was Douglas MacArthur) shimmering beneath his perfunctory wire, never amplified, to the Longs: "I deeply regret the attempt made upon the life of Senator Long. . . ." Of course, it came to pass that it was FDR who won four terms and was called dictator, not the country Kingfish, and FDR who, with bigger fish to fry, presided over the five years in which the mass murder of World War II supplanted individual assassination, in which the Cain in man turned upon Abel by the millions in the names of fascism and freedom. Dizzyingly apt then was Long's comment on Hitler: "Don't liken me to that son of a bitch. Anybody that lets his public policies be mixed up with religious prejudice is a goddamned fool. . . . There has never been a country that put its heel down on the Jews that ever lived afterward." For all its gaudy improbability, nothing Huey ever said was truer for our time.

• Finally, such as that the man who succeeded FDR was not Huey but Harry, and that it was Truman next in the gunsight-mind of assassins. Certainly not this time the mind of any smallish, landed-gentry physician but two Puerto Ricans who wanted freedom for their land—and whose desire burns still in the bombings of restaurants, of banks and of Government buildings.

Mercifully, the parallels stop there.

Oscar Collazo and Griselio Torresola did not understand in November, 1950, when they charged Truman's residence at Blair House with their hopeless pistols—indeed, could not understand as well as Weiss and Long would have—how fitting for a Kingfish's epitaph were the words of Senator Harry Truman in 1935 when he heard of Huey's shooting. Harry said, "The proper way for Louisiana to get rid of Huey Long is to vote him out."

In that sentiment, too often abrogated by politics' true fourth estate of violence, lies the vexing problem of American assassinations. It would be seen next in the futile attempt on Truman in 1950 and, too soon after, in the murder in Dallas that altered the mind of America forever about itself.

IV

DEATH IN DALLAS

*"The people will forget in a few
days and there will be another
President."*

—LEE HARVEY OSWALD,
November 23, 1963

For some, it was the muffled drums, the posthumous pulse of John
Fitzgerald Kennedy sounding in ceaseless cadence. For some, the hideous
yellow catering lift bellied against Air Force One, the somnambulistic
widow in bloody clothes, the bronze casket burnished by TV lights descending to the tarmac's ring of somber, famous faces. For some, the
clockwork quadrille of the deathwatch guard, or De Gaulle marching tall
behind the horse-drawn caisson, or John-John's farewell salute. For this
writer, it was Caroline's small right hand reaching as though for verifica-
tion beneath the covering flag to touch the unyielding surface of her
father's casket—"Daddy's too big for that," she'd said—there in the rotunda of the Capitol of the United States, kneeling next to her mother, that
at last brought into the mind with a bullet's force the irreconcilable fact
that the thirty-fifth President of the United States was dead, slain in Dallas
by, it was said, a punk with a mail-order rifle.

That, assuredly, was the message. However it came to each of us, collectively we learned that the truce of sixty-two years had been broken, that
a citizen had again murdered an American President and, pre-eminently,
that the event had caught us in a new world of instant mass communication that conveyed the images to us—the funereal tableaux, the people,
even the murder of the President's accused murderer—in a telethon that
threw us forever out of the slow-motion historical world of Lincoln and
Garfield and McKinley into our own hard-edged, video-taped nowness.
History for us had stopped. We were really there, so much so that a
half-hour after Kennedy was shot, 68 percent of his adult citizenry (more

101

than 75,000,000 people) had the word. So much so that by late afternoon of Friday, November 22, 1963, an estimated 99.8 percent of the American people knew their President was dead and that somebody named Lee Harvey Oswald, twenty-four years old, was suspected of the killing. Back in that other world, in 1865, news of the assassination of Abraham Lincoln —our first Presidential victim, whom Kennedy admired, to whom he was compared and on whose catafalque he lay in state—didn't reach Oregon until two months after John Wilkes Booth's act in Ford's Theater. But in our new world, its slain leader arriving at Andrews Air Force Base from the unlikely latitudes of Dallas, we all at once and as a nation knew and felt—were *made* in this age of media to know and feel, to participate in —a martyrdom for the handsome, bright, brash President who was so brutally murdered right before our eyes. For four days, a great national catharsis swept us clean of any dream that we were immune to this horror. It filled us with pity for the lovely First Lady, with fear for the future. We wept. Most of us, that is. A few did not, were glad John Kennedy was dead. A few were brought to thoughts of vengeance, notably a strip-joint operator in Dallas itself. A few stopped mourning to realize the martyr image was only one, a bluish picture that altered John Kennedy as much as the embalmer's cosmetics. Distorted the tough Irish politician, the whiskey baron's progeny, the philanderer. Covered over achievements like the Test Ban Treaty, the Missile Crisis, the assault on organized crime, the pending tax-cut bill and Civil Rights Bill. Prettified the dreadful and portentous failures like the Bay of Pigs.

Yet most Americans watched, wept and wondered what had happened in Dallas. How had this come to him? To us? We could understand our other assassinations, because history rendered them as somebody else's sorrow. We could objectify the attempt on Harry Truman back in 1950, the doomed charge by two Puerto Rican nationalists with pistols against a President's impregnable home, could admire their courage, even their cause of independence. But their attack had failed. The sniper in Dallas had not, and now there were the drums, the riderless horse, the caisson, the foreign leaders, the widow in black, the hard-faced brothers, the innocent children, over and over and over, and how could we begin to grasp how all that had come to be?

The assassination of John Kennedy would freight with significance almost all its circumstances, almost every person, place or event connected with it. That fact alone testifies to the killing's shock effect, to the resultant need to know what happened and, again, to the information blitz that provided the facts on which the myriad speculations and conclusions were built. But there was little gainsaying the facts themselves or what seemed to be facts, as they emerged during and after the national mourning.

For a start, John Kennedy didn't want to be in Texas that day. "I wish I weren't going to Texas," he told Pierre Salinger. And with reason. Though LBJ's presence on his ticket had helped him carry Texas in 1960 against Nixon—who was even then in Dallas meeting with some Pepsi-Cola executives—Kennedy knew 1964 could be different. The state's Democratic Party throbbed with disagreements. There was Kennedy's loyal liberal faction, a minority led by Senator Ralph Yarborough, who was anathema to the rightists like Governor John Connally, who was a onetime protégé of Lyndon Johnson and who was now a man with large ambitions that could be achieved only with the aid of Texas' rich right-wingers (some said Connally might jump the party soon and serve as Senator Barry Goldwater's running mate). Between them stood the Vice President, a consummate politician but bereft now of his Lone Star power base and apprehensive to the point of impotence over rumors that JFK might dump him in 1964. Only the President, his advisers told him, could hold things together. Hence the political trip to Texas, and hence the President's joy when, uncharacteristically, his wife said she'd go along. Texans surely wouldn't be rude to such a lady as Jackie.

Except perhaps in Dallas. That peculiar city was scheduled as the next-to-last stop on the visit. Only a motorcade to a luncheon speech at the new Trade Mart. Yet even that could be dicey. "Big D" bubbled with hate for the liberal Federal Government (Nixon got 63 percent of Dallas' vote) and any hint of its accommodation with Commies, Jews or niggers. It wasn't particularly fond of Catholics, either, being as it was 97 percent Protestant. It was active hate, too, passed around in sniggering jokes. Dallas led the nation in per-capita murders (72 percent committed with guns). It was home to "IMPEACH EARL WARREN" billboards, to the reactionary fulminations of H. L. Hunt and retired Major General Edwin A. Walker, to John Birchers, Minutemen and Christian Crusaders, to "K.O. THE KENNEDYS" bumper stickers and other signs of the Old Frontier. In 1960, a fun-loving bunch of Dallasites had tossed a cup of spit at Lyndon and Lady Bird, presumably protesting their alliance with the mackerel-snapping Kennedys. Adlai Stevenson had been roughed up in a crowd on UN Day just a month before Kennedy's visit. He'd considered warning the President about the mood in Dallas. But then, the President could have read it in the Dallas *Morning News*. That rightist paper had called him a Judas for his Test Ban Treaty and the Cuban fiasco, and its publisher, E. M. Dealey

—whose father had a plaza, built by the socialist WPA, named for him downtown—once had attacked the President's left-wing sellout policies at a White House get-together. It was at people like Dealey that John Kennedy's Trade Mart speech would be aimed. "Today, other voices are heard in the land," he would say, "voices preaching doctrines . . . which apparently assume that words will suffice without weapons, that vituperation is as good as victory and that peace is a sign of weakness." Kennedy would tell them that straight out and proceed on his way, although he hoped his plan to start withdrawing the advisers from Vietnam didn't provoke trouble while he was in Texas. Strange, they were so religious down there, but they didn't seem to remember a cause had to be just. His speech would conclude with the Bible's words, "Except the Lord keep the city, the watchman waketh but in vain."

Many were the premonitions suggesting the Lord wasn't keeping Dallas just now. A Democratic National Committeeman from Texas urged the President to cancel the Dallas stopover, and an editor in Austin, which was to be the last public stop before going to LBJ's Pedernales paradise, wrote, "He will not get through this without something happening to him." In Washington, Hale Boggs and Hubert Humphrey cautioned Kennedy about the trip (on November 21, Humphrey, with JFK on his way, told the National Association for Mental Health that the "wild men of reaction" were "deeply and fundamentally disturbed . . . the act of an emotionally unstable person or irresponsible citizen can strike down a great leader"). More directly, the calm J. William Fulbright said to the President, "Dallas is a very dangerous place. I wouldn't go there. Don't you go." But go he must, he decided, as a politician, to try to heal the factional wounds and to gain currency for the 1964 campaign. At 10:45 A.M., Thursday, November 21, the choppers lifted off the White House lawn for the twelve-minute hop to Andrews AFB and Air Force One. Two-year-old John-John rode along. He loved his father and airplanes, both passionately, and when the helicopters set down beside the graceful blue-and-white 707, he begged to go along. "You can't," the President said. Then, to his son's Secret Service guardian, Kennedy said, "You take care of John, Mr. Foster."

The Secret Service was supposed to take care of the President, too. With the ascent of Air Force One, their task became complicated. The security routines in Washington were fixed and proved. On the road, they were not. In San Antonio, Houston, Fort Worth, Dallas, Austin, men of the Protective Research Section had coordinated their plans with local police, checked out routes, secured buildings, examined their own and FBI files for homicidal threats. But they couldn't be sure. Dallas would be most difficult tomorrow. A long motorcade from Love Field to the luncheon in the Presidential limousine (they called it SS 100 X) and, even with the Lincoln's bubbletop on in bad weather, it wasn't bulletproof. The job was complicated by the President (the Boss, they called him, though his code name was Lancer). Like Abraham Lincoln, he detested the shield his bodyguards put around him. He was forever breaking out to plunge into crowds, shaking hands and giving away PT-109 tie clasps (hell of a commander, his rightish military critics snorted, lost his only ship), and, not long before, he'd told an agent to "keep those Ivy League charlatans off the back of the car." So there he'd be in Dallas, protected mostly by what they reckoned an inefficient police force; there where that very morning of November 21 some hatemongers had printed and passed out five thousand mug-shot handbills accusing the President of treason for not invading Cuba, for having Stevenson turn "the sovereignty of the U.S. over to the Communist-controlled United Nations"; there where in that morning's *News* and *Times Herald* anyone could read the route of the motorcade and its timing, even that it would go slow so all Dallas could see the President, riding along in an open car. Twenty thousand windows overlooked the motorcade's path, too many to watch, and when on November 18 the Secret Service's advance man, Winston Lawson, rode it in company with the Dallas office's Forrest V. Sorrels and Dallas police chief Jesse Curry, all three remarked how they'd be sitting ducks. Toward the end of the ride, turning from Main Street into Houston Street, Lawson saw an ungainly tan-brick building with concrete latticework marking its first floor and windows marching up past a ledge and final story to a big, blinking time-and-temperature Hertz Rent-a-Car sign. He asked, "What's the Texas School Book Depository?"

Lee Harvey Oswald could have told him. It was where, since mid-October, he had been making $1.25 an hour as a clerk (not enough to buy a rifle, he later told police), which meant pulling books out of boxes to match order forms and sending them downstairs to the offices of his boss, Roy Truly, who had criticized Kennedy. Inside, the warehouse wasn't what you'd expect of a repository of learning. Drab offices, a grimy second-floor lunchroom, two dusty freight elevators, claustrophobic storage space crammed with cartons, lit by 60-watt bulbs, surrounded by brick walls that dropped scabs of paint to the buckling wood floors. Up in the sixth story, they were relaying the floor, and the boxes were moved to the southeastern corner of the building, close to the windows overlooking Dealey Plaza's mock-Grecian peristyles and pergolas. Oswald worked up there sometimes. From the southeast window, you could see straight out to where

Main turned into Houston Street, then directly below where Houston turned into Elm Street, then right, where Elm Street curved to go through a triple underpass, the railroad tracks on top, and on out to the ramp up to Stemmons Freeway, the way to the Trade Mart. A superb view from an ugly building, where Lee did his menial job.

He'd been born in New Orleans on October 18, 1939, two months after his father's death, to Marguerite Oswald, a hulking, pouty woman who resented mightily the demise of this, her second husband. Lee grew up alone in and out of orphanages and relatives' homes, because his mother worked. But even though he slept with her in their various homes in New Orleans and Fort Worth until he was eleven, that didn't fill him with love. Marguerite's third marriage, in 1945, provided a temporary father until divorce ended it in 1948. But then his mother worked again. Lee protested her neglect by skipping school. Once he chased his half-brother with a knife, and another time threatened the half-brother's wife with a blade. It seems these defiances didn't satisfy, any more than did geographical changes. They kept moving, on to New York, then back to New Orleans. Though he was smart (I.Q. of 118), he quit school after the ninth grade and enlisted in the manly Marine Corps, as had his brother, Robert. Even in that homogenized milieu, something in him turned people off. Fellow Marines called him "Ozzie Rabbit," and thought he was intelligent and well informed but strangely withdrawn and secretive. Yet he did his duties (albeit court-martialed twice—once for possession of an unregistered private firearm, a .22 derringer that accidentally went off and wounded him, and once for gross insubordination, which included spilling a drink on an officer—a trick that earned him four weeks in the stockade). He acquired basic military skills. He qualified as Sharpshooter with the M-1, became a private, first class/aviation electronics operator, which meant he tracked aircraft on radar and scanned their radio signals, notably from the Atsugi base in Japan, where some U-2 flights over Russia originated. Lee liked Russia, or the idea of Russia. He'd discovered Marxism at fifteen, and two perceptions stuck with him: It was for the downtrodden, he saw, and hence antiestablishment; and it was taboo in America. Of Marx's complexity, of the moral subtleties of the dialectic, Oswald spoke little, though he did study the Russian language and profess *ad nauseam* to the gyrenes the wonders of the Soviet system.

After nearly three years, Oswald sought and was granted, on September 11, 1959, an early "hardship" discharge to go to Fort Worth and take care of his impoverished and disabled mother, now a resident there. Marguerite was not disabled long, apparently, since by October 16 Lee Harvey

Oswald was in Moscow trying to defect to Russia and become a Soviet citizen. As it turned out, he was successful at neither. Although he ranted to the U.S. Embassy and wrote letters forsaking his citizenship, he never forfeited his passport or completed the papers necessary to terminate his citizenship. He didn't become a Soviet citizen either, since he tired of their system within eighteen months and wanted to come home. He was delayed, however, by bureaucratic tangles until June, 1962. In between, he made an insincere attempt at suicide (to dramatize his sincerity about wanting to be a Russian). He was then assigned work at a radio and TV factory in Minsk, where he fell in love, was jilted and then rebounded to marry a pharmacist, the unhappy niece of a Minsk MVD official, on whom he fathered a daughter. He bought a shotgun and hunted a little, talked Marxism and continued fitful attempts at higher education (including a try at enrolling in Moscow's Patrice Lumumba Friendship University, unfortunately reserved for citizens of the Third World). In general, he lived what for most Russians would be a pampered life. His pay, as was customary with defectors, was supplemented. He was given a good apartment. But he didn't like the authoritarianism of Russia any better than Marine Corps discipline, perhaps felt insufficiently rewarded for his secrets (nothing that threatened U.S. security) or his devotion to Marx's cause. The difficulties of obtaining exit visas vexed him and he wrote to Senator John Tower for help. He beseeched his brother and mother for financial aid (Marguerite suggested capitalizing on the story of his defection—after Kennedy's death she ruefully remarked, "Moneywise, I got took"). With their help, patience and $435.71 in borrowed State Department funds, Lee Harvey Oswald, with wife and child, returned to the United States on June 13, 1962.

As we shall see detailed in the second part of the Kennedy story, the days from then until November 22, 1963, spun away from Oswald in a downward spiral. For now, it is enough to see their gross direction. Items: A succession of plebeian jobs, the best of which was as a photoprint trainee for a graphics company. Between jobs, unemployment checks—some obtained on spurious grounds. Increasing tension with Marina, who found him in his native land to be irritable, reclusive, sexually inactive, tyrannical and cruel. (Lee beat her and discouraged her attempts to learn English —Russian may have been their only remaining bond.) Separations from Marina, then feverish reconciliations. The interventions of their few friends (who, for example, paid for Marina's dental work and once helped her leave Lee), first in the Russian-speaking community of Fort Worth, then in Dallas. And last, Mrs. Ruth Paine, who in suburban Irving sheltered Marina and her two daughters (the second born October 20, 1963, at Parkland Memorial Hospital) during the Oswalds' intermittent separations from April until November. Mrs. Paine was herself estranged from her leftist husband and, before Marina moved in, the two women often exchanged sympathetic letters. Then, too, there were annoying interviews with the FBI, which was interested in the Oswalds' Russian connections, particularly midway in 1963, when Marina began writing (at Lee's request, she said) for visas to re-enter Russia and Lee went to New Orleans, then Mexico, apparently plumping for Castro and seeking permission to traverse Cuba on their way back to the U.S.S.R. And coloring all in Oswald, the day-to-dayness of bootless work, of reading Marxist texts and periodicals, of shifting from one rented quarters to another, with and without Marina as his marriage turned sweet and sour, of watching war movies on television, of penning letters—to the Soviet Embassy pleading for a visa or to the Communist Party pleading for utilization of his talents—and far from least of thinking up other names for himself, of photographically fabricating identification for these names, maybe for a dark purpose, maybe to alleviate the incongruity he felt amid these circumstances.

Indeed, flipping through that calendar, Lee Harvey Oswald could have recalled only a few luminous times.

There was January 27, 1963, when, using the name A. J. Hidell, he put ten dollars down on a mail-order snub-nosed Smith & Wesson .38 revolver ("the equalizer," Texans used to call the revolver) from a Los Angeles firm. The pistol was paid off in March.

There was March 12, 1963, when, as A. Hidell, he ordered for $19.95 a Model 91/38 Mannlicher-Carcano carbine (an Italian World War II surplus weapon, this one numbered C2766) and an Ordnance Optics Japanese-made four-power scope to be shipped to P.O. Box 2915, Dallas, Texas. Oswald did not order an M-1 advertised on the same page of the *American Rifleman* by Klein's Sporting Goods of Chicago, despite his familiarity with the weapon, perhaps because the M-1 cost $78.88 and his mother had tinctured him forever with frugality.

There were the days after March 20, when the weapons were shipped, that Lee, his wife said, sat alone with the rifle and practiced working the bolt, for hunting, he told her. She says she took two pictures of him, posed with rifle, revolver and copies of *The Worker* and *The Militant.*

There was April 10, when, Marina reported, Lee took his rifle from a concealed place near General Walker's home and fired a shot through a window at the general, who seemed to Oswald like Hitler and, therefore, fair game.

There were those occasional days in New Orleans, from late April to September, when he and Marina seemed reconciled, when he became obsessed with Cuba, when, after first seeking out anti-Castro men, he formed under aliases a chapter of the Fair Play for Cuba Committee, himself sole member, and passed out leaflets, and got arrested, and was celebrated in the papers, on radio and TV, became a media man.

There was his trip to Mexico City, from September 25 to October 3, when he called on the Soviet and Cuban delegations for visas to Russia via Cuba, but was rejected, in effect sentenced to the United States, to his renewed marital difficulties, to rage at the latest FBI interrogation of Marina, and to the needs of his child and soon-to-be-born daughter. Kindly Ruth Paine led him to the job at the Texas School Book Depository. After another marital scrap, he went to that job the morning of November 22 carrying a heavy brown-paper package. He told fellow employee Buell Wesley Frazier (a neighbor of the Paines), who drove him there, that it contained curtain rods for his hermetic rented room in Dallas' Oak Cliff section.

In their hotel rooms, John and Jackie Kennedy prepared for a big day. Yesterday had been sweet but exhausting. First the Washington departure, then the constant business on Air Force One (for instance, keeping up with the progress of the six Cabinet members flying to the Far East for wide-ranging discussions with our allies, including South Vietnam), the roaring welcome in San Antonio, where the crowds screamed "Jackieee" and made the President smile, the hop to Houston for more adulation and a perfunctory dinner speech and, throughout, the strain among Yarborough, Connally and Johnson, but ending at last with the flight to Fort Worth and its rainy-night welcome and the aging Hotel Texas. Friday, predictable as wind-up dolls, Jack would say a few words to the blue-collar faithful who'd assembled outside the hotel, and they'd have this chamber of commerce breakfast, and then leap the few miles to Dallas for the motorcade, the speech, the flight to Austin, to Lyndon's ranch, and by then they would be at the end of things, at the close of this November 22. Jackie chose a pink wool suit with a navy collar, a matching pillbox hat and short white gloves for the day.

The morning counted down. After the breakfast (such a triumph for Jackie it caused one reporter to ask JFK's assistant David Powers, "When are you going to have her come out of a cake?"), the Kennedys enjoyed that rarity of political trips, an unscheduled period. The President surveyed the Dallas *News*. Stories about the Texas Democratic rift. A quote

from Nixon, just then airborne from Dallas to New York, predicting that
JFK would drop LBJ from the 1964 ticket. And an ad, signed by the
American Fact-Finding Committee (Bernard Weissman, chairman), that
pilloried Kennedy for abrogating the Constitution, for substituting the
"Spirit of Moscow" for the Monroe Doctrine and, in general, for leading
the country to socialist ruin; to wit, allowing his brother "Bobby, the
Attorney General, to go soft on Communists, fellow travelers and ultra
leftists in America while permitting him to persecute loyal Americans."
Seemingly, the last meant people like Jimmy Hoffa, awaiting trial on
charges of jury tampering. The President explained to Jackie, "Oh, you
know, we're heading into nut country today," and added in free association, "You know, last night would have been a hell of a night to assassinate
a President."

Two hours later, SS 100 X made the turn, slowly, ponderously, from Main
onto Houston, approaching the Depository, and the President waved at
the Dallasites. The weather had cleared (the temperature was up to 68
degrees—"Kennedy weather," his aides called it) and the bubbletop was
off. Behind the car was Love Field, the encouraging welcome there ("Jackieee," they called, and the President shook hands by the fence), and the
unprecedented fervor along the route. "You sure can't say Dallas doesn't
love you, Mr. President," chirruped Mrs. Connally from Kennedy's left
front, next to her husband on the jump seats. "No, you can't," John
Kennedy replied. No one could. As politics, the trip was working. The
crowds along the route had grown bigger and more friendly. At one place,
the President had ordered his driver, William Greer, to stop so he could
get out and greet schoolchildren. The Secret Service agents winced. But
the President stopped a second time to talk with some nuns. A priest,
Father Oscar Huber, had hurried to see him, waved madly and thought
the President responded. Almost everyone believed the waves, the smiles
of Jack and Jackie were especially for them. The motorcade pierced the
commercial heart of Dallas by 12:20, proceeding in designated order: three
motorcycle cops; a pilot car; more motorcycle police; a white Ford lead
car with Chief Curry, agents Lawson and Sorrels and Sheriff Bill Decker
in it; then SS 100 X with Greer driving and Roy Kellerman, chief of JFK's
guards, beside him, and behind them the Connallys and, in the rear seat,
the Kennedys—two motorcycles flanked each side of the limousine's
trunk; next came the Cadillac convertible backup car, crammed with
Secret Service men, four more riding the running boards, all armed, one
with an AR-15 automatic rifle that was disturbingly close to Presidential
aides Powers and Kenneth O'Donnell, who perched on the jump seats;

behind them the Vice President's rented convertible, with LBJ and Senator Yarborough and the Secret Service detail headed by Rufus Youngblood; and behind them LBJ's backup car; and behind that the Dallas
mayor's car; and then the first press car, the "pool car," carrying Assistant
Press Secretary Mac Kilduff on the right, with Merriman Smith, UPI's
dean of White House correspondents, facing the radiotelephone in the
center of the dashboard, and an AP reporter, a Dallas *News* reporter and
an ABC correspondent riding in back. Trailing afterward were the photographers' car, the vehicles of lesser dignitaries, the VIP bus and assorted
extras in the motorcade's placid progress.

Down Main Street they'd come. The excited cries and squeals as the
motorcyclists swept past . . . "The President . . . he's coming . . . Jackie,
she's with him . . . the President . . . here he comes. . . ." And there he
was, passing the faces, the mouths open to cheer, waving as he came. Past
the windows of H. L. Hunt, who looked down from his high office on the
President. Past FBI agent James Hosty, who'd wanted a glimpse of the
Boss and whose burdensome case load included a couple named Oswald.
Nearby, at the Dallas *News,* a short, paunchy man born Jacob Rubenstein
but now named Jack Ruby sat discussing the ads for his night clubs, oblivi-
ous to the President slipping by below. Past the enthusiastic mobs on Main
Street, the obvious dangers there, all the Secret Service necks craning up
and around like spaceship antennae, scanning windows and faces until the
Lincoln reaches the right turn onto Houston, with the lead car just now
turning off Houston onto Elm, the crowds sparser here, some tension gone,
spread out, and the motorcycles at slow speed, their cylinders popping like
firecrackers among the cheers, while the young President and his wife
wave and SS 100 X makes its languorous turn onto Elm by the Depostory
into the zoom lens of a Bell & Howell movie camera held by a New York
garment manufacturer as out of place in his adopted Dallas as John
Kennedy. Abraham Zapruder held the camera steady on the limousine to
film his President and so filmed his President's murder.

It wasn't a difficult shot. Thousands of tourists have eye-measured the
distance from the southeast sixth-floor window of the Texas School Book
Depository to the spot on the pavement, about the fourth road stripe
down from the corner, just past a live oak tree fronting the Depository,
where the Lincoln was when the President was first hit. Thousands have
looked up as did Howard Brennan and Amos Lee Euins that day in fear
and expectation of seeing the gunman there, the one the Secret Service
didn't see, the long rifle barrel barely visible outside the window, then
disappearing. They look, and nod, and look again, and the Dallas cops

watching mutter about the goddamned Yankees out there getting their tonsils sunburned. No, it wasn't a hard shot. About 190 feet when the limousine cleared the oak tree and came into the scope.

Right then, if you were somebody who liked technical things, guns and electronics, say, you would have thought it all out, or had it stored in memory cells ready for use. You'd know that at 190 feet (or 63 yards), the four-power cross hairs made the target appear only about 50 feet away— a mere 17 yards, nothing compared with the 100-plus-yard ranges over iron sights used for rapid-fire training in the Marine Corps. You might know, with a quick rabbitlike intelligence, lots of technical things. That the Mannlicher-Carcano was accurate at short range. That the Italian NATO rifle team still used the carbine for meets. It was called "humanitarian," not because, as its critics later said, it missed, but because it put slugs where you wanted them, either to wound or to kill. Small slugs, 6.5mm, about a quarter of an inch, a little bigger than a .22, traveling, if the charge was fresh, at about 2,200 feet per second at 100 yards. Not extremely fast, not slow either. If the round wasn't fresh, the velocity could be less. The slug would tend to wobble or "go to sleep" within the first 100 yards, a tumbling that would be exaggerated if the slug hit anything. The slugs themselves could vary. Steel-jacketed, or "solid," with round noses, they'd blow through things leaving a nice clean hole. Copper-jacketed (lead thinly coated with copper), the round-nosed bullets were capricious. If they hit something hard, they'd likely deform. If something soft was encountered, they'd pass on through, their velocity decreasing, especially if the velocity was low to begin with, and probably start to tumble end over end and do strange things. Any policeman could tell you stories about bullets. Like about the .38 the would-be suicide fired against his right temple that entered the skin, glanced off the skull and tumbled around the forehead beneath the skin, finally ripping out over his left ear, leaving him dazed and life-loving.

All the rounds for this Mannlicher-Carcano had round-nosed, copper-jacketed bullets weighing between 160–161 grains. One was in the chamber as the target came into view. At least two more live ones lay in the magazine, probably in a clip, though they could, if you were sloppy or rushed, just be jammed in the magazine and forced up by the follower spring. A third might have been in the magazine, since three cartridge cases and one live round were later found. Or, if you believe only two shots were fired, one expended round might have been in the rifle's chamber when the shooter took the weapon out of the brown-paper bag and assembled it. If that hull was left there carelessly, it could have been the one shucked out, to be found with a dent on the neck that held the slug, the sort of flaw you get loading an expended cartridge case to practice dry firing and bolt manipulation. But you can dent a live round, too, not using a clip, so the spring forces the round up at the wrong angle before the bolt pushes the round into the chamber. If that round was live and dented in the chambering process, the dent might well cause the projectile to tumble from the start, doing odd things to whatever it hit, as a certain bullet in this instance was said to do. Anyway, the rifleman had at least three live rounds. Or he could have had four. Whichever, the first now lay awaiting its moment.

It came as the Hertz clock blinked 12:30 C.S.T. It came with the cross hairs low and a bit left. The cheap scope, unmatched to the rifle, threw the aiming point high and right. Any trained marksman experienced with that rifle would adjust for the error, a maximum of five inches high, three right at this range. The shooter would hold his sight picture down, too, because he was taught that with any target below and going away, the tendency was to shoot too high. The limousine's speed—only 11.2 miles per hour as later calculated—was no obstacle; the picture stayed the same and there wasn't much traversing to do. The pavement's slight declination toward the underpass would help the shooter, if anything, the limousine's downhill progress correcting a high shot. All that was needed now was a good "weld" of right-hand thumb to cheek, a short "sipping" breath, hold it and then squeeze.

Witnesses likened the first report to a firecracker. Many thought it was backfiring from the motorcycles. But the sudden, sharp *pop!* announced the Mannlicher-Carcano's slug, slamming low and a trifle right into the President's nether neck, so that his right arm, raised to wave, suddenly cramped talonlike and, joined by his left, clawed for his throat. In Zapruder's film, as the Lincoln glides from behind an obstructing street sign, we see, in the distortions of two planes and camera speed, his agonized movement, and, in our agony of attention, Kennedy's movements are so slow to us, it seems we ought to be able to see everything. . . .

. . . See behind the President in the back-up car the Secret Service men scowling at the noise, poised but uncertain, some looking backward, while the motorcycle outriders peer at the President, and Howard Brennan, a forty-four-year-old steamfitter, come to see his President, and Amos Lee Euins, a fifteen-year-old black schoolboy, look up from across Elm at the sixth-floor southeast window, a floor above and to the right of three black people watching the procession from the Depository, and think they see the rifle and the shooter, preparing for the last shots.

. . . See John Connally, holding his Stetson, turn quizzically to his left, then jerk back right in the start of a slump, while his mouth opens, cheeks puff, hair flies, as something hits him while the President behind him begins sliding leftward toward his puzzled wife, a leftward slide oddly stiff, until you remember he is wearing a surgical corset for his chronic bad back, and an Ace bandage twisted in a figure eight over his hips, so that he is propped upright like a shooting-gallery silhouette.

That was good, he's hit, now the bolt up, back, forward, down, good, smooth and quick, just track a little right, up a bit, there, hold . . . squeeze . . . Christ, where did it go?

. . . See the crowd's faces change from enthusiasm to confusion to fear, their cheers to screams, their hands from applause to grotesque stop-motion, as another shot seems to sound, this one shattering, maybe on the roadway or curb, a fragment hitting James Tague, who stands 270 feet away, near the underpass—and although later it can't be proved that this shot missed (or even was fired, though 83 percent of the witnesses reported three shots), people throw themselves down for cover, except the dumfounded or a peculiar man with an umbrella or those in buildings, like the blacks in the Depository, one of whom thinks he hears after the shots the tinkle of the cartridge cases on the floor above them.

. . . Watch the cops look up and around, see Roy Kellerman in SS 100 X twisting in wonder and driver William Greer owl-eying the road, and Clint Hill lurching off the back-up car and running for the Lincoln, while Dave Powers and Ken O'Donnell see the President falling toward Jackie, and, at the same time in LBJ's convertible, Special Agent Rufus Youngblood is turning to the Vice President, pushing him down.

Bolt it again, move that ˙icture up, that one looked low, there! Hold it there on the head, a little left with the cross hairs . . . now, squeeezze. . . .

Lastly, near the end of our time, we concentrate on Mrs. Kennedy. She is staring doe-eyed at her husband, knowing he is hurt, reaching for him, unconscious of John Connally's moaning "Oh, no, no, no" from the jump seat, of the crowd's shrieking disintegration, of Clint Hill rushing toward her, of everything except this hurt in Jack's throat. There is now no consideration of the heat, of cloying Texans, of fatigue, no recollection in sorrow or joy of her living children, of her poor dead baby Patrick buried in August, of Jack's wounding love affairs, of their poignant anniversary just two months ago, of her own flights for rest and succor to the Greek islands, not even of what a triumph she, the First Lady, has been on this journey, how much, for all his charm, in the end he *needed* her. There is only the hurt, and her hand on his elbow, and the confused image of the tanned face contorted, and then there is no more time.

It is Zapruder frame number 313. The Mannlicher-Carcano slug, high and right again, hits, fragments, blows a fist-sized hole in the upper-right side of John Fitzgerald Kennedy's head, and he is dead, at the speed of light, of brain neurons disconnected.

Nellie Connally described it as "like spent buckshot falling all over us, and then, of course, I could see that it was matter, brain tissue." Dave Powers said it "took off the top of the President's head, and had the sickening sound of a grapefruit splattering against the side of a wall." The rain of blood, tissue, bone shards fell on both sides of the limousine. It splattered motorcycle patrolmen Bobby W. Hargis and B. J. Martin to the left rear of the Lincoln, and dotted spectators beside and right of the car, and the Connallys, Greer, Roy Kellerman in front of the stricken President. Such facts were to be important in the future appraisal of the murder.

In the back seat, the only fact was the horror, the great gouts of blood John Kennedy's heart pushed out through his skull and onto his widow's dress, her stockings and gloves, across the red roses she'd been given at Love Field (Texas had run out of yellow roses for her). And suddenly Jackie is on the trunk of the Lincoln, probably in shock, scrambling after a fish-belly-white piece of her husband's skull that's skittering across the polished black surface, as though she could catch it and Band-Aid it back. Or perhaps she was terrified and escaping to Clint Hill, who now has made it to SS 100 X, has grasped one of the welded handholds and is pulling himself up against the belated acceleration of the Lincoln as Greer finally reacts and Kellerman barks into his mike, "We are hit. Get us to a hospital." Hill struggles up and pushes Jackie into the seat and looks at Lancer, his Boss, as the car screams away for Parkland Memorial Hospital, and he hammers his fist on the trunk in rage and frustration and loss.

It has taken six seconds. It's now 12:30:06 C.S.T. Panicked pigeons rise from the Depository's roof and see madness below. Officer Hargis rams a curb, flips off and charges with drawn pistol up an incline toward the grassy knoll, pergola and stockade fence west of the Depository. Faces turn toward the Depository. Abraham Zapruder, who has filmed the Lincoln until it went beneath the underpass, is screaming, "They killed him, they killed him!"

In the press "pool car," Merriman Smith has the radiotelephone. He shouts to the UPI operator, "Three shots were fired at President Kennedy's motorcade in downtown Dallas." He will hold onto the phone, onto his greatest coup, keeping it from the AP reporter for crucial minutes, but that is not important. Nor is the fact that soon after UPI came ABC Radio, then CBS's Cronkite interrupting, fittingly, *As the World Turns,* or last, the favorite, NBC's Huntley and Brinkley. What is important is that, within fifteen minutes after the event, most of us knew the President had been shot, and that, henceforth, the events would be as much what the media reported as what had happened. That fact will haunt all the murder's investigations. Smith's "three shots," for example. Though most people in the acoustical nightmare of Dealey Plaza reported three shots, some said four or five, even six. Mrs. Kennedy, Clint Hill, Zapruder reported only two, and the third bullet has been impossible to place. Thus, in the reports that followed from the separate worlds of Dallas and Washington, of investigation and grief, we should have acknowledged that no picture, however conscientiously projected, was complete or accurate.

We were all like the audience in a Nevada movie theater, whose manager brought up the lights and announced that the President, Vice President, governor of Texas and a Secret Service man had been murdered in Dallas and "We will now continue with our matinee feature." Except the feature *was* the murder of President John F. Kennedy and the reels were crazily playing at once facts and rumors, and resonances of both.

At Dealey Plaza, amid the confusion, motorcycle officer Marrion L. Baker looks up, dismounts and runs into the Depository, convinced the sniper is on its roof. He encounters Superintendent Roy Truly and asks which way is up. Using the stairway, because the elevators are somewhere above, the two men arrive at the second-floor landing ninety seconds after the first shot, in time to see Lee Harvey Oswald hurrying into the lunchroom. Drawing his revolver, Baker summons Oswald and asks Truly, "Do you know this man, does he work here?" Truly assures the cop Oswald is an employee, and he and Baker continue upstairs to the roof. Oswald, many believe, then buys a Coke, walks downstairs and exits the Depository at 12:33, leaving behind him the Mannlicher-Carcano, complete with a live chambered round, stuffed between two rows of boxes, the three spent cartridge cases, the brown-paper bag, his palm prints and a tuft of fibers from his shirt wedged in the metal butt plate of the carbine. He walks east on Elm Street, will walk for seven blocks and by 12:40 will board a bus but, taking a transfer (so thriftily), will soon leave it in the unusual traffic and ride a cab from the Greyhound bus station to Oak Cliff near his rented room. He'll walk to his room, too. By 1:03, he will leave, carrying his revolver in his waistband.

In that time at the Plaza, some order begins to come out of the chaos.

The Dallas police—all the Secret Service are with the motorcade, racing toward Parkland—have begun questioning witnesses. Eventually, over 190 Plaza spectators will testify, offering various ear- and eye-witness reports: of the number of shots; of men running out of the Depository, down the street or into station wagons; of smoke—gun smoke?—from sewers and from behind fences; of shots from the grassy knoll, other buildings, the railing above the underpass. But the consensus at 12:34 is, as the Dallas police radio log shows, the Depository (but, queerly, one of the two police radio channels is garbled—in the melee, a mike button is stuck, or, as critics say later, somebody is intentionally jamming those wave lengths).

At 12:35, Howard Brennan tells what he saw. At 12:36, Sergeant D. V. Harkness speaks with Amos Lee Euins. The schoolboy tells about the man in the window. The Depository is ordered sealed. At 12:44, fourteen minutes after the shots were fired, a bulletin is broadcast: "Attention all squads, the suspect in the shooting at Elm and Houston is reported to be an unknown white male, approximately thirty, slender build, height five feet six, weight one hundred sixty-five pounds. . . ." In his car, Officer J. D. Tippit hears the call and, soon after, the order to patrol the Oak Cliff section.

At Parkland Memorial Hospital, Jackie stands watching the hopeless attempts to resuscitate her husband. She knows. On the way, Clint Hill had heard her cry, "He's dead, they've killed him—oh, Jack, oh, Jack, I love you." He recalled how she hesitated to leave the gory SS 100 X until Hill's coat was draped over the President's exploded head. Then there'd been the run with the stretcher (God! Her roses were on his chest!) into Trauma Room Number One, in this dun-colored tailings-heap complex called Parkland Memorial Hospital. There, for the next ninety minutes, nothing made sense.

In the gray-tile sterility of the trauma room, the doctors looked at the body of the President. They see a white male patient, number 24740, gunshot wound, who is lean, tanned, 170 pounds, six feet, aged 46, back-braced and doomed. They try fluids and external cardiac massage and perform a tracheotomy by enlarging a wound at the base of his throat, but they, too, know it is useless. No one could live with so massive a head wound. Dr. Malcolm Perry—the surgeon who was soon to raise suspicion by telling reporters the throat wound could have been an entrance hole —ends the cardiac massage at 1 P.M. C.S.T. and, as a matter of record, Dr. William Kemp Clark pronounces the President dead. Lancer is unhorsed, and Camelot is finished. Jackie Kennedy kneels in the blood, the debris on the floor, and trembles in anguish, in prayer, but does not cry.

In a nearby room, sequestered by the Secret Service, paces the thirty-sixth President of the United States. He is shocked and fearful to realize that thirty-five minutes ago he could not even sway events in his native state—now he is the leader of the world's most powerful country. He knows that thought is in many minds, twinned, if you were a Kennedyite, with the odious but irrepressible feeling that this man Johnson (this Texan!) is a usurper. His words of condolence seem awkward to him. His wife tells Mrs. Kennedy, "I wish to God there was something I could do." For the Johnsons, however, there is nothing to be done, except what the Secret Service suggests. The agents, those who have not, out of loyalty or irrationality, stayed with the slain President, fear a plot, maybe even a coup. What better time than with the Vice President in Dallas too, and most of the Cabinet out of the country? Rufus Youngblood tells the new President they must go at once to the security of Air Force One and then as quickly as possible to Washington. LBJ agrees reluctantly, saying, "We don't know whether it's a Communist conspiracy or not." The President orders word of JFK's death withheld until they leave.

At the same time, the Secret Service and police have sealed the emergency area of Parkland Hospital, including the trauma rooms, where Kennedy lies dead and Connally wounded (the governor soon is taken for emergency surgery). The nurses' station serves as a command center. Telephone links are made with the White House communications agency in Washington, and, through it, with the world. Jack Kennedy's Gaelic brigade—O'Donnell, Powers, Lawrence O'Brien—try to do what must be done to comfort Jackie, to arrange matters for their dead chieftain. Secret Service men and military aides seek to impose order, calling key officials. They worry that LBJ doesn't know the code keys that will implement various defensive reactions, those carried around in the metal suitcase by a President's shadow—the "bagman," whose various packets contain codes to set up hotlines to world leaders or to implement nuclear attacks of several magnitudes. This "man with the satchel," Ira Gearhart, has been separated from both JFK and LBJ for some time in the strung-out chase to Parkland. He is with LBJ now, but LBJ hasn't been briefed. Suppose the assassination signaled an attack? In Washington, Secretary of Defense McNamara has placed U.S. bases on alert as soon as he heard of the shooting. The Cabinet plane, bearing Secretaries Rusk, Freeman, Dillon, Hodges, Wirtz and Udall, has been contacted (they turned back after confirming UPI reports).

Soon after his brother arrives at Parkland, Attorney General Robert Kennedy is reached at his home in Virginia by J. Edgar Hoover. Steelypale, Bobby then telephones his mother, Rose. The chilling word goes throughout the Kennedy family in Massachusetts (except to the patriarch Joseph P. Kennedy—the news is kept from him for fear of his health, to the extent that his son Teddy, arriving later that afternoon from Washington, rips out the wires of his father's TV set). When in a few moments Bobby will learn from Dallas of Jack's death, he will say, "He had the most wonderful life," and turn to the ordeal of organized grief.

Outside Parkland's secure area, reporters throng and speculate (including one, Seth Kantor, who will claim he saw Jack Ruby). The AP reporter issues a bulletin saying LBJ and a Secret Service man have been shot. Rumors mixed with facts multiply, divide and conquer the nation's attentions. In the Senate of the United States, Edward M. Kennedy learns of his brother's wound from a wire-service ticker. Richard Nixon hears of it from a New York cabbie. Sargent Shriver, who will plan much of the funeral, learns by telephone at lunch. They all want to know what's really going on, want to know that:

• At 12:57, Father Oscar Huber (who had waved at John Kennedy forty-five minutes earlier) and Father James Thompson arrive at the hospital. In the trauma room, Huber administers the last rites to the President (outside, reporters whisper, "It looks like he's gone. They've called a priest"). Father Huber assures Mrs. Kennedy that Jack's soul was still in his body, that the rite was effective. The widow thanks him. Outside again, Huber answers reporters' questions, hinting the President is dead.

• At 1:26, President Johnson, his wife, Chief Curry and the Secret Service detail break out of Parkland, that possible trap, and race to Love Field and Air Force One. They arrive seven minutes later.

• At 1:30, a Dallas undertaker named Vernon Oneal arrives in response to Clint Hill's behest with his best bronze casket (a Britannia model, eventually billed to the Kennedys at $3,995). Jackie has said, "I'm not going to leave here without Jack," and so John Kennedy's body is swaddled in plastic, his ruined head wrapped and cushioned with rubber bags until, mummylike, he is closed in his coffin. On his finger is Jackie's wedding ring, put there to keep him company on the last flight home.

• At 1:33, Assistant Press Secretary Mac Kilduff announces that the President of the United States is dead. In hysterical bulletins, the confirmation is flashed around the world. Reactions of all kinds come. Fidel Castro says, "Everything has changed," and today we wonder what, exactly, he meant. A high school student in Amarillo shouts, "Hey, great, JFK's croaked!" A retired Marine Corps general in Washington unwittingly echoes some Southerners after Lincoln: "It was the hand of God that

pulled the trigger that killed Kennedy." But those sentiments were excep-
tional. Mostly, America is stunned, grieving and worrying. The *Times*
reports New York is like a vast church. Weeping is widespread. Every eye
and ear is turned to television or radio. There is rage, too, of course. In the
White House, where mourning now must intertwine with planning for a
funeral and transition, a friend and adviser speaks for many: "I'd like to
take a fucking bomb and blow the fucking state of Texas off the fucking
map." That was before the last maddening Texas events occurred.

First came the battle of the body. With the dead President encased, his
widow, his guards, his aides, all want to leave this place of death, leave with
the awful sacks of personal effects needed for evidence. Secret Service
agent Richard Johnson wants to get to the FBI with this nearly perfect
6.5mm bullet found on a stretcher, probably Connally's, by a Parkland
employee and passed on to Johnson by the hospital's security chief. That
could (and would) be terribly important in a hypothesis later based on that
unusual bullet. They all *need* to leave. But Dr. Earl Rose, the Dallas
County medical examiner, says they cannot leave. Under Texas statute,
any homicide victim must undergo an autopsy, so that the rights of the
accused murderer are protected, and they cannot leave until that is done
(in retrospect, as we will see, perhaps the law should have been obeyed).
Dr. Rose blocks the emergency-area doorway, backed by a justice of the
peace. The President's physician, Admiral George Burkley, exclaims, "It's
the President of the United States!" Dr. Rose retorts, "You people from
Washington can't make your own law." And so, in death, John Kennedy
is the object of a struggle emblematic of that which, in life, he came to
Texas to resolve. This one Ken O'Donnell resolves. "It's just another homicide case as far as I'm concerned," the JP, Judge Theron Ward, opines. "Go
screw yourself," says Ken. "We're leaving." And they sweep through, led
by an angry Secret Service detail. Surrounding Jackie and the casket, they
brush aside a strange priest, who's waving a green bag containing a relic
of the true Cross (he's blessing the President). They muscle the heavy
Britannia into Vernon Oneal's hearse, and then the cars peel off for Love
Field. On Air Force One, the Kennedyites will find the Texans, and a
terrible delay (what if those bastards *impound* the body?), while LBJ waits
for Judge Sarah Hughes to swear him in (unnecessary, since he'd actually
been in power since John Kennedy was hit). Factionalism will fester there,
while Jackie Kennedy sits in the rear of the plane by her husband's coffin,
refusing to change from her bloody clothes, and the Irish Mafia kneel to
speak with her, wondering when in hell they'll take off, and admiring her
preternatural lucidity, while Texas accents sound faintly from the forward

cabin. People will eat vegetable soup and drink whiskey which doesn't affect them and be unaware of the other Texas thing happening out there in Dallas.

Around 1:03 P.M., just after the President was pronounced dead, Roy Truly has informed police and agent Sorrels that in his canvass of employees he's discovered Oswald, the same man who was in the lunchroom just after the shooting, is missing. Maybe he should be questioned. Certainly, the physical evidence should promptly be examined (by 1:22, the rifle mistakenly described at first as a Mauser will be found). Meanwhile, Oswald is walking away from his rooming house (strange, his housekeeper later said, she thought a police car came and honked, and then there was her tenant "O. H. Lee" on the street at a bus stop). He wears a light shirt, light jacket, dark slacks and his .38 Smith & Wesson Special—the cylinder may, like the rifle, have one expended round in it, and the bullets are standard .38 Specials, slightly small for the .38 Smith & Wesson Special, which has an odd-sized barrel diameter, a detail that would make slug identification difficult. At 1:15, less than a mile from the rooming house, Officer J. D. Tippit sees Oswald, who matches the radioed description of the Dealey Plaza suspect. What happens next is verified by nine witnesses, including William Scoggins and Helen Markham, who see the first act. They see Tippit's car roll up from behind the young man and stop next to him. The pedestrian goes to the right door, and the cop opens the driver's side and steps out, starting around the front of the car. As before, earwitness accounts of the number of shots differ. But the young, slight, dark-haired man soon identified as Oswald did, Tippit's autopsy showed, put four rounds into the cop. One drives a uniform button into his chest, another nicks the aorta, a third penetrates his torso and the fourth rips into the falling policeman's temple. Then the killer runs for several blocks. He empties four cartridge cases in some bushes as people watch. He jogs past a used-car lot, discards a jacket. Behind him, a witness is calling in the murder on Tippit's radio. Immediately, sirens rend the Oak Cliff quiet. The Dallas police have had enough. A shoe store manager named Johnny Brewer, on West Jefferson Boulevard, watches a young man duck into his doorway until a prowl car passes, then walk quickly into the Texas Theater (Tony Russell, starring in *War Is Hell*). Brewer later said, "He looked funny to me . . . like he had been running, and he looked scared." Brewer asks the ticket seller about the man and learns he didn't pay, and the ticket seller, like Brewer, thinks about the assassination and the sirens and calls the police.

At 1:45, while at Parkland the battle of the body rages, the Dallas police

—fifteen strong—fan through the theater, fingerpainted by the flickering heroics, until the lights come up and Brewer points out Lee Harvey Oswald. Officer M. N. McDonald strides to Oswald, orders him to stand and begins a search. "Well, it's all over now," Oswald sighs and, hitting McDonald with his left hand, snatches for the revolver with his right. McDonald slugs the suspect, grapples for the gun, and the rest of the cops pile on. In minutes, Lee Harvey Oswald is handcuffed and on his way to police headquarters. He has a contusion on the right side of his forehead. He complains about police brutality, claims he knows nothing about Tippit, about the President, seems wise to his rights and cunning (surely enough, police later think, for aliases, for knowing something about immigration and passport procedures). At headquarters, the homicide captain has in the meantime decided, based on the Depository circumstances, to arrest this Lee Harvey Oswald in Irving. But Oswald's already there. His interrogation begins. Secret Service agent Sorrels is there and the FBI's James Hosty (who, according to a lieutenant in Dallas' intelligence section, has just confided that the FBI had information "that this subject was capable of committing the assassination of President Kennedy"—that assertion will lie buried for years).

The networks identify the suspect at 3:23, and commentators immediately link Kennedy, Tippit and Oswald. In the hours to come, they'll have much more to report. Oswald will say, "Now, everyone will know me." He will be arraigned for Tippit's, then for the President's murder. He will try to reach a New York lawyer active in ACLU cases—it seems Oswald is a member—and fail. He will see his wife. And Marina will tell police she's found Lee's wedding ring in a cup at the Paines', where he'd left it early that Friday morning, along with almost all his money and, yes, they'd had another fight the night before. She'll know about the rifle in Paines' garage and about the pictures of Lee and his guns, thus drawing tighter the lengthening chain of circumstantial and physical evidence around "A. Hidell." She'll intimate he seems guilty by the look in his eyes. His mother, Marguerite, hearing over the radio of her son's arrest, will call Bob Schieffer, then a Fort Worth reporter (now CBS White House correspondent), and tell him she wants to sell her story of Lee. And, with plans already hatching for a lawyer (who'll turn out to be Mark Lane), she will join Marina in Dallas, their lodgings courtesy of *Life* magazine (which is also acquiring Abe Zapruder's film and to whom Marguerite will also say, "Boys, I'll give you a story for money"). Oswald will become the star of his own show, appearing before reporters to state his innocence ("I didn't kill anybody, no sir"), while his prosecutors prejudice the case by saying, as

District Attorney Henry Wade did, "I figure we have sufficient evidence to convict him." Indeed, just as a matter of law—ignoring the consequences—the case will become one of the most convoluted in American history, instanced at once by the discovery U.S. Attorney Barefoot Sanders made that no Federal law forbade assassinating a President. Thus Lee Harvey Oswald, if guilty, was just a plain old Texas murderer.

All that will occur, and all along Oswald seems to enjoy the game. Baiting the police, vouchsafing little, eating well and sleeping soundly. Happily for him, one supposes, he doesn't know he, too, is doomed. Jack Ruby has attended one of the press briefings. Jack is a police buff, with inferiority feelings born of failure. Adulation of guns and cuffs and power seems to alleviate those feelings, and he is, on Friday and Saturday, cruising police headquarters, radio stations and his clubs in alternating currents of funk and vulgar business enthusiasms, until—he will claim—he is overcome with pity for the Kennedys. At 11:21, Sunday, November 24, Ruby gut-shoots Lee Harvey Oswald to death in the Dallas police-building basement with a nickel-plated .38, on live television, as the accused assassin is being led away for transfer to the county jail. That development, too (how did he get in? why? who is he?), will fester in the nation's wounds. The wounds that Jackie Kennedy, en route home on Air Force One (codenamed Angel, aptly enough), resolved would be bandaged in the ceremonies of the three days to follow. That time, from the departure at Love Field until John Kennedy was laid to rest in Arlington National Cemetery on Monday, November 25, comes back to us as a series of vignettes, like figures on a frieze telling of an ancient tragedy.

There is Jackie Kennedy, on the airplane, vowing that America must realize what's happened. Another dress? "No, let them see what they've done." She said that often, stipulating with the plural pronoun that Lee Harvey Oswald for her was surely symbolic of the hatred that had killed her husband. The feeling motivated her decision to take the bronze casket off publicly. "We'll go out the regular way," she said. "I want them to see what they have done." And she wanted it known that she had sat by her husband all the way to Andrews Air Force Base, that she at the end possessed him totally. "Suppose I hadn't been there with him?" she asked. There could be no answer, perhaps because it seemed irrelevant in the divided atmosphere of Air Force One, where the Kennedy faction felt deracinated by the Johnson people, by the new President, who was doing what he must: take over the administration of the country. "The Government must go forward," he was to say.

Never was such division better demonstrated than in the next picture, the image that told us it had really happened. There at Andrews, we saw it through the camera's eye—the casket shoved into the lift, and Jackie and Bobby (who'd boarded the plane a moment earlier to comfort her) descending while the assembled dignitaries, shadowy figures beyond the floodlit airplane, watched or moved in hesitant strides to greet the survivors of Dallas, and a team of military men went forward to take the burden and put it into the ambulance. It was true. Jack Kennedy was in that thing. That was what we saw and remembered, not the new President, who, his pride hurt, did not even emerge from what was now his flagship until after the Kennedys had left for Bethesda Hospital, not the tall man who mumbled something about needing our help and God's before the stations began playing the hundredth recapitulation of the Kennedy years. Yet that man was the President now. While Jack Kennedy went to the autopsy room, Johnson and the advisers would go by helicopter to the White House lawn, then to the Executive Office Building for meetings and briefings (and Caroline and John-John, unaware yet, had heard the helicopters earlier ferrying VIPs to meet Air Force One and had rushed to the windows, crying, "There they are. Mummy and Daddy are home. . . . Daddy's here!"—their nanny tells Caroline later).

The autopsy itself should, it seems now, have been the next picture, at least for those qualified. But because it was not pretty, Robert Kennedy asked that the autopsy photos not be disseminated. (The Warren Commission never saw them.) Thus, although Kennedy's body was X-rayed, photographed, probed, examined for some three hours, the results—as we shall see in detail in the second Kennedy chapter—have been in dispute ever since, largely because: (a) there were discrepancies among the physicians' working notes, the FBI's initial autopsy report (written by laymen) and the doctors' final report; (b) based on the Kennedy autopsy and the time required to fire Oswald's carbine, an odd explanation had to be advanced for Connally's wounds—that a bullet (the one found on Parkland's stretcher) passed through Kennedy's neck and on through the governor's chest, and out, to fracture the Texan's wrist and end by wounding his thigh; and (c) rumors from Dallas—of more than one gun, of plots, of front entrance wounds—circulated an air of skepticism around the official version. Yet the gross findings were clear then and are now. One wound about five-and-one-half inches below the bony point behind the right ear, and about the same distance from the right shoulder joint. This opening, although it seems not to have been traced to its end, led between two strap muscles to the throat wound, apparently an exit for the slug, which continued on to Connally. Unfortunately, the exit had been obliterated by Dr.

Perry's desperate tracheotomy in the resuscitation attempts. About the second wound, the fatal shot, there was little doubt. Inward-beveled bone, metal fragments driven forward (like the ball that killed Lincoln) into the orb of the right eye. Massive, downward-slanting cerebral damage. Each fact clearly indicative of a shot from above and behind.

But we saw only the revised autopsy report, not the pictures, and when the autopsy was done and the new casket arrived at Bethesda—a plain African-mahogany model to replace the Britannia, damaged in the escape from Dallas—embalmers went to work to create the beautiful memory picture of the undertaker's trade. They dressed the body in a blue-gray suit, put mesh and artificial hair over the awful wound, brought color to the ashen flesh. They put a rosary in the folded hands. Jackie Kennedy would not like it, would say "It was like something you would see at Madame Tussaud's," and so the casket would stay closed for the obsequies. That, like everything else, caused speculation. Is he disfigured? Shot in the face? Is he really dead, or a vegetable someplace? But it was Jackie's will, as so much was, and it was consistent with her decision, reached at Bethesda, that John Fitzgerald Kennedy's funeral would be like Abraham Lincoln's. It was.

At 4:34 A.M., Washington time, Saturday, November 23, the dead President went at last back to the White House. The dawn promised and would deliver a rainy, blowy, maudlin day. A Marine honor guard escorted the widow, still in the same pink, blood-covered suit, and the dead Commander in Chief's brother, and the flag-draped-coffin to the East Room, where Kennedy would lie that morning, surrounded by the deathwatch sentinels, by four tall tapers, by the windows garlanded with black crepe, stark against even a lowering sky. Outside, thousands gathered to stare in silence at the White House and the black windows. Inside, Jackie looked again at her husband and murmured, "It isn't Jack."

The world knew it was. Westminster Abbey's bell tolled each minute for an hour, as it had done only for fallen monarchs. De Gaulle mused, "I am stunned. They are crying all over France." Italians marched in mourning. In Berlin, where Kennedy had announced, *"Ich bin ein Berliner,"* candles lit every window. The U.S.S.R.'s Andrei Gromyko wept. The world leaders came, some to visit the East Room, some as the President lay in state on Sunday in the Capitol's rotunda, all to walk on Monday behind the Kennedys, behind the caisson from the White House to St. Matthew's Cathedral, then to ride to Arlington for the burial. There were eight heads of state, ten prime ministers, most of the world's remaining royalty. Ninety-two nations sent delegations. Some 250,000 Americans came in person to file by Kennedy's body in their Capitol. One million flanked the route of the funeral cortege, the procession to Arlington. Countless millions watched it all on television. We saw, and saw repeatedly so that it became imprinted in us almost genetically, the last images of the Kennedy era.

The riderless horse, Black Jack, cavorting so that the saber, the boots reversed in their silver stirrups, jangled and flashed—it was as though he were possessed, or mounted by a presence only he could feel.

Those drums, accompanied by the hundred-to-the-minute mourning pace of the military units, moving behind the caisson to the band's slowed dirge of "Hail to the Chief," and to the melancholy skirl of the Black Watch pipers, on the way to the Capitol, to the cathedral, to Arlington.

Cardinal Cushing, the high priest himself, breaking from Latin into English at the Mass to say, "May the angels, dear Jack, lead you into Paradise," and the veiled widow weeps, until Caroline says, "Don't cry, I'll take care of you."

The Arlington moment when, the last ritual words uttered in the echo of Air Force One's wing-waggling last fly-by, the bugler who's blown taps thousands of times reaches for the highest note, and breaks, the sound like a catch in our throats, and Jackie receives the covering flag. Then she stoops to light the flame that's to burn forever.

Finally, the midnight visit to the grave with Bobby, that Monday, after a small celebration of John-John's birthday, when she sees the tokens—a Special Forces beret, a prayer card—against the mass of odd flowers, against the flame, and she looks down, perhaps thinking of her letter to Jack, of her son's scrawl, and her daughter's note, and a pair of cuff links and a scrimshaw Presidential Seal that now rest with Jack beneath the ground, against the coffin's silky lining where she'd put them. Then she looks up, turns to go—for the moment a secular saint. But one who will live another life, and return from it to mourn the murder of the brother-in-law so stern next to her. For them, it is not finished. For Jack Kennedy, it is.

Neither is it finished for us. Despite the feelings of the Kennedyites, the United States will go on. President Lyndon Baines Johnson has already met with the visiting diplomats and leaders, establishing himself. He has ordered the FBI to investigate his predecessor's murder vigorously. He must now prepare the budget, move into the Executive Mansion ("Where will I live?" Jackie had asked Bobby) and inaugurate his era. Vietnam's escalation is still in his future, but other killings lie close at hand. This man Ruby has killed Oswald, saying, "You killed the President, you rat," and then, "You all know me, I'm Jack Ruby." What's all that about? And there is Kennedy's killing. Who did it really? Things will have to be cleared up, for sure.

President Johnson's first impulse was to convene a Texas panel to look into these Texas matters. But the Justice Department, chiefly Nicholas Katzenbach, persuaded the President that this matter transcended state boundaries.

On November 29, 1963, by Executive Order Number 11130, President Johnson created the Warren Commission to investigate the murders of John F. Kennedy and Oswald. The Commission's official charge was to arrive at the truth wherever it was to be found. But it was also understood that this panel of distinguished Americans—Chief Justice Earl Warren, Senators John Sherman Cooper and Richard Russell, Representatives Hale Boggs and Gerald R. Ford, ex-CIA Director Allen W. Dulles, and the statesman-businessman John J. McCloy—would in its findings, if possible, preserve as a political necessity the respect for our institutions that was so vital in a period of transition and turmoil. The commission was also told to get it done fast. Unfortunately, the panel was insufficiently equipped for any of these tasks. Its members, perforce, were busy men unable to devote full time to the investigation (some attended as few as 20 percent of the hearings). It had no investigative staff, instead exclusively relying on the FBI (who had things to hide) and on a small group of young lawyers, who were being pushed constantly to investigate and to write the report as soon as possible. Even so, the Commission amassed information unparalleled in any investigation of any of our assassinations.

On September 24, 1964, the Warren Commission submitted its report to the President. In painstaking detail through millions of words, it laid out its proof that Lee Harvey Oswald and Lee Harvey Oswald alone had murdered John F. Kennedy. It described how he had done it. It assessed Jack Ruby as a disturbed man, a crazed avenging angel, who had acted alone. It recommended that killing a President be made a Federal crime. It criticized the FBI's handling of crucial information and witnesses. Overall, it sought to dispel the myths, the theories (many voiced in Europe) of conspiracy—executed by leftists or rightists or militarists or foreign operatives.

For a time, the report succeeded. Polls showed most Americans accepted the findings. It was endorsed editorially around the nation. The *New York Times*, as bellwether, wrote:

The Warren Commission report is a massive and moving document . . . it tells all that can now be learned about the deaths of the President and his assassin, Lee

Harvey Oswald. No comparable event in history has ever received such an exhaustive and searching examination while all the facts were fresh and witnesses available to testify. Those in this country and abroad who prefer devious explanations will cling to their theories of a sinister conspiracy. But those who can confront the truth with all its complexity and ironic force will recognize in the events in Dallas much that is symbolic of the irrationality of man's fate.

Within a year, those who preferred devious explanations and suspected conspiracies would take the field, armed with evidence even the mountainous report could not dwarf. The report, they said, was symbolic of man's irrationality. This murder must out, they cried, and the nation heard them.

ATTACK ON THE REPORT

*"A bad man shot my daddy in the head
with a rifle."*

—JOHN F. KENNEDY, JR.

Twelve years ago, just after release of the Warren Report, almost everyone knew who the bad man with the rifle was. Lee Harvey Oswald had
killed President John F. Kennedy. According to the report, Oswald, and
Oswald alone, had ambushed the President. Surely that was clear, documented in twenty-seven volumes that overwhelmed the early tremors of
suspicion about a plot and calmed the first wave of rumors launched by
the shock of the President's death and by the nearly incredible end of his
accused assassin. True, eccentrics like Bertrand Russell might immediately attack the report from abroad, but that was typical of the Old World,
where assassination conspiracies had for centuries been common. Not so,
most of us thought, here in the New World. With the exceptions of John
Wilkes Booth's band of anti-Lincolnites and Truman's two Puerto Rican
attackers, our Presidential assassins had proved to be lone, maddened
men. They were small, white, young, from disturbed homes and possessed
by a murderous cause. Was not Lee Harvey Oswald exactly that sort?
Could anyone reasonably doubt he *was* the bad man with the rifle?

Today, seven out of ten Americans believe Oswald was not the only bad
man. Since 1965, when the first serious attacks on the report were
mounted, skepticism about the Warren Commission's conclusion has risen
steadily. Many reasons have been offered. Perhaps the Cold War's climate
contributed, with its ceaseless talk of spy conspiracies, with Joe McCarthy
finding Reds under every rug. Or maybe, some say, our refusal to believe
was born in the exponential increase of madness in the land when the
murder of a President was followed by the lacerating atrocities of Viet-

nam, by more assassinations, by civil riots, by the crippling absurdities of Watergate; finally, by the disclosures of FBI and CIA crimes, until Americans, swirled in cyclones of cynicism, were ready to believe that anything was possible. Perhaps, others suggest, it has from the first been the sheer incongruity of that weak-chinned Oswald's bringing down the hero of PT 109 that galled us beyond belief. But these explanations beg the point.

The Warren Report is doubted because its responsible critics have raised vital questions about the Commission's procedures, evidence and conclusions. In what follows, we will look, as objectively as possible, at the key elements of the physical evidence and at the plausible possibilities of conspiracy, with the warning that the enormous amount of data on the Kennedy assassination prevents examination of more than the major elements and theories. For, if you reject the Warren Commission's theories, there are no simple answers.

Indeed, the central strength of the Warren Report is its monolithic character since its critics have no single alternative. For example, if you reject the Commission's findings in the matter of where guns were fired in Dealey Plaza, you have a wide choice. Or, if you reject Oswald as a solitary killer, you can choose conspirators from the Russians, Castroites, dissident elements of the CIA and FBI (with Oswald perhaps an agent for each and all), or the Teamsters-cum-Mafia-cum-CIA, or Lyndon Johnson, or H. L. Hunt–style Texas right-wingers acting for God and country. You can consider anti-Castro Cubans incensed over the Bay of Pigs, the Minutemen, the Klan, an embryonic military junta (assisted by military intelligence and key industrial leaders), the Dallas Police Force, or New Orleans homosexuals connected with organized crime and the CIA (the CIA is, predictably, most often involved in speculations on the assassination). You even have your choice of Oswalds. In many instances, the theories overlap in rings of persons and places rippling out from the central incident to encompass so much that one wonders if any conspiracy so huge could remain a secret. Three or four men, perhaps—but many more . . . well, why didn't they just wait and *vote* Kennedy out?

Yet the fact that the report's critics cannot agree on every specific point (except that Oswald alone didn't do it) should not disqualify their views, especially those buttressed by the persuasive evidence some have unearthed. If some of them are open to charges of being careerists out for a fast buck, or trendy egomaniacs, or paranoids in the twilight of logic, or erectors of vast clockwork systems in which human error does not exist and every act is linked with every other, then they are little worse than the Government itself, which through the Warren Commission failed to answer the question once and for all of who killed John Kennedy. It was, we must remember, the Government who had that responsibility and the resources to discharge it. It was the FBI who, out of guilt or vainglory, decided after Kennedy's death to cover up a threatening note of Lee Harvey Oswald's to agent James Hosty that fateful week in Dallas. It was the FBI, the Commission's staff and to a lesser degree, the Secret Service who, it seems, persuaded some witnesses to agree with the Commission's already-conceived view. It was the distinguished members of the Warren Commission who did not even view, let alone release, the crucial autopsy photos that show exactly how the bullets killed Kennedy. It was the Commission's failure to call certain witnesses or to credit only selected others that fueled suspicion of its findings. It was the Commission's questionable interpretations of ballistics, its strained reconstructions of the crime, its unwillingness to pick up beguiling threads of inquiry, its seeming blindness to the conspiratorial connotations of Oswald's odd life that aroused the critics.

But before we can talk of conspiracy, or of the one deranged Oswald, we must go back to Dealey Plaza, to the critical physical evidence. All theories begin with that.

Although it does not mean that Oswald killed Kennedy, there is little doubt he ordered the Mannlicher-Carcano that did slay the President. The handwriting on the order to Klein's Sporting Goods of Chicago and that on the order for a .38 Smith & Wesson revolver from Seaport Traders, Inc., of Los Angeles have been identified as Oswald's. Both documents bear the name "A. Hidell," which also appeared with minor variations on counterfeit identification found in Oswald's wallet after his arrest in the Texas Theater about 1:50 P.M. on November 22, shortly after Officer J. D. Tippit had been killed with the .38 Smith & Wesson. Both guns were shipped in March, 1963, to P.O. Box 2915, Dallas, which had been rented by a Lee H. Oswald, whose signature matched that of A. Hidell. It is not clear why he used this alias, whether out of murderous cunning, insecurity about himself or an attempt to link himself, at least phonetically, with "Fidel." Suggesting the latter (as his wife, Marina, did too) Oswald, in the spring of 1963 in New Orleans, formed a chapter of the Fair Play for Cuba Committee, himself as sole member and A. J. Hidell as president (Hidell also had a post-office box there).

In addition, among the identification cards found on Oswald were two clever bits of forgery, both in the name Alek James Hidell (in Russia, Marina said, Lee was called Alek). They were a draft card and a certificate of service in the U.S. Marine Corps, each made of prints from doctored photographic negatives that were pasted back to back. Oswald knew quite a bit about photography. In the Marines, he analyzed aerial photos and tracked U-2 flights. His best job in Dallas had been as a photoprint trainee with Jaggars-Chiles-Stovall, a graphic-arts firm. Then, too, after he was arrested, he told Dallas police that the photos they'd scavenged from Marina's lodgings in Irving, showing him posed with rifle, pistol and leftist publications, were fakes, that he knew someone had pasted his head on somebody else's body and shot a new negative. The Warren Commission expert said no, but other experts have said yes (the background shadows are inconsistent with the foreshadows, and the relative sizes of head and body are wrong). But none of that proves he killed the President.

Did Oswald even have the Mannlicher-Carcano with him that November 22 and did he ever practice with it? Marina said she remembered him working the bolt and squinting through the sight in New Orleans in May, 1963. She also said that on other occasions in Dallas she saw him clean it and work the bolt. Once, she said, he took the rifle concealed in a raincoat, saying he was going to practice shooting. A Russian friend of the Oswalds (they were often among the *émigrés* of Dallas and Fort Worth) testified that Lee told him of target shooting. One such target, according to Marina, was the virulently right-wing Major General Edwin A. Walker, at whom Lee said he took a shot with the Mannlicher-Carcano on April 10, 1963, after leaving a note in Russian for her with instructions on what to do if he were caught, along with the pictures of himself with rifle, pistol and *The Worker* in hand. (The gunman fired through the house window, missing Walker's head, not by much, and escaped. The slug was too mutilated to determine if a Mannlicher-Carcano had fired it.)

By far the most intriguing tale, though, is that of Oswald at rifle ranges. On several days in November prior to the assassination, witnesses at target ranges saw a man they said looked like Oswald. That would seem further to incriminate Oswald, were it not that other evidence developed by the FBI for the Warren Commission placed Oswald elsewhere. Were these witnesses simply mistaken, as eyewitnesses often are? Did they want somehow to participate in the crime of the century? It's been suggested by many leading conspiracy theorists—especially Harold Weisberg, Richard Popkin, Jim Garrison and Robert Sam Anson—that they may have been witnesses to the "second Oswald"—a look-alike who acted to attract attention to "Oswald," thus putting the frame tightly around the decoy. But serious consideration of that must come after some other matters. Again, did the real Oswald, who worked at the Texas School Book Depository, have his Mannlicher-Carcano with him at 12:30 P.M. on November 22, 1963?

The Warren Commission was satisfied that Oswald had taken the disassembled rifle to work that morning in a thirty-eight-inch-long brown-paper bag he had made earlier of wrapping paper and tape available in the Depository's shipping room. Oswald's right palm print and left-index fingerprint were detected on the bag. Buell Wesley Frazier, who drove Oswald to work that morning from Irving, said Lee had with him a longish, heavy, brown-paper package. Lee said it contained curtain rods. Even so, questions have since been raised about the bag. Frazier and his sister, Mrs. Linnie Mae Randle, both saw the package that morning when Lee came over. Lee even surprised Frazier by hurrying into the Depository ahead of him, holding the package upright with his right hand, the end seemingly tucked into his armpit.

However, both Frazier and Mrs. Randle repeatedly told the Commission's lawyers that the package they saw was no more than 27 inches long, whereas the shortest component of the broken-down rifle, the stock, was 34 1/2 inches long (too long for Oswald to have tucked in his armpit). There is also, critics claim, a question about when Oswald made the bag and got it to the Paines', where his rifle was kept—no witness recalled seeing the bag prior to the twenty-second—but, all in all, it seems clear Oswald could have transported his gun as the Commission says.

More important are the constellations of questions surrounding the weaponry and ballistics of the Kennedy murder, the brightest glowing around the famous "magic bullet." The theory of the Commission is that the slug hit both Kennedy and Connally and was finally found little the worse for wear on the Governor's stretcher at Parkland Hospital. Before that wonder can be explored come simpler considerations. First is the number of shots. Eight-three percent of the witnesses in Dealey Plaza who offered an opinion reported three. Only 7 percent said two (though they included Mrs. Kennedy and Secret Service men, notably Clint Hill). Very few reported more than three, tending to dispute investigators who believe there were several assassins.

Accepting the majority opinion becomes easier, if not necessarily correct, when we recall that three cartridge cases were found next to the wall under the sill of the southeast window on the sixth floor of the Texas School Book Depository. There, Dallas police photographs showed, were three boxes stacked to the west side of the partially opened window, allegedly to form a gun rest for the sniper. Other boxes along that side of the building concealed the shooter from anyone else who might be on the floor. According to Dallas police and FBI laboratory reports, only one of the three gun-rest boxes held Oswald's prints—the right-index fingerprint and left palm print. Another small box set back from the window had on it Oswald's right palm print. But, as many observers have noted, Oswald worked in the building, filling book orders from cartons, including those on the sixth floor. Why shouldn't his prints be there? In addition, if he stacked the boxes, why weren't his prints on all of them? Furthermore, there are other photos of the nest that show a different arrangement of boxes. Which, if any, were taken before investigators moved the boxes, and did those square with what people outside saw looking upward? The Warren Commission's best witness to Oswald in the window was Howard Brennan, a steamfitter who was seated on a concrete wall opposite the Depository. Saying nothing substantive about the boxes, he testified that Oswald was standing in the window with the rifle, leaning against the left sill—a flat impossibility, since the gunman would then have had to shoot through the window panes. Still, the testimony of other witnesses, especially that of the fifteen-year-old schoolboy Amos Lee Euins, suggests that there was at least one man seen in the window—as another witness said, "crowded in among boxes"—and that he had a gun.

When did he fire it, and how many times, and what did he hit? All the theorists, including the Warren Commission, have been forced to time the shots and to hypothesize about their effect, based on the film record of the assassination created by Abraham Zapruder, the Dallas garment manufacturer who had stationed himself and his zoom-lens Bell & Howell 8mm movie camera on a concrete pedestal at one end of the Plaza's northern pergola—a structure like a bandstand immediately west of the Depository and next to a grassy knoll that led up to a line of trees fronting a six-foot stockade fence. The fence screened a parking lot next to railway yards. Zapruder's camera, tests later showed, ran at an average 18.3 frames per second. Thus his film provides both a clock and a visual record of Kennedy's and Connally's reactions during the horror of those six seconds. Indeed, Zapruder's film might have put an end to all the speculations about Kennedy's death had it not been for a large traffic sign obscuring the exact location (hence time) of the first shot. As it is, the camera's speed, the sign's obstruction and the rapidity with which the Mannlicher-Carcano could be operated are among the variables that have plagued us. The Warren Commission's staff, as well as several independent and conscientious investigators, have tried mightily to unravel precisely what happened. But little is absolute except the mathematics. Only the Warren

Commission had access to Oswald's rifle. Its tests indicated that it could not be fired and rebolted in less than 2.3 seconds. (Tests made for this book, over iron sights at comparable distances with similar Mannlicher-Carcanos, allowed three accurate shots to be fired in as little as 4.4 seconds, though some of the sequences took as long as eight due to the erratic behavior of the weapon.)

So, for a three-shot firing sequence consistent with the Warren Report and the Zapruder film, the sniper must aim and fire the cartridge lying ready in the chamber, bolt a new cartridge in, re-aim, shoot and repeat this—all in less than six seconds (or a second more than the Government's minimum required time). Six seconds was all the time available, because the sniper's view of Kennedy's body from the southeast window of the Depository was obscured by a live oak tree from Zapruder frame 166 until approximately frame 210. Curiously, Kennedy was a fine target before that time, all the way down Houston Street and through the turn just below the window, yet no shots were then fired. There is a moment at frame 186 when a shot might have been fired through an opening in the foliage. Some observers believe one was fired about then, hitting the pavement at the rear of the President's car (several spectators thought, in retrospect, that they saw something splatter) and flinging fragments several hundred yards, one of which may have injured James Tague, who was standing on Commerce Street near the Triple Underpass. More probably, Tague was nicked in the cheek by something—a bullet fragment or chip of concrete —bouncing up from a Main Street curb about fifteen feet away. A section of curbing there, examined belatedly by the FBI, showed under spectrographic testing traces of lead and antimony, two elements common in the lead cores of bullets. No trace of copper was found, meaning the smear could not be from the first impact of one of the Mannlicher-Carcano's copper-jacketed rounds. If from a bullet at all (many articles contain lead and antimony), the smear had to come either from a Mannlicher-Carcano bullet fragment or from another bullet altogether. This last explanation is preferred by those suspecting more than one gunman.

Further complicating matters, Mr. Tague thinks he was hit at the time of "either the second or the third" shot (meaning, if Oswald was the lone gunman, either by what the Warren Commission calls the miss or by the fatal head shot). Yet Tague was a long way from the limousine—almost a hundred yards when Kennedy's head exploded. Would a fragment fly that far? Or was there another gun? Do we even know, assuming three shots were fired from the Depository, which of the first two missed? Unfortunately, it's impossible to determine from Zapruder's film, because by the time the President's limousine cleared the oak tree and offered the gunman a good sight picture, the car had also passed behind the street sign. We only know that by frame 225, when the limousine emerges from behind the sign, Kennedy has been hit. His hands move upward toward his throat, his shoulders hunch. In James Altgens' photo taken an instant later at frame 255, we see the Secret Service men crane back toward the unexpected firecracker pop, while Jackie grabs Jack's arm and Connally turns awkwardly to his right. This the Commission calls the first shot from the lone gunman and is the magic bullet. The second probably misses, it says. The third, about 4.2 seconds after Kennedy emerges from behind the sign, at Zapruder frame 313, blows out the right side of Kennedy's skull.

Several quick but significant questions about those shots. Could the 1941-vintage Mannlicher-Carcano, which was later found stuck between two rows of boxes near the descending staircase on the southwest end of the building, have all by itself killed Kennedy? Yes. At short range, with the 160-161-grain copper-jacketed bullets, it had more than the necessary penetrating power and accuracy, despite a tendency to shoot high and right (which defect could easily have been compensated for by anyone familiar with the weapon). Is it certain that three shots were fired from that window, as so many witnesses heard? No.

Kennedy may well have been the target of just two shots from there. Even though three expended cartridges were found, one casing was dented at the neck in a way occurring commonly when dry-firing a weapon. It is conceivable that Oswald took the rifle to the Depository with an empty hull in the chamber and a clip containing three live rounds in the magazine. Since one live round was in the rifle when it was discovered, that would mean only two shots were fired from the window, both hitting their mark, one maybe going on to Connally. Interestingly, no other ammunition for the rifle was found among Oswald's possessions, which may mean that he bought only one box (Lee *was* quite thrifty) and expended all but these three or four rounds in practice, less one maybe loosed at Edwin Walker. Or perhaps, a few sleuths whisper, an as yet unknown and stingy employer doled out these necessary rounds to Oswald, who had been enlisted in a Byzantine scheme to assassinate a President unaware that the final act required him, as gunman, to take the rap.

Anyway, the 6.5mm Mannlicher-Carcano found in the Depository (at first mistakenly identified as a 7.65mm Mauser, an error that fueled suspicions about a conspiracy, since it suggested two weapons) was directly tied to Oswald by only one palm print, lifted from the underside of the barrel, beneath the stock's wooden forepiece. No usable prints were found on the cartridge cases. Thus the assumption that Oswald used the rifle that day rests as much on his ability and opportunity as on the weapon itself. Was Oswald a good enough shot? Certainly, for a trained marksman, the distance was not great—about 175 feet when the President's limousine first came from behind the oak tree. Through the scope, it would look no more than 50 feet. Oswald had been trained by the Marine Corps, which boasts of producing the finest marksmen in the world (Charles Whitman, the "Texas tower sniper," was one such). Lee qualified as sharpshooter with the M-1, though he later dropped to the lowest end of the Marksman scale. Nelson Delgado, a Marine buddy, testified that he was a very poor shot. A stronger malediction came from a strange quarter. In February, 1964, a Russian KGB agent named Yuri Nosenko abruptly defected. One of his statements concerned Oswald, who, Nosenko said, while living in Russia was such a bad shot that when he went hunting, somebody had to go along to provide him with game. Nosenko also assured the CIA that Oswald was not a Russian agent, a possibility that Oswald's own defection to Russia and his espousement of left-wing causes since his return had raised—especially with Lyndon B. Johnson, who initially feared he was President by virtue of a Communist conspiracy (LBJ also feared a nuclear war should Oswald turn out to be a Russian spook). Exactly why Nosenko defected when he did is unknown, although from a Soviet viewpoint he went at an opportune time, just after Kennedy's death, bearing assurances that the KGB had nothing to do with it. Anyway, the verdict is mixed on Oswald's marksmanship prior to the Kennedy killing. Certainly he was a trained shooter at distances of up to 500 yards. An additional aid to his speed and aim, if he was in that window, might have been simple adrenalin.

Could he have fired the weapon three times within six seconds? In tests run for the Warren Commission's investigation, three National Rifle Association masters shot Oswald's weapon at stationary targets positioned at distances corresponding to Zapruder frames number 210 (175 feet), about number 252 (240 feet) and number 313 (265 feet). These experts even with the clumsy rifle succeeded two of six times in getting off three shots in less than six seconds. They hit the first and third targets consistently but often missed the second, because the aiming movement from first to second target required a change of firing position. In 1967, CBS News, as part of its first "inquiry" into the Kennedy assassination, had a tower and a ramp constructed, complete with moving silhouette, to simulate the heights and distances between the Presidential limousine and the Depository window. Marksmen in those tests, conducted with a rifle like Oswald's (and ours), could get the three shots off in time, and several hit the silhouette two or three times. Almost half of the tests, though, were invalidated because the rifle malfunctioned. (In our tests conducted with a Mannlicher-Carcano of the same type used by Oswald, malfunctions [either jamming or misfires] occurred more than 50 percent of the time.)

In sum, all we can suppose is that if Oswald had a good day and the rifle was working well, he could have made the shots. We can suppose, too, that the bullet fragments, and the magic bullet, came from the Mannlicher-Carcano. Two good-sized fragments, one from a bullet's nose and another from a base, were recovered from the limousine. Several other tiny pieces were retrieved from the automobile and Connally's wrist (X-rays showed more minuscule pieces in Kennedy's skull and in Connally's femur and chest). These fragments, the nearly pristine bullet found at Parkland and the cartridge cases were said by the FBI to have been fired from the Mannlicher-Carcano. Spectrography revealed only that the slugs had similar metallic composition—not surprising, since all were made in 1944 by the Western Cartridge Company of similar materials. Even these facts have been questioned by critics of the FBI investigation (the Warren Commission had no investigative staff and was forced to rely on Hoover's men). One skeptic asks why tests were not done to see if the magic bullet went through human tissue, both Kennedy's and Connally's. Or if conclusive neutron-activation analyses were done, for example, on Kennedy's shirt and coat, through which the magic bullet supposedly passed, to determine if metallic residues found on the back of the garment marked that passage all the way through and, if so, whether the residue was identical in elemental composition with the bullet. Similarly, the spectrographic tests linking Connally's wrist fragments with the wondrous bullet have been challenged by various investigators, most effectively by Weisberg and Howard Roffman.

Apparently nothing in the case can be taken on its face. Not even that Oswald was on the sixth floor and had access to the window. The Commission's witness on that crucial point was Charles Givens, a worker in the Depository who said he saw Oswald about noon November 22, walking from the southeast corner of the *sixth* floor toward the freight elevators that are on the building's north side. Surely such testimony would be beyond debate were it not for the fact that Givens first told the FBI that he had seen Oswald on the *first* floor before the shooting—a story he stuck to until April, 1964, when intensive interrogation by Commission lawyer David Belin brought forth the new version. Also, since published FBI documents show that Mrs. R. E. Arnold, a secretary at the Depository, thought she might have caught a glimpse of Oswald on the first floor around 12:25, Givens' revised testimony is most questionable.

Can it be *proved* that Oswald was on the sixth floor, in or near that window? Three eyewitnesses—Brennan, Euins and an Arnold Rowland—had good long views of a man with a gun there. But eyewitnesses are frequently mistaken. Predictably, such witnesses offered contradictory stories; e.g., as to just which floor the gunman was on, how tall he was, how long the rifle was, even as to whether he was alone. Rowland, for example, later told the FBI and the Commission he'd seen two men, a rifleman in a *southwest* window and an elderly black man in the southeast (three black men did watch the motorcade from the fifth floor below the nest and after the shooting pointed up at the southeast window above them). Another witness, Mrs Carolyn Walther, whom the Commission never called to testify directly, said she saw the gunman and, beside him, another man with a shorter weapon, but they were on a floor lower than the sixth. This point—whether or not Oswald was accompanied—cried for proof. For a time it seemed that photography would produce an answer. Twenty-two photographers stood in Dealey Plaza with film in their cameras that might be invaluable in solving the murder. One was Robert Hughes, who stood a block away from the motorcade shooting a 8mm movie. As the fateful turn onto Elm Street began, Hughes's camera recorded the southeast window of the Depository. Could close examination of those frames reveal how many waited in ambush? One answer came in a second CBS inquiry into the killing. Computer studies of the shape, contrast and depth of the tiny images (a fraction of a small frame, taken 100 yards away) by the Itek Corporation showed yes, there was movement (hence the gunman) and no, there was no other human being there. But Itek's findings generated skepticism. Itek has as its president a former CIA man, and is it not the CIA that, we learned, hired news correspondents as informers, including Sam A. Jaffee, once of CBS, who said it seemed to him quite possible that the CIA had got him hired by CBS in the first place? If the CIA could get people hired at CBS, could it not also influence the content of broadcasts? If the head of Itek was with the CIA, could Itek's report to CBS have been influenced, particularly since 60 percent of Itek's business was for the Government? The questions are unanswerable.

Another movie, this by Orville Nix, aroused high excitement because it seemed to show a rifleman perched on a car parked directly behind the concrete wall bordering the pergola near the grassy knoll. Edward Jay Epstein, whose book *Inquest* first illuminated the Commission's procedural inadequacies, brought this theory to national prominence, while another critic, Jones Harris, who'd discovered the malevolent figure, proceeded, with UPI's help (UPI had bought the Nix film for $5,000), to subject the film to the greatest possible scrutiny. That's right, they sent it to Itek. The conclusion was that, because it lacked depth, the figure was really a shadow and the car was parked far back of the pergola. Harris then decided that Itek and UPI had collaborated to suppress the discovery of the real assassin. To answer this, Nix's poor-quality 8mm movie was once more analyzed, this time at Caltech. The results received in February, 1975, supported the Itek findings but did not rule out the possibility of a grassy-knoll assassin. As of today, some theorists see three assassins aligned on a walk descending from the knoll toward Elm Street. Two of these, it's said, resemble Watergate plotters E. Howard Hunt and Frank Sturgis. So it seems the more we know, the less we know. Any bit of evidence about John Kennedy's murder so fascinates investigators that, spider-like, they spin out of it immense webs of intrigue. One more example now.

In an Altgens photo of the motorcade, if we look past the puzzled Jackie and the President just reacting to his first wound, we see peering out of the Depository's broad entranceway, hard on the right, a face that mightily resembles Oswald's. As soon as the picture was released, people asked if it was Oswald, for, if so, Oswald could not be the killer. Thorough investigation, however, established that the man was Billy Nolan Lovelady, an employee of the Depository. Lovelady himself said "Yes, sir," when asked if that was he. But this was questioned, because an FBI photo of Lovelady showed him in a red-and-white-striped short-sleeved shirt, quite unlike the dark, long-sleeved shirt seen on the man in the doorway. (Oswald, when arrested, was wearing a shirt very like the one on the man in the doorway.) Eventually, Lovelady said he did wear the dark shirt on November 22 but wore the striped shirt for the FBI picture. However, a different photo seems to show him in the doorway wearing yet another dark checked shirt, again raising suspicions about who was where. This shows how any given piece of information or misinformation can awaken suspicions of startling longevity.

No suspicions in the assassination have had a greater or more deserved life span than those surrounding the next mystery—the magic bullet. The thesis, as formulated by Commission attorneys Arlen Specter and David Belin, was simple if farfetched. A bullet penetrated Kennedy's neck, transited the muscle layers, exited at the throat, went on to punch an elliptical hole in Connally's back, there shattering the Texan's fifth rib, before exiting below the right nipple to tear into the back of the right wrist, exit at the palm and finish the remarkable odyssey by lodging in the left thigh and finally falling out to be discovered on Parkland's stretcher. All this with only moderate flattening and the loss from its base of no more than 2.4 grains of metal. (That is possible if unlikely: Only about 1.5 grains of metal either were removed from Connally's wrist or were seen by X-ray to be still embedded in his chest and femur. But Weisberg maintains the metal missing from the bullet's base was cut out by the FBI for testing and was thus *never* in Connally.)

When the wild theory of the bullet's path was proposed, responsible investigators howled. How could it be? More importantly, *why* must it be? Did not the initial FBI and Secret Service assassination reports themselves clearly say that three shots were fired, the first hitting the President in the back, the second striking Connally and the third slamming into Kennedy's skull? Why must there be a magic bullet at all? The answer again came from Zapruder's camera. Quite simply, given the time needed to fire the Mannlicher-Carcano, the film showed that unless one bullet struck both the President and the governor, there had to be more than one assassin. Had to be because between Zapruder frame 225, when Kennedy clearly has been hit, and frame 237, when Connally unmistakably reacts to his wound, there isn't time to reload and fire Oswald's carbine. What was more perplexing, there seemed to be too much time between the reactions of Connally and Kennedy for a single bullet to have penetrated both men. Never mind the bullet's physical condition. Here was scientific proof of a conspiracy, not to mention duplicity by the Commission (such as ignoring the FBI and Secret Service and saying that Connally had suffered a "delayed reaction" to the bullet marauding through his body).

This contention again brought sophisticated optical analysis to bear on Zapruder's movie. The latest, conducted by the ubiquitous Itek, indicates that Connally may be reacting to his wound as early as frames 223–226, a sixth of a second in which a flipping motion begins in the right hand, with which he holds his Stetson. Other theorists ridicule the suggestion, saying they see no sign of distress in Connally until almost a second after Kennedy is seen reaching for his throat. And how can he still be holding his Stetson in frame 235 if a bullet was coming out of his palm? No firm answer can be given. Men in combat often react late to wounds. Deer run through by high-powered arrows often look up quizzically, then return to grazing before they react to their mortal wound. Yet Connally himself has always vowed he was hit by the second shot, because he heard the first before feeling his wounds (you can't hear the bullet that hits you, since sound travels at only 1,100 feet per second, half the speed of the 6.5mm rounds). It is "inconceivable" that he was hit by the same bullet that hit Kennedy. His wife agrees, saying she heard the shot and she and Connally started to turn toward the wounded President, and then the Governor was hit. Of course, this also implies two gunmen, for even if a first shot from the Depository missed the car and that was what Connally heard, how then was the President hit *before* Connally unless by another gun? Certainly, it could be that the Connallys are mistaken. In that case, return for a moment to the physical evidence. Could the notorious bullet do all that the Commission asks of it?

Numerous ballistics tests have been made with 6.5mm Mannlicher-Carcanos to determine if any bullet could do so much and yet end up mostly unmutilated. The Army fired Oswald's carbine at blocks of skin-covered gelatin and chunks of animal flesh to simulate Kennedy's neck wound. It concluded that the projectile lost little velocity or stability (good penetrating power is characteristic of these quarter-inch slugs), thus accounting for exit holes only slightly larger than the entrances. Testers also fired through a goat's chest cavity, producing back and rib wounds similar to Connally's and slugs a bit more mutilated than the magic bullet. Another test on a cadaver's wrist yielded a much more mutilated bullet but also a much more damaged wrist, which indicated to the Commission that the Parkland bullet struck Connally's wrist at relatively low velocity. One would expect that from a bullet that had already transited two bodies. Similarly, as the Commission held, the elliptical and ragged entry and exit wounds in Connally argued for a bullet that had begun yawing due to striking Kennedy first. These results at once were attacked. For example, if the exit wounds in the neck tests were larger than the entry holes, how did that fact fit with Dr. Malcolm Perry's insistence right after the shooting that the wound in Kennedy's throat could have been an entry hole? (That, unfortunately, could not be tested; Dr. Perry had enlarged the "puncture" wound in a futile tracheotomy.)

Inevitably, many more tests were staged and most of them reaffirmed what we've known since the beginning of firearms: Bullets can do funny things, sometimes shattering in cloth, sometimes getting through a pine-board unscathed. But this point is crucial and efforts to fathom its mystery continue. Dr. Milton Helpern, the former medical examiner of the city of New York and one of the most experienced forensic pathologists in the world, once said, "I cannot accept the premise that this bullet thrashed around in all that bony tissue and lost only 1.4 to 2.4 grains of its original weight." Dr. Cyril Wecht, forensic pathologist and coroner of Allegheny County, Pennsylvania, believes not only that the bullet would have been more deformed but that the trajectory of the shot as projected through Kennedy, given the positions of the two men as adduced from Zapruder's film, makes it impossible for it to have hit Connally. Instead, Dr. Wecht hypothesizes, the bullet that transited the President went over the limousine driver's shoulder and beyond (maybe fragmenting and hitting Tague), and then another gunman hit Connally an instant later. Other noted pathologists, including Dr. James Weston, former president of the National Academy of Forensic Sciences, claim it's quite possible the bullet did all that the report specifies, and besides, it is impossible to deduce precise trajectories from studying wounds.

Gun buffs have long been curious. Could the dented cartridge have anything to do with the magic bullet? Suppose that round had been jammed in the chamber and fired. The dent might cause the projectile to wobble to Kennedy, penetrate, yaw, lose velocity, and travel on to rummage around Connally's body. But it's very difficult to chamber such a dented round, and what if that round, as the critic Josiah Thompson has suggested, had never been fired in Oswald's rifle, and instead had been planted by a conspirator to frame Oswald with all three shots? Suppose, then, one of the 1944 cartridges had lost some zip, was in effect "downloaded." That could cause low velocity and strange ballistics. For their part, scientific folk wonder if neutron-activation tests on Connally's clothes might show if that bullet struck him, leaving the telltale residue. Such tests would reveal in parts-per-million accuracy if the copper traces matched the magic bullet. Unfortunately, Connally's clothes were washed or dry-cleaned before such tests could be made. What about Kennedy's bloody shirt and jacket, two evidentiary items of paramount importance? The Government's reports on them—extracted through Weisberg's Freedom of Information suits—confirm that spectrography revealed traces of copper around the rear holes, indicating that a copper-jacketed bullet had pierced them. The report insists it was the superbullet. Yet, it seems, *no* tests tie *those* copper traces to the magic bullet. Nor are there, according to these documents, any traces of copper or lead alloys at the front of the shirt collar where, according to the report, the bullet exited. Finally, it seems, based on recently obtained reports, that sophisticated neutron-activation tests were done on the magic bullet and other recovered fragments—but that the FBI, for whatever reasons, has suppressed or distorted the results to conform to the single-bullet thesis. So there remain unanswered questions about the magic bullet—and, as we'll see, about Kennedy's clothes. For now, all we can know is that if that bullet did what the report's theory requires, it was, indeed, a magical projectile.

So magical that one theory maintains it never was fired through anything but cotton, was instead part of a plot calling for the deceptive bullet to be planted at Parkland Memorial Hospital—the better to incriminate Oswald, the patsy. (Oswald did say, "I'm just a patsy," while in custody.) Didn't the respected journalist Seth Kantor and a witness named Wilma Tice swear they saw Jack Ruby there just after the shooting? He could have done it and, as part of a plot, would deny it later at his trial. Penn Jones, a Texas newspaper editor who has followed a skein of mysterious deaths befalling witnesses, was at the hospital, too, and he has said that in the chaos there, a lot could have happened. Thus there is debate over whether the bullet really was found on Connally's stretcher. A hospital engineer named Darrell Tomlinson, who found the bullet, first thought it was on Connally's stretcher, but later couldn't swear it was the Governor's. Some people thus theorize that the bullet fell out of a shallow wound in *Kennedy's* back, a wound that has been covered up by the Government because its existence would again prove the conspiracy the report had to dismiss for reasons of domestic tranquillity and world peace.

For those convinced of conspiracy, however, easier hypotheses were at hand. Some of them just *knew* the fatal shot came not from the Depository but from the right front, from the grassy knoll. First, they say, more than half the witnesses in Dealey Plaza who had an opinion on the direction of the shots said they came from the knoll or the stockade fence. Wilma Bond's photographs showed people reacting as if shots had come from there. These included motorcycle policeman Bobby Hargis, who charged the knoll, and Presidential aides such as Dave Powers and Secret Service men such as Forrest Sorrels, who was riding in the car ahead of Kennedy's, and numerous ordinary citizens. These opinions have been bolstered ever since the assassination by photos and statements, most of which were debunked by the Commission, whose members in several instances failed to question the witnesses or to investigate in detail the evidence advanced for an assassin on the knoll. For example, Zapruder frames 313–316 unmistakably show the President's head moving backward and to the left as he suffers his killing wound. Robert Groden, an optics technician who is skeptical of the Warren Report, has subjected Zapruder's film to prolonged examination. His blowups and intensifications of these key frames have convinced many people, particularly among college audiences who see the film under the auspices of some assassination careerists called the Assassination Information Bureau, that unless Newtonian laws of motion have been repealed, the shot had to come from the right front. This evidence is a staple for knoll-assassin believers. They are not persuaded otherwise by Itek's recent conclusion that Kennedy's head (and most of his brain matter) is first driven forward, very fast, then backward much more slowly. They do not believe that Jackie pulled him leftward and backward, thus changing the head's direction. They do not accept the fact (established in tests with skulls packed with tissue simulants) that a "jet" effect, a hydrostatic propulsion due to the skull's explosion, threw Kennedy's head back. Rather, they point out that Officer Hargis, who was riding escort to the Presidential car at its left-rear fender, was splattered with blood and brain. That Officer James Chaney, looking at Kennedy from his motorcycle near the right fender, said he saw "the President struck in the face." That Deputy Sheriff Seymour Weitzman found part of Kennedy's skull, perhaps the same piece that Jackie had scrambled onto the trunk of the Lincoln to try to recover, on the *south* (left) side of Elm Street. That Secret Service agent Clint Hill and eyewitness Charles Brohm saw what they thought was impact debris flying to the left and rear of the car (it seems to have been recorded, too, on Nix's film). That agent Hill and his colleague Roy Kellerman, who was riding in the right front seat of Kennedy's car, said the fatal shot sounded funny, like a double bang-bang (and Hill thought there had been only two shots, the second in the head). No, they think the shot had to come from the right front, from another kind of gun, perhaps one loaded with explosive bullets (eerily, there is a rumor that in early 1963 some members of the CIA asked a research-and-development man to sketch an exploding round for a 6.5mm Mannlicher-Carcano).

Other photographs, too, conjured men on the grassy knoll. Groden has to his own satisfaction identified two shadows in the Zapruder film as more snipers. We have seen the speculations based on the Nix film. Another photograph, taken by Mary Moorman, who stood about fifteen feet from the President's car, seems to show a man with a gun standing behind the stockade fence about fourteen feet from its corner. The Moorman photo, taken approximately one-fifth of a second after Kennedy's head exploded, has been studied intensely. Some experts say the figure is a shadow, others that it is a shadowy assassin.

S. M. Holland, a railroad switchman, who was standing on the Triple Underpass when the shots were fired, believes in a grassy knoll gunman. After the shots he hot-footed it to the parking lot and found muddy footprints behind the fence. It looked to him like one or two men had paced back and forth behind a car. Holland is positive he heard shots coming from the knoll, although Dealey Plaza's conformation makes it equally likely that he could have heard echoes.

Holland's story, which he told repeatedly to sundry assassination buffs including the Warren Commission, fits nicely if circumstantially with that told by Lee Bowers, who was ensconced in a railroad switching tower set well back in the parking lot behind the fence and knoll. The morning of the assassination, Bowers says, he saw a sequence of three cars enter the parking lot. Car number one was a 1959 Olds, he thought, blue and white with an out-of-state license, a Goldwater sticker, and red mud splashed on it. Next came a 1957 black Ford, with a man in it who seemed to be talking into a microphone. Each of these cars exited shortly after coming into the lot. Last came a Chevrolet, also bearing red mud and a Goldwater sticker. This car moved toward the Depository and the last Bowers saw it seemed to pause "just above the assassination site." Bowers also said he saw two men, one middle-aged and heavy-set, the other young, wearing a plaid shirt or jacket, standing fifteen feet apart by the fence just before the gunfire began. When that happened, Bowers said, his eye was drawn that way by something peculiar, "a flash of light or smoke or something."

The claims of Holland and Bowers excited other investigators, even if they failed to convince the Commission that something strange might have been afoot. For a time it seemed the tale of Julia Ann Mercer would tie the stories together. Miss Mercer said she was driving by the Depository the morning of November 22, and was forced to stop because of a green Ford pick-up truck with "Air Conditioning" lettered on it which was parked half up on the Elm Street curb. A heavy-set man slouched over the wheel, while a young man in a plaid shirt took what appeared to be a gun case from the truck bed and ambled up the grassy slope toward the Triple Underpass. That was strange, she said, since there were police watching all this. The Warren Commission wasn't curious enough to call Miss Mercer as a witness, perhaps because subsequent investigation suggested her memory was faulty. There was a truck broken down there, and workmen in it, but no one took anything like a rifle from the truck, at least according to a Dallas policeman who stopped to assist the men. So the Mercer story could not corroborate the impressions of Holland and Bowers (the "heavy man" and the "young man" reappeared again, though— one witness, and only one, said they were the team that slew Officer Tippit).

The railroad yards themselves inspired another grassy-knoll speculation, for it was from them that the three famous "tramps" were rousted after the murder and marched across Dealey Plaza, where they were photographed. The tramps seemed too neatly groomed to be bums, and they were never booked or questioned about the crime. Thus, some believe, they had to have a role in Kennedy's death. Two major theories have been offered. The first, proffered by an egregious duo named Michael Canfield and Allan Weberman, supposes that two of the three men are Frank Sturgis and E. Howard Hunt. (This means, of course, Sturgis and Hunt cannot be seen in Nix's film on the grassy knoll.) It seems they were in Dallas to assist in killing Kennedy because of the President's "betrayal" of the anti-Castro Cubans during the Bay of Pigs debacle. More dubious evidence lies in the fact that Richard Nixon was in Dallas that morning, too, thereby implying an early relationship with the men later to be hired as President Nixon's Watergate plumbers. The second hypothesis states that the tramps are Americans who trained Cuban exiles, partly under Hunt's direction, and then decided to remove the President who had turned away from liberating Cuba. Both versions exhibit the free association that the most fanatic assassination theorists use to weave huge patterns of conspiracy. For example, one of the tramps is also now said to be Jack Youngblood, a reputed mercenary who is also now said to be privy to who had Martin Luther King killed.

Other theories include the suggestion that conspirators had hollowed out the grassy knoll and then cut down the President from there. Former New Orleans District Attorney Jim Garrison and Penn Jones say a gunman lurked in a sewer and on signal plugged the President. Much more intriguing is the "umbrella man." Although the day was warm and sunny, a single neatly dressed man stood and watched the President being murdered, while holding an open umbrella above his head. After the killing, he stood watching the motorcade, trailing the dying President, disappear down Elm Street, then folded his umbrella and walked calmly away. He was the only person so shielding himself. Could some manipulation of his umbrella have been a signal for shooting to begin? Or did the man have a gun built into his umbrella? Was he acting in concert with a man one assassination theory calls a "communications man," another figure in a photograph who appears to have a "two-way radio" in his back pocket (and who has been identified as a man now a patient in a mental hospital)? It's possible that he was just an eccentric, but the Warren Commission never looked into this.

It did, however, look into and dismiss as meaningless a story three witnesses told of two men, seen at different times. One man, heavy-set, was said to be in a Depository window, then hurrying away from the Depository and finally entering a station wagon driven by a young black man. The other, younger, was seen by Deputy Sheriff Roger Craig, running out of the Depository's Elm Street entrance, down the gentle slope and into a light-colored Rambler station wagon (easily identifiable by its rooftop luggage rack). The driver of the wagon, according to Craig, was "very dark complected, had real dark short hair and was wearing a thin white-looking jacket." Craig said he tried to reach the car to question the men, but the crush of people prevented him, and then the wagon took off down Elm.

Many people believe these witnesses are describing other assassins, because they could not be Oswald. He was, the Warren Commission Report says, taking a bus and a taxi toward his rooming house. The heavy-set man could be the "Saul" who has confessed in Hugh McDonald's recent novelistic account of the case that he killed Kennedy for money, with Oswald as a patsy. The younger man could be the second Oswald, out on his appointed rounds again, this time as a killer in the Depository. The driver of the station wagon could be a Cuban exile or, if you prefer, one of Castro's men avenging the assassination plots the CIA-Mafia connection concocted for the Cuban leader in the early sixties. Or they could have been part of a Texas right-wing plot—at least according to some people, who find interesting (if illogical) connotations in the facts that H. L. Hunt's son Nelson Bunker Hunt apparently contributed money for a scurrilous anti-Kennedy ad that appeared the morning of November 22, and Jack Ruby had driven one of his strippers to Hunt's office the day before, and Mrs. Paine had a light-colored station wagon. Craig himself now is dead, under strange circumstances, as are more than fifty people who allegedly knew something about Kennedy's death. (The actuarial odds against that were calculated at 100 trillion to one.) Of course, if half a hundred or more people were involved—especially from as many disparate groups as have been suggested—it's likely that so huge a conspiracy probably would come apart in time, Joe Valachi–style. But two or three men would need only their anger and a gun. Is there any hard evidence of a second gunman?

The ultimate evidence was the President's body, but the autopsy was botched from start to finish. At Bethesda Naval Hospital on November 22, a team of pathologists conducted the autopsy under conditions of stress, shock and pressure, which apparently caused them to omit some valuable procedures (e.g., dissecting the neck—or back—wound). Two FBI agents named James Silbert and Francis O'Neill observed the autopsy. Their report said of the President's back wound, "The distance traveled by this missile was a short distance inasmuch as the end of the opening could be felt with the finger." The agents also called it a "back" wound rather than a neck wound and said the downward angle was 45 to 60 degrees, a trajectory inconsistent with the 20-degree angle from the Depository's sixth-floor window. Secret Service man Kellerman, also present, said the wound was probed and Lieutenant Colonel Finck, the forensic medicine specialist, told him there was no outlet. How, then, could the bullet that made this wound have hit Connally? Furthermore, the FBI men said the doctors were puzzled because they could find no bullet in the back wound, and so Finck and another pathologist, Commander Humes, said "it was entirely possible" the bullet had worked its way out and fallen on a stretcher. How did the report's defenders answer this? The same way they answered so many other things that didn't fit: They said it was a mistake. The FBI and Secret Service agents were laymen, after all. Besides, by morning the autopsy physicians had conferred with the doctors at Parkland and confirmed that the tracheotomy had obliterated Kennedy's throat wound. That gave them the exit wound for the bullet, though it ignored the possibility the wound marked a bullet's entrance. The fact that the wound couldn't be probed was explained by saying the muscles had closed, a contention strongly resisted by pathologists like Wecht. To those critical of the Commission, the conflicting reports smacked of *ex post facto* reasoning, and textual analysis of Commander Humes's draft autopsy report does show substantial word-tinkering to ensure support for the single-bullet theory.

Another puzzle was the sketch of Kennedy's wounds made by the third physician, Commander Boswell. There the wound is shown not in the neck, about two inches right of the spinal column, but well down on the back (Secret Service agent Glen Bennett, riding in the backup car, said he saw Kennedy hit "four inches down from the right shoulder"), so low that to exit at the throat, piercing the shirt collar and nicking the tie, the bullet would have had to go *upward.* Some theorists still maintain that the front of the shirt and the tie were damaged by surgeons, not by bullets. Is Boswell's sketch mistaken? The doctors say yes, as to location. The sketch was merely a rough. The measurements are found noted on it, placing the wound 14 centimeters (5.6 inches) down from the right mastoid process (the bony point behind the right ear) and 14 centimeters from the tip of the right shoulder. Right in the neck. In any event, the report's supporters say, we have X-rays and photographs of the body which indisputably locate the wounds.

Surprisingly, these visual records were never seen by the members of the Warren Commission. In 1968, awash in criticism of the report, Attorney General Ramsey Clark secured permission for three pathologists and a radiologist to examine the X-rays and photos. They confirmed that the President was shot twice from above and behind, the one bullet most probably going through his neck and out his throat, and the other blowing a large hole in the right side of his skull. A few years later, Wecht examined the materials, the first alternate-theorist to do so. He grudgingly accepted that finding, while reiterating that there might be fragments from other bullets in Kennedy and that the finding did not *per se* preclude another gunman. Wecht also wanted, during later surveys of the material, to examine Kennedy's brain, which should have been preserved for sectioning so a pathologist could trace the exact paths of all bullets and fragments. Thus it was we learned the ghastly fact that the President's brain is missing or hidden.

Even without that cerebral aid, Dr. James Weston has said he has absolutely no doubt after examining all available autopsy materials that John Kennedy was hit by only two shots, both from above, behind and slightly to the right. One went through the neck. The other entered the skull, distinctly beveling the bone inward. Put this statement beside the aforementioned ballistics tests linking such wounds to the Mannlicher-Carcano, and the fact that the fibers of Kennedy's shirt and jacket bearing copper residue are pushed inwards, and the report's conclusion seems inescapable.

Except there is something still that frets mightily about that jacket and shirt, regardless of the body's wounds. Consider first that, as anyone with a jacket and shirt can determine at home, in order for the holes—about five and a half inches down from the collar top—to align with the wound in the neck, the garments would have had to ride up about three inches. In simulating the situation, it is difficult to cause a shirt—let alone a heavier suit coat—to ride up that far. Also, photographs of the President at the instant matching the magic-bullet shot show Kennedy's shirt and jacket seemingly unbunched. And even if the clothes had ridden up that far as the President waved, they would have doubled over, which means that a bullet would have perforated at least one garment three times. It didn't. Then there is the disconcerting fact that the holes *do* line up with the wound shown on Commander Boswell's sketch. Finally, one must note the peculiar holes beside the shirt collar's button. They are sharp-edged and elliptical, not ragged or puncturelike, leading people to guess that they, perhaps the tie's nick, too, resulted at Parkland from cutting away the President's clothes to give him air. Then there would be no magic bullet coming out at the throat and there would be another gunman—something even Weston's unequivocal statement does not eliminate.

The shirt and jacket alone justify a new investigation. They constitute physical evidence that contradicts the Warren Commission's theory. For that matter, we have seen several other questions—such as, was Oswald on the Depository's sixth floor?—that a skillful defense attorney could have used to challenge the Government's case. True, the circumstantial evidence indicating Oswald as the lone killer is strong, but scattered through it, stubborn as fossils, are implications that he may not have been alone. And beyond the physical evidence lie hints which, if susceptible to proof, would make Oswald more than the Warren Commission would have him, more than the desperate little youth who grabbed for glory out of frustration with his life, his wife, his country's capitalistic mode.

Therefore, to arrive at the end with any understanding of the John Kennedy riddle, we need a summary of the chief conspiracy suppositions, if only to judge how believable they might be.

VI

DANGER FOR THE PEOPLE

*". . . most assassinations in the United States
have been the products of individual passion or
derangement. . . . Despite this, the public, in
reaction to the assassinations, has sometimes attempted to tie the assassins to political movements or conspiracies."*

*—Report to the National Commission on the
Causes and Prevention of Violence*

We seem to find endless fascination in John Kennedy's assassination. The
number and variety of conspiracy theories surrounding it testify to its
powerful, long-lingering aftershock. It appears we do not, or cannot, or
will not believe the Lee Harvey Oswald alone slew that gifted young
President. An event of that magnitude, we seem to believe, must have
been caused by a plot of equal magnitude.

The feeling doubtless has been exacerbated by destinal quirks: The
murder of Oswald himself before he could be tried, the sense of deprivation arising from our sad acknowledgment that Kennedy's historical place
will forever be marked more by promise denied than by accomplishment
realized. Perhaps most of all by the vapors of disillusionment still rising out
of Watergate, condensing to form in a few distraught Americans the most
fearsome shapes, clouding their minds from reason, so that Kennedy's
assassination is seen as part of all our recent misfortunes—of Vietnam and
Nixonism and all injustice—and so is truly and horribly fateful.

Nonetheless, many sane citizens suspect a conspiracy. Certainly the
theories exist, some exhaling a legitimate if frightening plausibility. What
follows is a roster of current notions that Oswald did not alone kill John
Kennedy.

The Oswald–Ruby–Tippit Connection: An old theory, forged in the belief that Ruby and Tippit knew Oswald and had conspired with him to
kill the President, probably for right-wingers in Dallas' law-enforcement
and/or local government circles. Tippit's job was to kill Oswald after Lee

154 Assassination in America

incriminated himself in the murder of the President, thereby completing a perfect crime. This accounts, the theorists say, for the police car that came to Oswald's rooming house around 1 P.M. after the assassination. The car stopped and its horn honked, said Earlene Roberts, the housekeeper there, but Oswald had left and was walking several blocks away. The car then must have found him, and Tippit called Lee over to the car. But Oswald, one story goes, suspected the plot and shot Tippit down, so the cops tried again in the Texas Theater to kill him. (There *was* a suspicious click like a gun's during the struggle to subdue him.) When that failed, the plotters decided to have Ruby kill Oswald. Jack was well known both as a minor criminal and as a genial host to the police force ("You all know me, I'm Jack Ruby," he cried after killing Oswald), and he may have been assured that he'd be sprung one way or another. That promise accounts for Ruby's silence about the plot for the three years after the killing, for his insistence that he killed Oswald out of pity for Jackie Kennedy, that he became the avenging angel totally on his own. Or Ruby himself was scared of retaliation. Didn't he tell Earl Warren and other Commissioners when they visited Dallas, "Gentlemen, my life is in danger here"?

Evidence for this theory is nearly nonexistent. Unsubstantiated tales have placed Tippit and Oswald in a diner near Oswald's rooming house (also the neighborhood Jack Ruby lived in), and Tippit and Ruby, and maybe Oswald, huddling at Ruby's Carousel Club. This last is feasible. We know Ruby was a police buff, forever hanging around cops and police headquarters, especially during the madness attending Oswald's arrest. But some say Jack probably liked cops because he had a long rap sheet and wanted as many law-enforcement friends as possible (interestingly, Ruby did say one cop told him the night of November 22 that Oswald should be cut in ribbons). Nothing solid associates Ruby with Tippit, or Oswald with either, despite some lingering questions about the killing of Officer Tippit. These assume importance because if Oswald did kill Tippit the chain of physical evidence linking him to the assassination of John Kennedy becomes well-nigh unbreakable. One query was inspired by Acquilla Clemmons, who said she saw *two* men, one heavy-set, the other Oswald-like, approach Tippit, and then watched the young one shoot the cop. The Warren Commission didn't question Ms. Clemmons, probably because FBI reports cited inconsistencies in her account and because nine other witnesses put Oswald at the scene or fleeing it (and his gun did kill Tippit).

Then, was there something funny in the way Oswald was discovered in the movie theater? Did a mysterious stranger point him out, in the dark, to the cops and then vanish, as Robert Sam Anson says? No, according to many witnesses. Johnny Brewer, a shoe-store manager, who was already tense from news of the assassination and the sirens screaming toward the Tippit slaying scene, became suspicious of Oswald's furtive behavior in front of his store and trailed him to the theater. Brewer and the cashier decided to call the cops. When the police came, the house lights were put up and Brewer pointed out Oswald in the back row. Did the cops try to kill Oswald there? It's uncertain. The click may have come from Oswald's gun, which contained a discharged cartridge case—left either from the Tippit shooting (he discarded four others at the scene) or from target practicing. The hammer might have fallen on that. Or the noise could have been imagined, or the hammer could have been struck in the struggle, or it could have been a cop's gun. No one checked those service revolvers. In any event, Oswald was not killed by the police, but by Jack Ruby. How did Ruby accomplish that? Although it's claimed that one of Ruby's many police friends—he was said to know half the force—tipped him off when Oswald was going to be moved from police headquarters to the county jail, it's unlikely. The precise moment of transfer kept changing due to epidemic confusion up to the fateful time itself. It seems Ruby just took the notion at about 11:20 Sunday, November 24, and sauntered in at the moment the guard stepped away to direct a car from the ramp up which Oswald's vehicle would come. Then, was Oswald's look as Ruby lurched toward him one of recognition and fear? Who can know? Certainly of fear, but no one has proved Oswald knew Ruby.

In sum, most of the circumstantial evidence suggests Oswald alone killed Tippit. That doesn't deter the theorists. Harold Weisberg claims a witness named T. F. Bowley said he called in the shooting on Tippit's radio at 1:10—too early, the theory goes, for Oswald to have gotten to the spot from his rooming house, so Tippit's killers had to be Mrs. Clemmons' ephemeral pair, or someone in on a plot to frame Oswald. Still, there is no firm evidence that Tippit, Ruby and Oswald were conspirators, either alone or at the behest of a Minuteman-style bunch of vigilantes. With his dying words, Jack Ruby said he did it all by himself (skeptics maintain he was dying only because somebody infected him with cancer). Jack probably had the last correct words on the matter.

The Clay Shaw–Jim Garrison Carnival: Nothing had ever aroused the demimonde of assassination buffs like the announcement in February, 1967, that Jim Garrison had solved the Kennedy murder case. The assassination had resulted from a conspiracy headed by Clay L. Shaw, a director of New Orleans' International Trade Mart, a respected citizen of liberal

views, a homosexual, and the man who had met with Lee Harvey Oswald
and a man named David Ferrie to plan the murder of John Kennedy.
Assassination theorists, even a man who believed the world was run by a
conspiracy of intellectuals called the Illuminati, descended on New Orleans. Garrison opened his files to them, and everybody swapped information. This time they would see the truth.

What they finally saw was the Dienbienphu of official assassination inquiries. Here was a big man ("the Jolly Green Giant" the press called
Garrison), with a staff of investigators, with the power of subpoena, with
money and manpower and a cause, all the things the theorists had said
they needed, who was about to fall from high seriousness to low farce,
taking a passel of legitimate and illegitimate speculations with him.

Garrison's case seemed simple. Shaw, Oswald and Ferrie had met in
New Orleans, planned the murder and Oswald had executed it, but been
set up as the scapegoat by his fellow conspirators. As for the Warren
Report, Garrison said it was "probably the greatest fraud ever perpetrated
in the history of mankind," and the perpetration of that fraud no doubt
was due to "the one who has profited most from the assassination—your
friendly President, Lyndon Johnson." With such *élan* did the prosecution
proceed. The trouble was, their witnesses, or many of them, seemed either
crazy or dishonest. There was Charles Spiesel, a New York accountant,
who said that in May, 1963, he attended a party and heard Shaw, his old
war buddy Ferrie, and other men discuss how to kill Kennedy (high-
powered rifle with telescopic sight) and how Ferrie, an expert pilot, could
fly the killer to safety. Spiesel's credibility was challenged, though, when
he admitted he had been harassed and hypnotized over the past sixteen
years by fifty or sixty people, against whom he'd filed a $16 million lawsuit.
Then there was Vernon Bundy, a junkie and burglar, who said he'd seen
Shaw and Oswald on a Lake Pontchartrain beach in June, 1963, while he
was there shooting up. Oswald had dropped some of his pro-Cuba leaflets,
Bundy said. It all seemed fine had not cross-examination revealed that
Bundy was testifying to get a break on his own sentence, and had told
fellow inmates he was undecided quite how to fabricate his story. There
was Dean Andrews, a portly lawyer who told both the Warren Commission and Garrison that Oswald had visited his office about five times, and
that after the assassination a man named "Clay Bertrand" had called him
about representing Oswald in Dallas. However, at the Clay Shaw trial
when asked if the request to represent Oswald was a figment of his imagination, Andrews testified, "I have tried to say that consistently."

There was star witness Perry Raymond Russo, who said he'd seen "Clem

Bertrand" in 1963 at Ferrie's apartment, along with the pilot's bearded roommate "Leon Oswald," where the conversation centered on "three-sided triangulation" for the assassination, on "diversionary" shots, on the need for a patsy, and on an escape to Mexico. This testimony exhilarated those who thought Garrison had solved it, until it came out that Russo's recollections had emerged only after several sessions with Sodium Pentothal and hypnosis, a fact the defense belabored while establishing that the "conspiracy meeting" was just a bull session, that Russo never heard "Oswald" or "Bertrand" agree to kill Kennedy, and that he really couldn't positively identify Shaw as a man he'd seen with Ferrie until the defense "turned him on" (negatively) by asking if he believed in God.

With such witnesses, the few genuine Garrison gems couldn't shine much. Some folks from Clinton, Louisiana, testified that one cold day in late August or early September, 1963, they'd seen Oswald, Ferrie and Shaw in their town. Oswald even got a haircut, and asked about work at a mental hospital near there. The Clinton folk may have been mistaken about the weather—the Meteorological Service said it had been 90 degrees—and uncertain about Shaw until Garrison's men brought them to town to see the man, but they clung to their story. Unfortunately for Garrison, that didn't prove conspiracy. Nor did other testimony that Shaw and Ferrie were seen together at an airport, or that David Ferrie had come by Oswald's former New Orleans apartment shortly after the assassination. Garrison's prosecutors did their best to discredit the report, bringing in Wesley Frazier, Marina Oswald, Abraham Zapruder and Roger Craig, but nothing availed—not even gruesome repetitions of the Zapruder film designed, it appears, to make the jurors want to convict *somebody* of this heinous crime. But they acquitted Clay Shaw. Jim Garrison lived on to become an ex-district attorney (currently again appearing around the country giving assassination lectures), and the cause of finding conspiracies suffered a monumental setback. A shame, many felt, because some worthwhile leads surfaced, like a possible connection of the CIA with the assassination business. Garrison was convinced "the Company" knew something about JFK, and he accused it with vigor, hoping to ignite interest and figuring that since the spooks wouldn't defend themselves publicly a Congressional inquiry might result. But the Shaw trial stopped that, and it wasn't until 1975, when we learned that Clay Shaw and David Ferrie *had* been contract employees of the CIA, that Garrison's accusations made sense. We also had the makings of another plot.

The CIA–Mafia–Big Labor Conglomerate: This theory starts with David Ferrie. The multifaceted Ferrie, besides being a pilot, was a homosexual (he and Shaw *did* know some of the same people in that world), a gun enthusiast, and was said to be involved in training anti-Castro commandos for the CIA. Altogether, an active little man, albeit afflicted with a disease causing his hair to fall out. Ferrie worked betimes for a lawyer who handled the business of Carlos "The Little Man" Marcello, the alleged godfather of Mafia operations throughout the Southwest ("a respectable businessman," Garrison once said). It was Ferrie who reportedly flew Marcello home to New Orleans from Guatemala City after Robert Kennedy in his campaign (others called it a vendetta) against organized crime had Marcello deported.

Therefore, Marcello might have detested Robert Kennedy. He also had reason to hate Jack Kennedy, who not only concurred with his brother's attacks on citizens like Marcello and Jimmy Hoffa, but also had blown the Bay of Pigs, losing the brotherhood's Havana casinos and whores and numbers and dope forever to the puritanical socialist Castro. A cool $100 million a year in gambling alone. It was even reported that Marcello had been heard at a mafioso meeting musing over getting a nut to kill Jack Kennedy, maybe thereby ridding himself of both Irishmen at one stroke. Hoffa, too, had supposedly said, in 1962, he'd like to take Bobby Kennedy out. When Jack Kennedy was killed, Hoffa did not grieve, nor is it probable that Marcello did. After all, the two were said to have mutual interests, some nice Mob-labor arrangements, perhaps involving Teamster pension funds for posh resorts, dope from Southeast Asia (a booming business unless Kennedy really intended, as was rumored, to cool off Vietnam), and juries who were hostile to Hoffa.

But where does Ferrie fit in? First, Ferrie was rabidly anti-Castro. So, too, seemed to be the otherwise leftist Lee Harvey Oswald for a spell during his stay in New Orleans from late April, 1963, until late September, 1963. In August, Oswald offered his services as a trained warrior to some prominent Cuban exiles. Could Ferrie have met Oswald around then as Garrison claimed? One informant, who later retracted his statement, said Ferrie not only knew Oswald but had trained him on a sniper's rifle and had visited him in Dallas. Other rumors had the teen-aged Oswald a cadet in Ferrie's Civil Air Patrol squadron. But there was no hard evidence for any of that. Ferrie himself couldn't help. He was found dead—the coroner said of natural causes—six days after Garrison named him as a conspirator. The most that can be said is that Ferrie might have heard of Oswald. Lee was on television and radio during August, 1963, this time as a sane and articulate spokesman *for* Castro. The publicity resulted from Oswald's leafleting in behalf of his Fair Play for Cuba Committee in front of Clay Shaw's International Trade Mart. Another coincidence, probably, just as Lee Oswald's ideological flipflop may have reflected only a psychopathic craving for attention. But that didn't invalidate the questions. Was he Marcello's nut, or Ferrie-Shaw's patsy? Did anything weld all this in New Orleans, this center of various Cuban connections, to the events in Dallas?

Jack Ruby does, say some theorists. He was not just the little-league strip-joint, always-a-hustle buffoon who tried everything from managing a twelve-year-old black dancer named Sugar Daddy to peddling weight-reducing devices. Not just the man who loved dogs and couldn't be trusted with a secret, not just the sentimental slob who could *cry* over a peeler's problems yet liked beating drunks and carrying wads of dough and a pistol —no, he was also involved with big labor and, through them, with organized crime, and, through that, with killing John Kennedy. The line begins in Chicago, where since adolescence Jacob Rubenstein (our Jack Ruby) associated with very rough trade, notably as secretary of the Scrap Iron and Junk Handlers Union. Ruby was questioned but released after the union's founder turned up shot to death. The union fell to Paul Dorfman, an ally of Jimmy Hoffa during the 1950s in Hoffa's fight to succeed David Beck as Teamsters president after Robert Kennedy and the McClellan Committee drove Beck from office. (Bobby once ruefully remarked he had made Hoffa all he was.) Ruby next turned up in Dallas running night clubs. Some police there, it's said, suspected that, despite appearances, he was a utility man for the Chicago Mob, acting to bribe authorities, coordinate some gambling operations and facilitate narcotics traffic between Mexico and points north. It's reported the FBI in Dallas thought enough of Ruby in 1959 to ask him to inform on any shady dealings he ran across. Most important to this theory, if Ruby's activities were genuinely sinister, they surely would have been known to Marcello, whose turf Texas was.

From that point, the theory inflates to make Ruby a hireling of those who might have done in Kennedy. Had not Jack Ruby in the good-old pre-Castro era of 1959 spent ten days in Cuba, partly at a hotel-casino allegedly operated by some of Marcello's business acquaintances (the notorious Lansky brothers), and specifically as the guest of Lewis J. McWillie, a Dallas gentleman once described as a gambler and murderer? Didn't rumors, checked out by the CIA, have Ruby visiting Cuba again in 1962, from Mexico, and if true was it not possible Ruby was running errands for the Mob, maybe even negotiating about their now defunct interests? Didn't Ruby also visit McWillie, who was now violently anti-Castro, in Las

Vegas, where lots of Teamster and Mob business is conducted? And weren't there still more rumors that Jack Ruby had visited Israel as a Teamster representative, in a delegation of American trade unionists, and there contacted an Israeli labor official who was reputed to be a deep CIA agent?

For those given to such questions and their hypothetical answers, the game was deliciously complicated by the presence in Dallas on November 22 (in the Dal-Tex Building on Dealey Plaza, from which many think shots were fired) of one Eugene Hale Brading, an event whereby the organized-crime angle becomes more acute, sharpened by association with conservative business interests. That's because Brading, visiting Big D to see oil men while on parole in California, seemingly dropped by the offices of the Hunts the same afternoon of November 21 as did Ruby, and like Ruby, this Mr. Brading had long tendrils back to Mob activities. Could he have collaborated with Ruby and Oswald in an assassination? (Brading has said he only went in the Dal-Tex Building to use the telephone.) Despite the quantum leaps of logic necessary to assume that the Mafia, labor and Hunt-style right-wing businessmen could stay in bed together long enough to conceive and bear this plot, some conspiracy lovers believe the possibility is there. The string of circumstances is stretched! Marcello/-Hoffa to Ferrie/Shaw to Ruby/Oswald. And all doubtless aided by the CIA, the theory goes on.

That allegation comes through the unholy alliance of Mafia and CIA that without question began during World War II to help secure Sicily for the Allies. It's widely thought the arrangement worked so well it was continued until in the early 1960s the CIA called on Cosa Nostra chieftain Sam "Momo" Giancana and his underling Johnny Roselli for help in doing away with the nettlesome Fidel Castro. Then ensued the now famous assassination schemes (and the laughable proposals, such as to wreak chemical havoc on Castro's beard). Furthermore, beneath those facts lie others which don't yet fit in the puzzle. To wit: Sam Giancana's murder a few days before he was to tell what he knew about the CIA assassination plots, and Roselli's recent demise in vintage gangland style, complete with burial at sea in a weighted oil drum. The scandal of Judith Campbell Exner's affair with the assassinated President in view of the detail that she was Johnny Roselli's girlfriend, making people wonder if Kennedy knew about plots against Castro, and did he approve, and if he was killed in retaliation. The CIA's silence on speculations about its possible role, active or passive, in Kennedy's death, which some theorists take as a sign of guilt, others as a signal that the Mob has enough on the CIA's nefarious carryings-on to blackmail the agency. All interesting, but the key question remains: Why didn't Ruby, if he knew anything, speak up during the three years he lived after Kennedy's death? Because he knew nothing more? Because he feared reprisal (although he knew he was dying)? Theorists wonder why Ruby didn't even mention who Lee Harvey Oswald might really have been.

The Agent Oswald Question: No theory has received greater play than that Oswald was somebody's secret agent. Russian. Castro-Cuban. Anti-Castro-Cuban. CIA. FBI. Or even a double agent for any two of the above. It is the central thesis. It is fed by numerous curious occurences, and no amount of caviling can make it go away. One can only judge for oneself.

To support the Russian-agent idea, theorists proclaim: that Lee defected to Russia with minor radar secrets, and was an avowed Marxist both before and after; that Marina Oswald's uncle was connected with Soviet intelligence, so maybe she, too, was an agent; that Lee spent most of his Russian stay in Minsk working in a radio factory, supposedly with Cubans; that Lee was in the hospital for twelve days in early March, 1961, during which time he might have been conditioned to kill Kennedy or had radio components (yes!) installed in him, becoming a transistorized Manchurian Candidate; that the Oswalds had little trouble leaving Russia, a rarity for defectors and their wives; that the Oswalds spent much time among Russians in Dallas, any one of whom might have been a deep-cover Soviet agent; that Yuri Nosenko's defection seemed designed to convince the United States that Russia had nothing to do with the assassination (the Soviet leaders did go to a lot of trouble to establish that Oswald was not a KGB man).

Nourishing the Russian-agent theory are the CIA files released not long ago. They reveal that during his trip to Mexico in September, 1963, Oswald talked with a "consul" who was actually a KGB man working in that agency's *13* or "liquid affairs" department—that is, in the bureau containing the Soviet's own assassination plotters. The same CIA documents show that prior to Oswald's arrival in Minsk there had apparently resided there another Marine defector, who may have associated with the same young Russians as the Oswalds and who certainly was a CIA informant. Such facts inspire logical questions: Was Oswald sent to take this other defector's place by the CIA, or naval intelligence? Or was he a KGB agent, even a double agent? Did Khrushchev's own opinion, frequently expressed, that Kennedy fell victim to right-wing Americans who'd framed Oswald so as to blacken left-wingers, really conceal the fact that the Russians had sent Oswald to kill Kennedy? That last seems most unlikely, especially in the atmosphere of détente advocated by Kennedy after the Cuban missile crisis. And arguing against any Russian involvement is the sheer insanity of Khrushchev's ordering Kennedy killed. If discovered, that ploy could leave the world a smoking hulk.

To support the Castro-agent theory, there is almost no irrefutable evidence, physical or otherwise, except Oswald's New Orleans huckstering in favor of Havana, and the supposition that Castro ordered the assassination out of anger about the Bay of Pigs and the mafiosi running around his island trying to kill him. Lyndon Johnson, not long before his death, opined Castro might have been involved. Castro himself decried the murder and, fearing Oswald's pro-Cuba mouthings would tie it to his regime, put his intelligence network on full alert. He may then have learned that three of his agents in Mexico may have interviewed Oswald when Lee was trying for that visa to Cuba. But no one now knows exactly what Castro did find out about the assassination.

Recently, two gentlemen from Las Vegas have intimated there exists solid proof that Castro ordered Kennedy's death. Robert Maheu—who acted as intermediary between the CIA and Giancana/Roselli, and who served as Nevada regent for Howard Hughes (another man with beguiling CIA ties)—has hinted the CIA knows Castro orchestrated the assassination. The editor of the Las Vegas *Sun*, Hank Greenspan, has told reporters he has such proof safely locked away. (Indeed, Greenspan's information cache has been alleged to have been a target for burglary by the White House plumbers, perhaps either for the goods on Castro or, possibly, incriminating data on Hughes's $100,000 gift, channeled through Bebe Rebozo, to President Nixon.) Thus far, however, the proof remains to be seen. A fundamental question remains, too. Would Castro have risked killing Kennedy when, if his plot was discovered, it might have sparked an invasion making the Bay of Pigs look like a yachting exercise? In fact, if anybody wanted to overthrow Castro, they should have tried to pin the assassination on him. Why didn't anti-Castro people do just that? Which brings us to the next hypothesis.

First, there is some evidence that Cuban exiles and their American allies in the CIA-run commando schools schemed to do away with Kennedy. But it's fragile stuff. A woman named Silvia Odio, the daughter of Cubans imprisoned by Castro, told the Warren Commission staff that on September 25, 1963, three men visited her in Dallas. They came from New Orleans. Two seemed to be Latin and the other was the omnipresent "Leon Oswald." One of the men suggested "Oswald" could help in the underground activities against Castro. Mrs. Odio—whose testimony was corroborated by her sister—said the next day one of the men called her to say "Oswald" was a former Marine, an expert rifleman, and possessed of the opinion that "President Kennedy should have been killed after the Bay of Pigs." This was hearsay, but the rest of Mrs. Odio's story merited attention since Mrs. Odio unhesitatingly identified photographs of Oswald as the man who visited her. The Commission thought that couldn't be. They'd satisfied themselves that on September 25 their Oswald was on a bus from New Orleans to Mexico, in quest of the visa he wanted to Cuba. But the FBI was told to investigate Odio's story in more depth.

Late in September, 1964—the report was already written—the FBI reported they had found a Loran Eugene Hall (whose spoken name resembles "Oswald," especially if you're hard of hearing). Hall claimed he had visited Mrs. Odio that day with two other men, neither of them Oswald. Later still, the other two men denied it, and in time it was revealed not only that Hall retracted *his* story, but that Hall was a well-known anti-Castro American (reportedly associated with Frank Sturgis) who told Jim Garrison that he'd been at a meeting during which the assassination was discussed by CIA contract employees. The mind reels, and the suppositions still go on.

There is Robert McKeown, an admitted gunrunner from Texas, who says Jack Ruby once visited him to talk about providing arms for Cuban-exile commandos. Not only that, Lee Harvey Oswald himself once visited McKeown with another man to dicker about four high-powered rifles. Unhappily for conspiracy buffs, people familiar with McKeown question his veracity. Move, then, to Nancy Perrin Rich, wife of a former gunrunner, who said she was with Jack Ruby and an Army colonel at meetings held to arrange arms shipments to Cuba. Mrs. Rich, though, may have been angry with Ruby at the time for slapping her around when she worked at his Carousel Club.

Ceaselessly, the carousel of speculations spins. Recently an electronics engineer, bankrupt bon vivant and indicted counterfeiter named Robert Morrow published a book purporting in James Bondish breathlessness to solve Kennedy's murder by pinning it on anti-Castroites and, yes, Clay Shaw. The motive: the Kennedy Administration's break-up of a scheme to ruin Castro's economy by flooding the island with bogus pesos. Now it happens that Morrow, his artist-wife and a prominent anti-Castro exile named Mario Garcia Kohly *were* arrested in 1963 for just such counterfeiting. There's no doubt, too, that the Kennedy brothers did discourage anti-Castro activities after the failure of the Bay of Pigs expedition, instead urging a Caribbean détente, and so it's possible that the attack on the counterfeiting scheme was the last straw, that it so enraged anti-Castroites and Shaw that—as Morrow's book claims—the whole cast of Kennedy-assassination characters (Ruby, Tippit, Ferrie, maybe some Watergaters like Sturgis and Hunt, and several others) somehow cooperated in killing the President. Morrow even claims he bought three Mannlicher-Carcanos (of the rarer 7.32mm caliber, a modification of the standard 6.5mm) for the assassination teams in Dealey Plaza. He also asserts that he and David Ferrie flew into Cuba for the exiles, that he and Jack Ruby ran guns, that Oswald early on was picked as a patsy (Lee supposedly also served as a courier for the conspirators coming home from his Russian exile), and that Oswald trained as a commando near New Orleans under Ferrie *et al.* before winding up the dupe in Dealey Plaza.

As is customary with such solutions to the crime, little in this book beyond what anybody can find in published sources is verifiable. All Morrow's chief characters are dead, beyond proof or libel. In the end, all we know for sure is that Morrow was a counterfeiter with friends among dispossessed Batistaites, a combination that to some cynics might suggest the plot to print phony pesos was as much for personal gain as for political idealism. Like so much else, it seems the truth is beyond knowing.

So, of course, is the matter of whether Oswald was a CIA agent. Many theorists believe the CIA is everywhere in the Kennedy story, for that matter everywhere, period. Mae Brussell, an excitable lady who publishes the *Conspiracy Newsletter,* is quoted as saying the CIA was involved in the assassinations of John Kennedy, Martin Luther King and Robert Kennedy, besides all the foreign leaders, and were also busy setting up fronts like the SLA and IRA, all the while recruiting agents as far-flung as I. F. Stone and Nicholas von Hoffman. Obviously, Ms. Brussell and her sprouts, Paul Krassner and Dick Gregory, are extremists. Calmer analysts see CIA tracks only in specific places. They assume that if the Russians, as Yuri Nosenko said, thought Oswald was a CIA agent, then maybe he was. What happened, some suggest, is that the CIA contacted Oswald and told him while in the Marines to become a Marxist. Then defect, marry into Soviet intelligence, find out what you can, and come on back. A perfect mission for an amateur spy. But no, say other theorists. What really happened is that the CIA arranged an early hardship discharge for Oswald (the Marines say it was routine). Then a switch was made. The real Oswald was put on ice while a CIA phony Oswald took his place as a defector. After nearly three years in Russia the CIA's phony Oswald came back and the real Oswald took his place.

The line of reasoning for all this is too tortuous to recount here, but some salient notions bear mentioning (we will ignore Marguerite Oswald's claim that her son was an agent who had died in his country's service and so should, like Kennedy, be buried at Arlington). For instance, the visa stamps in the passport Oswald carried when he defected show him getting from England to Finland at times when there is no commercial airline flight. So, it's said, he had to go by CIA "black plane." Concerning passports, it must also be noted that in New Orleans Oswald applied for a passport one day and got it the next. Strange, eh? But then twenty-four other people who applied that same time also got their passports. What about the fact that Oswald's height and eye color vary widely at different times as recorded on Marine Corps records, passport applications, FBI files and police autopsy records? To Anson *et al.*, this surely is evidence of multiple Oswalds, maybe of a plot by elements of the CIA to set up the real Oswald as a decoy. Likewise, theorists point out, the official Dallas police photo of Oswald shows a man quite different in facial structure from the chubby-cheeked youth pictured in Minsk. Further, one photo of Marina and Lee in Russia shows him very little taller than his five-foot three-inch wife, although *that* Lee Oswald's passport has him five eleven and the Lee Oswald measured in the Dallas morgue was five foot nine. Such contradictions are not inexplicable. Clerks make errors, people do fib about their size, photo angles can be deceptive, and a face's fatness or thinness can change. The ear shape does not alter though, and the ears of the Dallas-Oswald, the Marines-Oswald, and the Russian-Oswald all match. What's most remarkable is that all these happenings should congregate around the assassin of an American President.

It's also odd that Lee Harvey Oswald should in September, 1963, decide to go to Mexico, there to seek, according to the Warren Report, a visa for Cuba and permission to re-enter Russia. The Warren Commission thought Oswald's domestic life was so bad, and his commitment to Marxism so strong, that he had decided this was his only course (Marina said Oswald had considered hijacking an airliner to Cuba, but she demurred). Oswald stayed in Mexico, the report says, for a week (his tourist cards show that) seeking the visa, but being rebuffed by both countries despite his sympathy for them as evidenced in Minsk and New Orleans. (Nosenko said the KGB ordered the Soviet Embassy in Mexico to refuse re-entrance to this perplexing man.) Oswald then, by the report's reasoning frustrated and angry, returned to Dallas, to his menial jobs and deteriorating marriage, and soon he killed the President. So had Oswald any connection with the CIA?

Only by implication, apparently. For instance, when the FBI found out about Oswald's Mexican sojourn, they asked the CIA if they might have a picture of Oswald visiting the Cuban or Soviet Embassies. They asked because the CIA had hidden cameras recording most visits. A picture came that showed a burly man, about thirty-five, who looked nothing like Oswald. The photo galvanized the CIA-theorists. The man had to be (a) another Oswald, (b) the mysterious assassin named Saul, (c) Oswald's CIA contact or "baby sitter," (d) another conspirator. The CIA has vehemently denied this, saying they sent a picture of an unidentified man who *might* have been this Lee Harvey Oswald the FBI was inquiring after. That answer has puzzled those skeptical of CIA explanations, and the release of CIA papers pertaining to the photo request have accentuated the bewilderment. In one memo, apparently to the FBI, the CIA writer refers to the mysterious man as "a certain person who is known to you." Does that mean Oswald, the suspect? Or some other criminal character unrelated to the assassination (as the CIA says this mystery man was unrelated)? Or just what? We still don't know. Theorists then asked about the photograph: Is it possible that the CIA had no substantial dossier on Oswald, a known defector and Communist sympathizer? That they didn't know what he looked like? Wasn't this burly man, then, somebody who said he was Lee Harvey Oswald, and hence, might he not have been a co-conspirator? Admittedly, a good question.

Another item was the story of "D." "D" was a Latin agent who declared he saw Lee Harvey Oswald in Mexico City accept $6,500 to kill the President. "D" said Oswald received the money in the Cuban Consulate from a tall, slender black man with dyed red hair (theorists at once recalled witnesses who said they saw such a man in the Depository), and then exclaimed he sure was man enough to do the job. A titillating story, but after prolonged investigation and questioning, "D" admitted he'd made the whole thing up. His story vanished into the maw of other rumors about Mexico, about Oswald flying there secretly in September for his assassination instructions, about clandestine meetings there with CIA operatives, about Chinese Communists plotting there with Cubans to kill Kennedy, about E. Howard Hunt coordinating the assassination from Mexico.

Finally, we are left only with the possibility that Oswald worked for the CIA, but with no proof. William Colby, former CIA Director, said Oswald certainly did not work for them, and that the Agency had only rudimentary information on the man. The FBI was responsible for minor defectors, Colby said.

Then, the indefatigable critics ask, was Oswald with the FBI? Certainly he was in contact with them. Oswald's notebook contained the name, phone number and license number for FBI agent James Hosty. The Bureau says that is because Hosty had the duty of interviewing Marina and Lee to see if they were hard-core Communists. It's also true that Oswald delivered a threatening note to Hosty just before the assassination, which Hosty or somebody ordered destroyed. The FBI alleges that the note referred only to Oswald's anger about the harassment of Marina. Does that mean the FBI covered up the note's existence until it came out in 1975 only because it made them seem lax? They were, of course. Everybody wonders if the note didn't threaten the President. Even the suspect Dallas police reported that Hosty, within two hours after the killing, said he knew Oswald was capable of committing the crime. If so, why wasn't Oswald locked up? Especially if, as former FBI clerk William Walter alleges, there was a special Teletype sent November 17 from the FBI's Washington headquarters to the offices in Mobile, New Orleans and Dallas warning that an attempt might be made to assassinate the President on November 22, by a "militant revolutionary group." The FBI says they have no record of such a message, though they admit they received information from the Miami police department about a wire-tapped conversation involving a plot by white racists to kill the President with a rifle sometime soon. Why with these warnings didn't the FBI corral Oswald? The most cynical critics say because somebody in the FBI wouldn't have minded seeing Kennedy and his pushy brother eliminated. Bobby was encroaching on Hoover with his organized-crime crusade, and Jack, Hoover knew from wire taps on Giancana, was womanizing in a most un-Presidential way, leaving the Chief Executive open to blackmail which might endanger the nation. Enter Oswald, whom the FBI had over a barrel.

Again, there is no proof of these ghoulish stories. The Teletype Walter swears exists has never been found. It could have been suppressed, like Oswald's threat to Hosty, but Mr. Walter was questioned by reporters at least twenty times about the message's existence and given a lie-detector test. He failed it. Another influential story, generated by a reporter named Lonnie Hudkins, proclaimed Oswald *was* an FBI informant. As proof Hudkins even offered Oswald's "pay number": S-172. What's not widely known is that Hugh Aynsworth, another reporter and long-time student of the Kennedy killing, simply made up that number because Hudkins was continually bugging him for inside stuff on the case. Of such stuff are assassination nightmares made.

In sum, while there are several leads that should be thoroughly reinvestigated, there is nothing that now proves Lee Harvey Oswald was anybody's agent other than his own. That may seem anticlimactic. A climax might come if we could learn what the CIA, for example, really knew or knows about Lee Harvey Oswald. The Agency's former employees like Victor Marchetti, co-author of *The CIA and the Cult of Intelligence,* are sure William Colby did not tell the whole truth in saying that until Oswald visited Mexico the Agency had almost nothing on him. Two of the seven Warren Commission members—Allen Dulles and John McCloy—were, respectively, a former Director of the CIA and a founder of its World War II predecessor, the OSS. And like the FBI, the CIA was checking up on itself. It could be climactic, too, if the FBI, who hurt its believability by destroying pertinent documents, and who we now know had its own "dirty tricks" division to harass the likes of Martin Luther King, would open *all* its files on the Oswalds and their acquaintances. It would help if the FBI's investigation for the Warren Commission—the *only* investigation—was supplemented by another conducted by a responsible, representative and independent group of American investigators with no sins to cover up, no case to prove, no political masters to please, no ideology to protect.

Only then will these serious speculations and suspicions be either confirmed or confounded. We may even then be free of the more idiotic notions that distract us from the plausible alternatives to the Warren Commission's Report.

Free of George O'Toole's contention that "psychological stress evaluations" of six words of Oswald's show he's not guilty, a position ridiculed by polygraph experts who say if their machine, which measures six galvanic responses, can't be trusted, how can analysis of a tape-recorded voice? Oswald himself turned down a polygraph test.

Free of former Colonel Fletcher Prouty's belief in a gigantic plot in which the CIA, FBI, Teamsters, Mafia, Defense Intelligence Agency, National Security Agency, Army Intelligence and the Warren Commission itself are "all pawns" of a mammoth cabal "able to influence the travel plans of the President, the Vice President and a Presidential candidate (Nixon) and all members of the Kennedy cabinet . . . powerful enough to have orders issued to the Army, and able to mount a massive campaign to control the media during and after the assassination . . . able to have Jack Ruby kill Oswald and to transfer jurisdiction of the murder from Texas and then to effectively control the outcome of the Warren Commission."

Free of Hugh C. McDonald and his "Saul" the Assassin, that unnamed, unavailable, unverifiable killer who may well have sprung from McDonald's head along with the author's belief that the Russians are giving us the flu by firing small germ-infested rockets into the jet stream.

Free of the nut stuff, of the paranoia, of the fantasizing about the malevolent forces that control our destiny. *We* should control our destiny, as much as possible. We should make one last effort to find out if Oswald was a pitiable young man whose closet was stuffed full of big ideas—"Hands off Cuba!," "The Road to Socialism," "The Coming American Revolution" —but whose small life hemmed him in, defeated him until, to justify himself, he took history by the horns and killed our President. Or if he was an agent of our own institutions, or of some foreign antagonist, or of a small group of ourselves, of Americans who succumbed to the black, unreasoning hatred and violence that John Kennedy knew was the greatest danger to free men.

We must also admit that knowledge is finite, and truth is not synonymous with data, that the metaphysical fact is we may never solve the mystery of John Kennedy's death. Even so, we should try, for many reasons. We might scourge the ideological ghouls who mistake Dealey Plaza for all of America. We might in finding out who killed Kennedy partially heal our own hearts and minds so grievously afflicted then and ever since by an insidious feeling of mutual guilt. And we might learn more about who kills our leaders, and why. Surely we cannot want less than that.

VII

WAITING FOR THE INEVITABLE

> *"This thing with me will be resolved by death and violence."*
>
> —MALCOLM X

> *"I'm not fearing any man. . . . Mine eyes have seen the glory of the coming of the Lord."*
>
> —MARTIN LUTHER KING, Jr.

John Kennedy's unfathomable death created in many Americans an ominous expectancy. If that could happen, anything was possible. We sensed that the potential for political murder had been only partially discharged with Kennedy. Somehow it was still suspended above the nation, a nearly palpable menace awaiting its moment. Who would be next? we wondered.

The answer surprised us. Our next two assassination victims were not, as always before, powerful white politicians. Instead, the assassins struck black reformers. Black men, in fact, who in different ways—the one as incendiary, the other as dreamer—were protesting the injustices they believed white politicians had caused or tolerated.

The first to die, Malcolm X, put his bitterness succinctly. Of Kennedy's assassination he said, "Chickens coming home to roost never did make me sad: They've always made me glad." The chickens Malcolm had in mind were not just in ghettos; he felt they had also winged in from Southeast Asia and the Third World. It didn't matter that Kennedy at the time of his death was preparing wide-ranging civil rights legislation or that his inheritor, Lyndon Johnson, was sponsoring bills that in time would inspire some black leaders to hail him as the greatest civil-rights President since Lincoln.

That was not enough for Malcolm, nor for King. They wanted justice now, freedom now. Like the preachers' sons they were, they exhorted their disciples to demand just that. But before they could see those demands met, each was dead and his cause soon faltered. Assassination had

171

again removed a leader and deflected, perhaps thwarted, his movement. For those who kept faith with Malcolm and King, it was small solace that the ultimate effects of their deaths were unknowable. Better to turn to assassination's companion constant, the question of just who killed them and why.

With Malcolm it seemed simple. On Sunday afternoon, February 21, 1965, three men attacked him while he was addressing a congregation of his Organization of Afro-American Unity in the Audubon Ballroom, at 166th Street and Broadway in New York. The assassins were well drilled. Two stood up about eight rows from the rostrum. "Don't be messin' with my pockets," one hollered, and while Malcolm asked them to cool it, his bodyguards moved toward them. Then smoke billowed from a man's sock soaked in lighter fluid and set afire in the aisle. As Malcolm and his four hundred followers stared at the confusion, a man rushed the stage with a sawed-off, double-barreled, 12-gauge shotgun wrapped in a gray jacket. The blasts caught Malcolm in the chest, blowing him backward over a chair. Two other men moved up and pumped shot after shot from a .38 and a .45 into his body before all three ran to escape. Two made it, but a bodyguard's pistol felled the third. The crowd outside broke his leg and would have killed him if police hadn't come to his rescue. They soon identified him as Talmadge Hayer, a.k.a. Thomas Hagan.

In the ballroom, Malcolm was dead. His pregnant wife, Betty Shabazz, wailed over his body, and another woman keened, "Oh, black folks, black folks, why you got to kill each other?" That was it, obviously, Malcolm's lieutenants were sure Elijah Muhammad had ordered the killing and that trained killers from the Fruit of Islam, the Black Muslim's strike force, had carried it out. Sixteen months before, Elijah had suspended Malcolm from the Muslims, ostensibly for his remark about Kennedy, but really, they thought, because he feared the startling charisma of Malcolm, feared that Malcolm's new organization would attract more blacks than the Muslims and, above all, feared that Malcolm would tell what he knew about *sub rosa* Muslim activities.

Malcolm himself had thought the Muslims might kill him. They were responsible, he'd said, for the fire-bombing of his house just six days before he went to the Audubon. That was their gratitude for all he'd done. He'd built the Muslim organization in New York. He'd enrolled their most famous recruit, the young heavyweight Cassius Clay. He'd articulated for them the black man's rage as no one had. "If ballots won't work, bullets will," he had once proclaimed, and now he feared he was to be the proof of that sentiment. That seemed ironic. He, born Malcolm Little, the man who in his youth was convinced that white racists had burned his home and killed his father, who as Big Red (for his reddish hair and light skin, the legacy of a "white rapist" grandfather) had gotten through zoot suits and processed hair, through dealing cocaine and grass, through burglary and six years in the slammer, where he'd learned about Islam and become converted, and then made it up close to Elijah's side, this man was now to be killed not by the "white devils" he excoriated but by his onetime brothers. Even Malcolm admitted they had reason. After he'd left the Muslims, he accused the sixty-seven-year-old Elijah of sexual promiscuity (anathema to Muslims) with teenage "secretaries" and declared he would, if threatened, tell what he knew; for example, about deals the Muslims had made with the Ku Klux Klan and the American Nazi Party to separate contested territories into black and white hegemonies. There were rumors, too, that Elijah's sect had, like the Klan, accepted money from H. L. Hunt, who likewise thought it a capital idea to keep black and white apart. Such things could badly damage the sect. "This die is set, and Malcolm shall not escape," Elijah opined. No wonder that Malcolm wrote, "Some of the followers of Elijah Muhammad would still consider it a first-rank honor to kill me."

It had apparently happened. Soon after the shooting, police arrested two Black Muslims as Hayer's accomplices. Thomas "15X" Johnson was eventually tried as the shotgunner. Norman "3X" Butler was charged with being the other gunman. Both had reputations as enforcers for the Muslims (at the time of Malcolm's assassination, Butler was out on $100,000 bond for shooting another Muslim defector). In 1966, the three were convicted of murder and sentenced to life. A rougher sort of justice moved faster than that. Within thirty-six hours of Malcolm's death, the Muslims' mosque number seven in Harlem burned beyond repair, and for months after, Malcolm's allies publicly, if futilely, threatened to kill Elijah. But at least everyone agreed: The Muslims—at least some Muslims—had assassinated Malcolm X.

That verdict still seems fair, even considering that no firm evidence ever led beyond the three accused assassins (Elijah repeatedly denied any personal or organizational responsibility). Of course, there were rumors of other people who wanted Malcolm dead. His half-sister thought the "power structure of the West," maybe the CIA, might have done it because if Malcolm had lived, he would have changed American society so much. James Farmer, former CORE director, said Malcolm could have been killed by Harlem narcotics interests because of his crusade against drugs (Malcolm remained a Moslem, adhering to their strictures about intoxicants). Others have said, yes, but it was the Red Chinese who did it, or maybe Turks or Arabs, all of them exporters of drugs that were heavily used by blacks, a habit Malcolm hoped to end. There were also speculations that he was betrayed by his bodyguards, most of whom had once been Black Muslims. But no proof of any of those conspiracies emerged, and they entered the limbo of incredible assassination theories.

We were left with the irreducible fact that Malcolm X was dead. Many called that good riddance, remembering his hysterical rantings against whites, his calls for a separate black nation, his exhortations to blacks to buy guns and "get the white monkey off your back." Yet near the end, Malcolm seemed to have changed. He professed a new idealism. Trips abroad and a pilgrimage to Mecca had convinced him of the need for a brotherhood of all the oppressed instead of a war between the darker and paler races. Ironically, that perception may also have helped doom Malcolm. Dark whisperings had it that Moslems in the East had decided to give money to Malcolm's organization rather that to Elijah's, a prospect that could have provided another motive for removing Malcolm.

Nevertheless, Malcolm persisted in assailing the Muslims, saying among other things that their doctrines produced "zombies." He said he was glad to be free of his hysteria, of "the sickness and madness of those days . . . it's time for martyrs now. And if I'm to be one, it will be in the cause of brotherhood." Unfortunately, he did not die in brotherhood's name but in a climate of violence that his early hatemongering may partially have made. Only his magnificent autobiography suggests what he might have become in other climes. Most sadly, the violent weather was to hold, a fact deplored at the time of Malcolm's death by King, who ruefully said such violence "is not good for the image of our nation and not good for the Negro cause." That was three years before Memphis, where King became a genuine martyr to brotherhood.

It was there, of course, that Martin Luther King and James Earl Ray came to be paired as saint and criminal in the pantheon of American assassinations. Yet as with Lincoln and Booth, Kennedy and Oswald, there are vital questions surrounding that pairing, so many that we truly know only two things.

First, we know that at 6 P.M. on April 4, 1968, King leaned on the railing of the balcony of Memphis' Lorraine Motel into the sights of a .30-'06 rifle. One minute later, a bullet ripped through his right jaw and into his throat and body, killing him with a single shot which ended his dream of social equality, which burned Detroit and Washington, which launched a worldwide search for his killer and which eventually brought in a skinny petty-criminal escaped convict and lifelong loser variously called Eric Starvo Galt, Harvey Lowmyer, John Willard, John L. Rayns, Paul Bridgman, Ramon George Sneyd, but known to us soon and ever since as James Earl Ray.

Second, we know that even if Ray did kill King—there is a reasonable doubt that it could be proved—he was victimized by judicial irregularities, the cover-up of important facts in the slaying and a failure by the FBI and Memphis police to investigate thoroughly the possibility of a conspiracy.

To understand those two things, we must begin with Martin Luther King. King was in Memphis to lead a protest march in support of Local 1733, the nearly all-black union of garbage and sewer workers. The thirteen hundred men had gone on strike in February, asking for a fifty-cent-an-hour raise, workmen's compensation and an insurance program. Memphis officials refused. Inevitably, trouble built. The town seethed with race hate. Memphis' black leaders called for King, the Nobel apostle of nonviolence.

On March 18, King arrived from Anaheim, California, where he'd given a speech two days before. (Ray, then underground in Los Angeles, had noticed it.) In Memphis, King exhorted fifteen thousand people to join in a work stoppage. It happened, but the agent was a freak snowstorm, not aggrieved citizens. One plan frustrated, King consented to lead a march on March 28.

It was a disaster. Militant youths, the Invaders, broke King's nonviolent rules and some windows. They looted stores, touched off a riot in which police killed a seventeen-year-old boy. Cops moved in, plucked King and Ralph Abernathy and others out of the melee and took them to the fashionable Rivermont Motel. (During the post-Hoover revelations of FBI harassment of King, we found that the Bureau discussed leaking the news that King was staying in a white establishment, to embarrass him. In turn, one of Ray's attorneys speculated that the FBI really wanted to drive King out of the Rivermont to the Lorraine, where he could be more easily killed.) Anyway, things were more volatile than ever. Could King come back for a second march if they'd cool off the kids? King again agreed. They'd march on Friday, April 5. Thus it was that King returned to Memphis from Atlanta on April 3, and checked into the black-owned Lorraine Motel. Lots of people knew it, what with the TV and radio coverage. In room 306 he worked, unaware that a bullet awaited him the next day.

Did James Earl Ray fire it? The physical evidence proves no more than that Ray was involved in King's assassination—something he has admitted, asserting, "I personally did not shoot Dr. King, but I believe I may be partly responsible for his death." Furthermore, other evidence—which Ray's 1969 guilty plea (forced out of him by his lawyer, he says) prevented from being introduced in court—suggests to many a conspiracy as much as it does a lone killer. In either case, King was at the Lorraine on April 4. Where was Ray?

For a time, no less than three hundred feet away, in a rooming house on South Main Street. The room—5B, in the north section of the double building—was a flophouse special featuring a chipped iron bedstead arched at each end like a leer. On the bed was the April 4 edition of the Memphis *Commercial Appeal.* In it was a report of King's speech the previous night, of his vow to march, and more, of an incandescent prophecy. "Some began to talk about the threats that were out, of what would happen to me from some of our sick white brothers. . . . Well, I don't know what will happen now. We've got some difficult days ahead. But it really doesn't matter with me now. Because I've been to the mountaintop!" Then his people heard him say, "Longevity has its place. But I'm not concerned about that now," and then on, his voice building, until he shouted, his broad face varnished with sweat: "So I'm happy tonight. I'm not fearing any man. 'Mine eyes have seen the glory of the coming of the Lord!'" The adulation washed over him. It must temporarily have cleansed him of the fear he'd recently admitted to close associates and friends, the fear that festered with every threat on his life since the first attempt in 1958, with every confrontation, with the fact of his surveillance by the FBI (and by the Memphis police, even now, as he spoke and, at the motel, from a fire station across the street). He may also have shed for the moment his correct suspicions that J. Edgar Hoover's animosity had led to illegal wire taps, to a nasty letter suggesting that he commit suicide, to the gossip spread about his alleged sexual misbehavior.

All that may have been. But it is sure that the next day anyone in room 5B could push aside the gold-and-green-flowered plastic curtain and see the balcony fronting room 306 at the Lorraine. Ray may have looked there, for certainly he was in the room at times, between 3:30 and 5:30 on April 4. However, no one would have taken a shot at King from that window. You'd have to lean halfway out for any sort of accuracy. But there was a bathroom next door to 5B. From it, a man could get a clear diagonal shot across the weedy, bushy back yards and Mulberry Street, if he could get the rifle out the window and stand in the cratered bathtub, with one foot up on its edge. And if he weren't interrupted. In this rooming house, the toilet got a lot of use, as it does in places inhabited by heavy drinkers. One such lived directly next door, in 6B, named Charles Quitman Stephens. Charley had seen Ray around 3:30 on the afternoon of the fourth, he later said. He'd come out into the hall when Mrs. Bessie Brewer, the manager, was showing that fellow 5B after he'd rejected a room without a view of the Lorraine. Stephens told police and newsmen that he could also identify Ray as the neat, "sharp-faced" man whom he'd seen in the failing twilight run down the hall after the shot, carrying a bundle, running, he thought, from the bathroom, which had been locked at different times between 3:30 and the shooting. Oddly, his common-law mate, Grace Walden, said Charley had to be wrong, that the running man she'd seen through her doorway looked nothing like Ray and that Charley didn't see the man until he was clear down the hall, rounding the corner for the stairs.

Could it have been Ray? No one denies he *was* in the rooming house. Or that he had with him a .30-'06 Model 760 Remington Gamemaster pump-action rifle fitted with a Redfield 2 × 7 telescopic sight. About four o'clock, he'd also bought a pair of Bushnell 7 × 35 binoculars at the York Arms Company a half-mile away, perhaps for observing King. The binoculars, along with the rifle (one spent casing in the chamber but *none* in the four-shot clip), several other .30-'06 cartridges, including five military rounds, a green-and-brown bedspread, a Browning rifle cardboard box and a 15" × 20" blue-plastic overnight case filled with toiletries, a white T-shirt (size 42–44), a pair of darned gray-and-white-paisley undershorts (size 34), a transistor radio, two cans of Schlitz, a pair of pliers, a tack hammer and the *Commercial Appeal* make up the famous "bundle of evidence" that Ray is said to have dropped in the door of the Canipe Amusement Company at 424 South Main Street after the fatal shot.

Ray—or, more properly, Ray as John Willard, the name he'd given Mrs. Brewer—also seems to have been in the bathroom. His palm print, the police said, was on the wall above the bathtub, right there where he'd leaned to get into the tub to take the shot. The scuff marks of shoes were clearly visible in the tub, too, and there was an identifiable Ray fingerprint on the rifle and scope. In room 5B, the FBI picked up fibers from the bedspread, as well as hair samples, the straps from the binocular case and other bits of physical evidence proving that Ray had been there.

Altogether, the weight of physical evidence against Ray seemed persuasive. A week after the killing, suspicious Atlantans directed the police and FBI to what turned out to be Ray's 1966 white Mustang, loaded with clothes and a Polaroid camera and even a white sheet. The same car was said to have been parked by Canipe's when King was killed. Ray, the thinking went, used it to escape, driving from Memphis to Atlanta, before abandoning it in favor of a bus to Cincinnati, a train to Detroit, then on to Toronto and Montreal, a plane to London, then to Lisbon and back to London, where he was caught in June, 1968. Authorities did prove it was Ray's car, after they proved it was Eric Starvo Galt's and that Galt was Ray. Establishing that could not convict Ray, however, especially since he has affirmed he bought the car (although once saying it was *after* the killing). That tireless assassination researcher Harold Weisberg believes he has evidence showing puzzling things about the car. For example: that it was almost bare of fingerprints, although there were several of Ray's left in Memphis; that there were cigarette butts in the ashtray, but Ray didn't smoke; that there was mud on the passenger side, but Ray was supposedly alone; that there was a white sheet on the back seat and some of the clothes didn't fit Ray. As we'll see in tracing alternate theories of the crime, these items could be important if verified, something Weisberg and other buffs have not yet accomplished (and something other students of the crime say is impossible because Ray alone did it).

But, to return to the car, it truly was odd that no all-points bulletin had been issued to stop a white Mustang. Guy Canipe said he had watched one roar past his door after he'd seen someone drop the bundle. The Tennessee State Police said they never got a request for an APB, and the Memphis police said that was because they had no proof the "young white male, well dressed," in the white Mustang had killed King, even though, yes, they had at 6:08 broadcast a local call to stop such a car. Trouble was, there were at least four hundred white Mustangs in Memphis and, besides, after the killing, there was a phony CB radio broadcast about a wild chase up in northeast Memphis with a white Mustang running away from a blue Pontiac, with three white men shooting at the Pontiac.

Police explained that as a schoolboy prank, coming too late (at 6:35 P.M.) to be part of conspiracy. It was interesting, though, that the broadcast diverted attention from the southern routes out of Memphis, which Ray admitted he took.

Besides the fingerprints and the car pointing to him as King's murderer, eyewitnesses identified Ray as the man who, on March 29 in Birmingham (fresh from Los Angeles via New Orleans, Selma and Atlanta), had purchased a .243 Remington Gamemaster, had ordered it fitted with a 2 × 7 variable-power scope, had bought some cartridges and had given his name and address as Harvey Lowmyer, 1807 South 11th Street, Birmingham. The next day, though, Lowmyer took the rifle back to the Aeromarine Supply Company and asked for a heavier one, a .30-'06, because his "brother" had said the .243 wasn't big enough for the deer hunting they planned to do in Wisconsin. The clerk, Don Wood, gave Lowmyer the same Remington model in a .30-'06, fitted it with the scope, exchanged cartridges and put everything into a Browning box, because the scope made the rifle too wide for the Remington box. Lowmyer seemed grateful, Wood said. So was the FBI, since through the rifle and Wood they could identify Lowmyer, Galt, Willard and Ray as the murderer, because hadn't that .30-'06 killed King?

That would be contested in later proceedings, since FBI ballistics expert Robert Frazier (who had worked on the John F. Kennedy killing, too) would say only that the deformed slug was "consistent with" the rifle—a meaningless statement, since the same would be true of any of millions of .30-'06s in America. Then, too, some firearms-identification texts and experts suggest the slug was not too mutilated to link with a specific weapon, since a full three-eighths inch of its base remained, or a "perfect evidence slug," as Ray's first lawyers called it.

Actually, all that was certain was the shot itself. The police saw its effects from their observation post in the fire station. Someone put King in his sights at 5:59 as he stepped out onto the balcony and leaned on the railing for a chat with his colleagues and disciples gathered below in the Lorraine's courtyard by the white Cadillac that was to take him to a soul-food supper. There was the driver, Solomon Jones, and his aides, the Reverends Andrew Young, James Bevel and Hosea Williams and Jesse Jackson just come down the metal staircase from the balcony. There they all were, gazing up at King, as he was shot, and they saw their spiritual leader jerk to his right, then fall backward to lie in the blood pumping from a fist-size hole in his right jaw. The slug tore downward and to his left and severed his spine and all his major nerves, killing him as a functioning human being in that one instant. The police swarmed from their posts into the Lorraine, but it was too late. King's disciples pointed across Mulberry Street, but no one was caught.

In the first shock of King's death, while disturbances rocked 125 American cities, speculations about his killers reverberated. Perhaps partly to forestall such talk, Attorney General Ramsey Clark, after consulting with the FBI and President Lyndon Johnson, flew to Memphis, where, the morning after the killing, he announced that the killer had left behind a remarkable amount of physical evidence, that there was no evidence of a conspiracy and that "all of our evidence at this time indicates that it was a single person who committed this criminal act."

That was debatable, but Clark's statement seemed expedient in the inflammable racial and political situation. Nothing in the physical evidence of Canipe's and 5B *excluded* two or more assassins. But Clark did not want to repeat the morass of doubts Oswald and Jack Ruby and Clay Shaw and the rest had created. Better to announce at once that one man did it, then let a massive investigation take place in secrecy. It *was* massive, since at the end, when they brought in Ray as the lone killer, it was the result of the work of three thousand FBI agents, the police of several countries and about $2,000,000. Who was this elusive man, and had he actually done it alone?

James Earl Ray was the kind of man for whom Martin Luther King spoke. Poor. Pissed off. Imprisoned in a world he never made. From his beginning on March 10, 1928, until now, in the Tennessee State Prison, Ray's life taught him to get before you're gotten. His father was a shiftless sort, a menial laborer, good mostly for siring nine children on Ray's hapless mother before leaving her so she could complete an ugly ruin with alcohol. The Ray children grew up in an agony of embarrassment and poverty. Eventually, Jimmy and his brothers Jerry and John became criminals. One sister went mad. Even so, as a teenager, Jimmy Ray seemed to have a nail-hanging hold on America's vertical mobility. He learned the leather-dying trade in Alton, Illinois, and was neat, shy with girls, polite, reliable and frugal as hell. Then, just as World War II ended, he lost that job. Six weeks later Ray joined the Army (on the enlistment form, he said his father was dead). After basic, he became an MP in Germany (and, some say, admired the defeated Hitler's racial policies), an occupation that didn't inhibit considerable boozing, a little dope, lots of fighting and trouble. In December, 1948, Ray was discharged for "ineptness" and "lack of adaptability to military service."

From then until he was arrested for the King murder, Ray was a Sammy Glick of the nether world, scrambling for all he was worth. If he ever heard anything like the messages of peace and brotherhood coming from a black Baptist minister and his son, Martin, in Atlanta, his twenty-year record doesn't show it:

January 1, 1949: arrested Alton, Illinois, for traffic violation.

July–December, 1949: $1.10-an-hour laborer, Chicago rubber factory.

1949: 90 days, Los Angeles County Jail, burglary of typewriter.

April, 1950–May, 1952: one-dollar-an-hour laborer at various Chicago firms.

1952: convicted of robbing Chicago taxi driver; served two years in Illinois State Prison.

September, 1954: charged with burglary, Edwardsville, Illinois.

March, 1955: arrested with an accomplice and convicted for stealing and cashing U.S. money orders in Hannibal, Missouri; sentenced to three years in Federal prison at Leavenworth, Kansas; released April, 1958.

April, 1958–October, 1959: odd jobs, St. Louis, Alton and thereabouts; used some aliases; suspected of robbery of Alton store but never charged.

October 10, 1959: with an accomplice, robbed a Kroger supermarket in St. Louis; caught in 20 minutes with $120 in loot; acted as own attorney at end of trial, and sentenced to 20 years in Missouri penitentiary at Jefferson City, Missouri, under habitual-criminal statutes; accomplice got seven years.

November, 1960: unsuccessful escape attempt, Missouri penitentiary.

March, 1966: unsuccessful escape attempt, Missouri penitentiary.

April 23, 1967: escaped from Missouri penitentiary.

June 8, 1968: arrested in London as Ramon George Sneyd, a Canadian, for the assassination of Martin Luther King.

Clearly, only the last event varies the pattern of small-time thievery. King's murder also differed in that a rifle was used. In his robberies, Ray had sometimes brandished a pistol, but he'd never fired it. After his escape from the Missouri penitentiary, he carried a pistol, was captured with one on him. But, other than in his Army basic training twenty-two years before, there's no evidence that he used a rifle. Why would he choose one to kill King? It's been suggested that in prison Ray was entranced by Oswald's feat, that maybe he went to school on it and decided on a long-range murder for a troublemaker he hated. George McMillan, whose book assumes Ray's guilt, quotes men in stir with Ray as saying he was rabid about "Martin Luther Coon" and vowed to get him. McMillan also claims Ray's brother Jerry said that Jimmy, who often contacted Jerry after his escape, was wild for Wallace and that on the morning of King's assassination, he got a call during which Jimmy said, "Big Nigger has had it." (Jerry has denied these statements.) McMillan further says that Ray financed his postescape peregrinations with money made in prison and sent outside to Jerry, about $7,000 in all.

How much of this is incontrovertible? The escape itself—Abernathy thinks "Ray may have been let loose" to kill King—*was* peculiarly successful for Ray. He hid in a box carrying loaves of bread, was trucked outside the walls and then left the truck. The authorities afterward put out a routine $50-reward leaflet, but it carried photographs of someone else's fingerprints—another detail that suggested to some that if Ray had been let out, he wasn't supposed to be caught. However that may be, it was true Ray's previous escape attempts hadn't gone so well.

Convicts at Missouri we have interviewed said Ray was laughable in those adventures, once playing the "mole" and hiding in ventilators, only to crawl out hours later into a guard's arms. Another time, he tried to scale a wall with a pole but fell back into the yard and hurt himself. (After the King affair, when Ray was finally transferred out of solitary in Nashville into the medium-security Brushy Mountain prison, he again tried to escape. This time he hid in a steam tunnel and got scalded out; he had picked the wrong tunnel—the other one in the yard led outside.) As for his wheeling and dealing at Missouri, one fellow inmate said, "He was the kind of guy who'd bring in ten dollars' worth of dope and sell it for twenty. This is while some guys are making ten grand a year in pills." But other convicts have said Ray made plenty, and his prosecutors point out he needed only about $11,000 to do all they claim Ray did.

Was Ray the kind of con who could plan and execute the King murder, then escape to three foreign countries? It's true you can learn a lot inside the walls about new identities and passports. In the months before King's death, Ray did travel in Canada and Mexico, as well as extensively in the United States. Yet before, he always had been a bungler. Dropping evidence at Canipe's would be his style, but eluding all the FBI agents would not. Perhaps, then, he was so deeply motivated by racism or something that he became inspired. Certainly, both in prison and out, Ray exhibited deep inferiority feelings, which he tried to allay through weight lifting, dance lessons, bartending lessons, hypnosis lessons, even plastic surgery, which changed the distinctive shape of his nose, and maybe they finally all worked to make him more confident and efficient. Or, some suspect, such activities were simply aids to the new identity he needed after killing King.

But was Ray a racist? His brothers admit they are. Jerry openly displayed his feelings, once working for J. B. Stoner, a hypermisanthropic Klansman, who helped form the black-hating National States Rights Party and whom Jerry tried to retain as a lawyer for Jimmy after Ray's guilty plea netted him ninety-nine years. John Ray also admits he dislikes blacks. As for Jimmy, he refused to live in the integrated "honor" dormitory at Leavenworth. While loose in Los Angeles, he volunteered in March, 1968, to work for Wallace (Jerry, again, supposedly said Jimmy thought if King were out of the way, Wallace could more easily be elected). He had a barroom fight over "niggers" there, and also wrote for information on emigrating to Rhodesia. A John Birch leaflet (along with a map, said to hold Ray's fingerprint, on which were marked the locations of King's church and home) was found in a room in Atlanta allegedly rented by Ray just before the killing. And in England, after the assassination, Ray reportedly made inquiries about signing on as a mercenary in Rhodesia or the Congo. Yet those facts, however suggestive, don't prove Ray killed for race reasons. A man who spent seven years in the Missouri penitentiary with him has a different feeling about that:

"I'd say he was about as close to me as he was to anybody, which wasn't too close. He was an extreme introvert. He didn't mix . . . he was only interested in gettin' out. Any fucking way he could . . . he couldn't stand the lockup, he hated it. Time drove his shit, just to speak frankly. You know about King, let's assume that Ray was down South . . . well, he goes on down there and he talks to two or three politicians, who are pretty influential people, and they could probably convince me that they could get me out of it or get me out of the country. A guy gets pretty fucking desperate out there on escape, you know. In my opinion [if Ray did kill King], it wasn't out of any racist motive. If he was a racist, I can honestly say I never heard this guy, not one time did I ever hear him, say one word about or against a black man or a nigger. Not one time. He wasn't hostile, but now, man, you know it was there. His smile came easily. But he had a temper. That great little ingratiating smile was pretty superficial."

We know that a man can smile and smile and be a villain. We can also believe that Ray, like many poor whites, didn't always have the kindest feelings toward his black brethren. We know he was a thief—"penny ante" his warden said—and one apparently possessed by the severe inferiority and antisocial feelings that, it's suspected, have in others generated a fantasy of greatness achieved through murder. We know that both as a child and grown-up criminal he created alibis. Does all that add to the murder of Martin Luther King? And if Ray alone did it, why?

There are, as with our other assassinations, several possible answers. The first is Ray's own, most of which he sold after his arrest to an Alabama writer named William Bradford Huie for money to pay for his defense (Huie's publication of much of Ray's tale in *Look* before the trial date would these days be considered prejudicial, a point stressed in Ray's petitions for a new trial).

The second comes from those who adhere to the official account of the case. The remainder emanate from people who are sure Ray could not have done it as the State maintained, and so—as with John Kennedy's murder—pursue every rumor, trace every lead and speculate at length about each and every. Moreover, all these versions are complicated by questions about the case's judicial and investigative procedures.

Ray's account to Huie is basic. Documented in I-followed-Ray's-foot-prints style, Huie's version portrays a bold and ingenious criminal who comes to the bad end of being framed by a mysterious man called Raoul. (Huie himself first believed that story of conspiracy, but then concluded Ray had done it by himself.) The story admits most of what the State of Tennessee would try to prove, differing only in the crucial detail of where Ray was when King was murdered. On that point, in fact, Ray has switched several times, as we'll see. But the rest was clear in his mind.

We track Ray as he escapes on April 23, 1967, and, probably with his brother John's help, makes his way to Chicago (McMillan believes that the next day, Jimmy told John and Jerry he was going to kill King). There he worked for two months in the kitchen of a restaurant. To his employers, this slim, quiet man was John Rayns, a model employee who didn't seem at all to mind the blacks he worked around. When he quit in late June, the owners were sorry to see him go, but they wished him well at his new job in Canada.

But Ray didn't go directly to Canada. With $450 and a $200 Chrysler—whose title, with his temporary driver's license, gave him a bit of tenuous ID—he went to the St. Louis area, where brother John had a saloon. When the Chrysler broke down, he sold it and bought a $200 red Plymouth.

In Canada, Ray/Rayns then became Eric Starvo Galt. Huie believes Ray chose the name after passing the city of Galt between Detroit and Toronto. However, there is an Eric St. Vincent Galt in Toronto, a writer, whose middle initials, St. V., when scrawled in signature, look like Starvo. Did Ray get that odd name there and, if so, why and where was he looking at Galt's signature? It's possible he sought out Galt's signature as he later, after King's death, supposedly sought out Canadians who resembled him and whose names he could use in getting a passport.

Anyway, he first headed for Montreal, where he hoped to find a Canadian citizen to act as guarantor of a passport that he could use to get someplace "from which I would never be extradited." He didn't know then that his information, maybe garnered in prison, was out of date: Canadian law no longer required such a guarantor. He did know he needed money. To get it, he told Huie, he robbed a whorehouse on July 18, though he later admitted it had been a supermarket.

After the robbery, Ray bought some glad rags, sent for some sex manuals, enrolled in a locksmithing correspondence course and went to the renowned Gray Rocks Inn in the Laurentian Mountains, where he met and seduced a beautiful Canadian divorcee who he hoped would swear he was a Canadian citizen.

Ray admits all this, but he adds "Raoul." And Raoul is all. If he exists, a conspiracy exists. According to Ray, he hung around "the boats" in Montreal, looking for a way out of the country. He frequented a waterfront tavern called the Neptune. He says there he put out word that he might be available for nefarious goings on, if fairly riskless, since he needed capital and a "good ID." One day, a sandy-haired, mid-thirtyish French Canadian named Raoul showed up, saying he might have some things for Galt to do, just little things at first, mind you, but then more and bigger, ending with lots of cash and all the papers Galt might need to get away to places with no extradition treaty with the United States, say Rhodesia or wherever.

And so, Ray told Huie, began the association with Raoul that continued sporadically over the next eight months until he told Ray to meet him in Memphis on April 4 on South Main Street, where, Ray says, Raoul or somebody must have killed King.

Does Raoul exist? The prosecution said no, that Ray was a loner. No Raoul, just Ray suddenly turned clever, and if their best eyewitness, Charles Stephens, couldn't exactly say it *was* Ray he'd seen running from 5B—and his mate had said no, the man was blond, stocky, older than Ray, in an Army jacket and plaid shirt—look at all the circumstances.

The circumstances—true or false—unreel like a cops-and-robbers movie down to the shot that blew away King. And as though proving the ambiguous, ironic nature of the King case, both Ray's script and his accusers' subtitles are created mostly from the same sources: Ray's account to Huie and the work of such thorough writer-investigators as Gerold Frank and Harold Weisberg. The star, James Earl Ray, comes on first:

I'm Eric Starvo Galt in August 1967, smuggling packages(heroin?)for Raoul into the U.S., modest fee, $750, then being told to sell the old Plymouth and go to Birmingham, Alabama, where Raoul would meet me, get the better I.D., give me money, a suitable car, and if I needed Raoul, here was a New Orleans telephone number. Raoul said there was $12,000 in it eventually, 'course it was risky in the U.S., but things hadn't worked out with the passport.

No, the opponents say, not that way. He went alone to Chicago and signed the Plymouth over to Jerry, and then went by train to Birmingham, where he took dance lessons, lived in a rooming house, bought a white Mustang for $2000 cash, got a Galt driver's license, bought surveillance-style photo equipment, movie stuff, just living there until October seventh.

Raoul met me in Birmingham. We bought the car after I found it and he OK'd it. He gave me $500 to live on and $500 for camera equipment he described to me, told me to lie low and stay out of trouble. I got Galt I.D. for driver's license and car registration.

Uh-uh. Ray was living on his prison and robbery earnings and probably wanted those cameras—he bought a Polaroid, too—for pornography, to make money. He was just indulging himself, building up his self-importance, and he may really have liked being in Wallace country.

I left Birmingham October sixth and went to Nueva Laredo, where Raoul met me, and we smuggled a tire full of something across the border, and he gave me $2000 in 20s and said he'd need me for other jobs, to keep in touch via that New Orleans number, why not stay in Mexico awhile and I said fine, there or Los Angeles.

Bull! Ray just lazed about in Mexico, mostly Puerto Vallarta, making it with three different whores, posing as a writer, setting up to smuggle a bunch of grass into California.

I'd like to go back there when I get out. It was good; I even proposed marriage to a woman, but it didn't work, so I left with some marijuana but got rid of it before crossing the border.

He took it into L.A. by himself and those halcyon Mexican days were spent as much as anything else with that Polaroid photographing himself, because he was obsessed with wanting to be in the Ten Most Wanted criminals, with his picture in all the post offices; he was so insecure, see, like Oswald, and he was studying his photos so he could get his prominent feature—the end of his nose—altered by plastic surgery, so when the great crime occurred, he couldn't be recognized.

Sure, I stayed in L.A. from November 18, 1968, until March 17, 1968. Had two apartments at different times and took bartending and dancing lessons, because if I lived in South America, they'd come in handy. Stuck with the locksmithing. Applied for two jobs but didn't have a Social Security card. Tried to learn about self-hypnosis; that's where those self-improvement books I had in England came from. Told the telephone company I was a Wallace worker so I'd get a phone quick to use looking for a job. Had trouble over race with some people in a bar called the Rabbit's Foot.

Hell, he told them since they loved niggers so much, he'd take 'em on down to Watts and see how they liked it. And he inquired about going to Africa. The hypnosis was strange; he actually gave that hypnotist his real name, since he believed he'd tell the truth when hypnotized, anyway.

I left for New Orleans December 15, after Raoul wrote me at General Delivery, saying come for a conference, they had a job for me. Charley Stein rode with me —he's the cousin of a girl I met—to take his sister's kids back to L.A. The ride was a favor, but I made them register for Wallace before we left. Anyway, I saw Raoul and he told me to be ready for a job in two or three months, hinted that there was some big businessman involved. He gave me another $500 in 20s.

Typical lie. He went because he was into some solo deal and Charley Stein saying he made several long-distance calls to New Orleans along the way doesn't change it, since he always kept in touch with Jerry, anyway, so maybe the calls weren't to New Orleans. And Raoul never wrote to him. He decided to go just the night before they left because he called that morning and canceled his appointment with the hypnotist, so again, no Raoul.

On March fifth, I had the tip of my nose cut off so I couldn't be recognized in any of those deals, because Raoul wrote in February and said the deal was on for about May first, the one we'd talked about, running guns, so I was to meet him in New Orleans about March 20 and finally I'd get the 12 grand and papers.

Sure, that was about when he decided to kill King; it was building in him, all the Wallace hatred, the desire to make the top ten, and Ray had heard enough when King was in L.A. March 16 and 17 and he'd had the nose job, so he stayed out his rent like the tightwad he was and took off to go find King and shoot him.

So, that's the way it is, the possible script for each, and the frames click madly as Galt leaves L.A., he says, driving to New Orleans and getting word there to meet Raoul next in Birmingham, so he started out, except, he vows, he got lost and had to spend the night of March 22 in Selma *(Wrong!* the accusers say, *you were stalking King, who had been in Selma);* then he's off for Birmingham and Raoul and then to Atlanta to that dumpy rooming house, where we heard about the gun deal *(No! You were alone and pursuing King, marking his haunts those days on a map)* . . . then faster, faster, the images melting . . .

I bought the .243 and then exchanged it like Raoul told me, in Birmingham the twenty-ninth and thirtieth *(You did it alone!),* and then went by slow stops to Memphis, just me, with this gun they were going to use for a sample, Raoul said, for the buyers, in Memphis, who'd take that kind and hundreds of cheap foreign rifles *(Sorry! You went back to Atlanta for King but found he would be in Memphis the fourth, so you went the third).* . . . No, no, Raoul met me near Memphis in a Mississippi motel on the second and took the rifle and told me to go the third to Memphis and stay at the Rebel Motel *(Yes, you did, but you got there the third, signed in—we have your handwriting—and found where King was and went the next day to kill him).* . . . No, Raoul came to room 5B with the gun *(But Mrs. Brewer doesn't remember anyone asking where Mr. Willard's room was)* and I went to South Main, I've told you, and bought the binoculars, and about five o'clock he sent me out for a beer so they could make the deal, and I went to Jim's Grill downstairs *(You can't describe the place and no one remembers you there)* . . . and then I was on the sidewalk and heard this shot and here came Raoul and dumped the bundle and jumped in the car and covered himself with that white sheet and we took off, then stopped a few blocks away and Raoul jumped out, the last I saw of him, and I was scared and took off. *(You say that? Why, then, did you through your lawyers change your story later and say you were at a filling station with the Mustang, getting a low tire checked?)* OK, I made up that sheet business and told it to Huie because I was scared, trapped, Huie was pressing me to confess so his book would sell, but I can prove it, there's a filling-station attendant and some others who'll say they remembered the car and me, at about six o'clock; no, I didn't kill King, didn't fire that shot.

And then, freeze frame of King falling.

Every scene after that is anticlimactic, although as fascinating as the conflicting tales. Ray admits he drove alone to Atlanta the night of April 4, and abandoned his car. He then went his circuitous way to Canada, arriving in Toronto on the eighth. He lived again in rooming houses, in which he read of the riots, the grief, the universal condemnation of King's murder (if Ray or someone had expected most of America to applaud, he was disheartened). Ray says he was fleeing in fear that Raoul and those who had set him up would now come and kill him, that he hadn't even known King was dead until he heard it on his Mustang's radio.

Fleeing he certainly was, and in ways the prosecution said were conwise and the conspiracy buffs say are sure signals he had help. Again, he needed money and an ID, and some way to get them. Ray has said he went to the library and looked up several Toronto births for 1932, finally choosing two names and, giving his rooming-house address, applied for birth certificates in their names—Paul E. Bridgman and Ramon George Sneyd. He picked 1932 to approximate his age. To verify a general resemblance, he floated in their neighborhoods and made sure they were of medium height, medium weight, dark-haired. A clever scheme. Too clever for Ray, the conspiracy theorists say, especially since Sneyd—in whose name Ray easily got a passport through a travel agent—was a policeman, and did not that imply an international conspiracy? Some people wonder, too, about Bridgman's story that he got a call from someone who said he was checking to see if he had a passport. But Ray said he did that.

In any event, on May 6, Ray as Sneyd flew to London on a $345 twenty-one-day excursion ticket. He cashed in the return portion and went on to Lisbon, there to try to escape to Angola as a mercenary. It was none too soon; by then the world knew that Galt, Lowmyer and Willard were really James Earl Ray. His picture had been in the papers, and police of several countries had been alerted (if, as the prosecution says, it was fame he sought, he must have been gratified). Even so, it had taken the FBI a long time—until April 19—to identify Ray, despite the mound of evidence at Canipe's. In fact, it hadn't been until April 18, after agents came upon Ray's room in Atlanta and his thumbprint on the map, that they started checking the fingerprint files of Federal offenders. Ray was among them because of his money-order caper. Of the 53,000 cards, his was the seven-hundredth up. Lucky FBI. But, it was later asked, why hadn't they immediately checked the serial number on the portable radio left in the bundle? They'd have found that Ray bought it in the Missouri pen and that would have told the Bureau who had dropped all the stuff. Maybe then he would have been picked up sooner. Or did someone not want him picked up, as many have suspected?

Yet he was picked up. There was nothing for Ray in Portugal except beer and whores, so he went back to England on May 17. There, it's said, he suffered headaches and lived in cheap hotels while trying, through a *Daily Telegraph* reporter, to get information on mercenary recruiting centers in Belgium. Apparently almost broke, Ray on June 4 robbed a savings bank of $240. On the eighth, he went to Heathrow for a flight to Brussels, but there Detective Sergeant Phillip Birch of Scotland Yard, on the lookout for someone using Sneyd's passport with Ray's picture in it, brought his hand down firmly on Ray's shoulder. It was finished. Ray handed over his cheap .38 and was taken to prison, where one man reported he uttered some of the few pitiable words anyone ever heard him say: "Oh, God, I feel so trapped."

That was true, in many ways. Take the judicial irregularities as one dimension of Ray's dilemma. His extradition from England—to which he agreed upon advice of counsel, though he could have declared King's murder a political act and so avoided extradition—was based on the questionable affidavit of Charles Stephens and the inconclusive ballistics and firearms evidence. Ray's return to the United States and subsequent imprisonment were of dubious constitutionality, and showed how scared the Government was running. The first was accomplished in an Air Force C-135 with Ray strapped to a seat and surrounded by curious Government cops. He was then stripped, searched, manacled and transferred, in an armored truck, to the Shelby County Jail, where for eight months he lived in a special cell section that was continually floodlighted, monitored by TV and shuttered from the sense of day and night by quarter-inch steel plates. Guards always watched him (Ray and his attorneys had to lie down in the shower facility and whisper to keep from being overheard while planning his defense). He had special tasters for his food, and his mail and messages to lawyers were censored and even copied, with the copies going to his prosecutors in the Attorney General's office. The Gulag Archipelago couldn't do much worse, Ray's defenders say. The extraordinary treatment continued after Ray's guilty plea. Until recently, he was kept in solitary. It also seems clear the authorities once intended to send him to Springfield, Missouri, where Ray feared he would be declared insane and be put into START, a by-Orwell-out-of-Skinner behavior-modification program. But Ray with the help of his counsel and interested newsmen managed to abort that.

Attorneys themselves have been a problem for Ray, one he has exacerbated by his jailhouse lawyering. He first wanted F. Lee Bailey (an index of his sense of importance), but when Bailey declined, Ray got Arthur Hanes, Sr., the mayor of Birmingham back in the Eugene (Bull) Connors, cattle-prod and fire-hose, sick-the-dogs-on-the-niggers days. Hanes is a good lawyer. He successfully defended the Klannish killers of Viola Liuzzo, and he maintains he could have done the same for Ray. Hanes and his son investigated Ray's story as much as they could preparing the case, and both thought it possible there was a conspiracy. But it wasn't the key to their defense. They had detected largish holes in the state's circumstantial evidence, and they would attack those. But Ray fired the Haneses in November, 1968, two days before the trial was to start.

The reasons were unclear. Cynics think he did it to postpone the trial until George Wallace could be elected that month and then pardon him. More probably, the reasons lie, as Ray has suggested, in the Catch-22 agreement under which Hanes worked. Hanes actually was paid by William Bradford Huie, who was financing Ray's defense by gathering and publishing information that indicated Ray was guilty. Thus Ray may have decided that Huie *needed* him guilty, since the profit potential for Huie's articles and books depended on their being a killer's inside story. So couldn't Huie accordingly influence his partner's, Hanes's, conduct of the trial? Jerry Ray claimed he told Jimmy that Huie offered him $12,000 to get Jimmy to stay off the stand; i.e., not to say he was innocent when Huie had decided Ray was guilty. Whatever the case, Jimmy decided to fire Hanes.

For their parts, both Hanes and Huie say that's nonsense. Hanes says he had a fine case, and Huie says a fair trial would have helped his book, no matter the result (as it was, Ray's guilty plea prevented a trial and turned Huie's book into a big loser).

Whatever the truth, Ray got his postponement, and into the case at Jerry Ray's behest strode Percy Foreman, the famous Texas criminal lawyer who boasted he'd won more cases than Clarence Darrow, had lost only one killer to the electric chair, and that was just, because his fees were punishment enough for any criminal. Now the fur would fly. Except that several things happened. First, Foreman entered an agreement with Huie and Ray for his fee, supposedly $150,000. Second, Foreman says he then found the state had a terrific case (Hanes violently disagrees, saying Foreman never even *looked* at his files), and so Ray was going to the electric chair unless he pleaded guilty. Finally, the famous trial lawyer appeared in court in March, 1969, with his sheepish client, and, instead of a furious legal battle, the onlookers saw the pro-forma rigmarole of Ray agreeing with the fifty-five stipulations the state had marshaled that said James Earl Ray alone had killed Martin Luther King. Was Mr. Ray guilty? "Yes, legally guilty, uh-huh," came the reply. That was that, except for a potentially exhilarating moment that died aborning when Ray rose up and said no, he just couldn't agree with Ramsey Clark and Mr. Hoover that there hadn't been a conspiracy.

Nothing more was said. Foreman immediately departed Memphis, taking with him the $9,000 left from Huie's original $40,000 in payments to Ray. He left behind several questions. Was it true, as Ray claimed, that Percy had coerced him into the guilty plea—"You'll bar-be-cue, boy!"— even put pressure on Ray's family to influence Jimmy to cop the plea? Why hadn't Foreman spent more time on the case? (He was with Ray only one hour and fifty-three minutes in the first seventy days of preparing the defense, though he saw Jimmy a lot in the days preceding the plea, the better to railroad him, Ray's advocates think.) Had Huie convinced Foreman that Ray was guilty? It's true Huie was summoned by the grand jury —Ray's several attorneys have questioned what precisely the writer told the grand jury about the Ray case. Had not Foreman, as Ray's lawyers have since alleged in various proceedings, provided adequate counsel for Ray (by way of invidious comparison, Foreman not long ago was acquitted of charges in Texas that he and two of H. L. Hunt's sons conspired to bribe private investigators who'd wiretapped Hunt executives)? Finally, was Ray justified in his accusation—related by John Ray—that Foreman had told him the trial judge would grant no more continuances, that Ray couldn't fire Foreman and so he had no choice but to plead guilty, unless he wanted to be left only with the public defender?

Those questions and many others have inspired Ray's various post-Foreman lawyers to battle for a new trial. They note that three days after his guilty plea, Ray wrote to the trial judge asking for a new trial, consistent with Tennessee law. Anti-Ray folks think, of course, that's just some more maneuvering by a professional convict and jailhouse lawyer who knows how to use the system, just as he knows how to keep the pot boiling about all these other nonexistent conspirators. Ray's request was, however, rejected under odd circumstances. His trial judge had died shortly after Ray's guilty plea, an event that under one Tennessee law seemed to guarantee Ray a new trial for the asking. Yet the successor to Ray's trial judge denied the petition for a new trial, claiming the voluntary guilty plea overrode the statutory provision for a new trial should the incumbent trial judge die. Of course, Ray has maintained to this day that his plea was *not* voluntary, and that the denial of another trial is consistent with what he feels is a governmental and judicial cover-up in his case (some Ray supporters even suspect that his judge did not die of a natural heart attack). Legal opinion is still divided over the matter, so that the only indisputable fact is that since then Ray has tried through a succession of attorneys, including the racist Stoner, to secure a new trial on the murder charge (and to secure compensation for allegedly libelous statements published by Huie and others). The grandest attempt thus far came in October, 1974, at a U.S. District Court evidentiary hearing that had been ordered by a U.S. Court of Appeals, who'd found that Ray's judicial record reeked with "ethical, moral and professional irregularities" and that "Ray's attorneys, Hanes and Foreman, were more interested in capitalizing on a notorious case than in representing the best interests of their client." Thus James Earl Ray again appeared in a courtroom, but in February, 1975, despite the success Ray's defense team had in reintroducing vital questions on the evidence, the District Court ruled against the petition. For many, that didn't vitiate the case's questions.

For example, there remains the weakness of Charles Stephens' identification of Ray as the man in the rooming house. (The police, by the way, sequestered Charles after the killing, providing him with bed and booze, while his wife, Grace Walden, was put away in a state mental hospital, still contending Charley was wrong.) If more were needed to impeach Stephens' testimony, Ray's lawyers interviewed a taxi driver named James McGraw, who said he was dispatched to 422 1/2 South Main Street to pick up Charley at "about 5:30" and found him too drunk to walk, so he left. McGraw also told a defense investigator that he had parked double in front of Jim's Grill—where, in one of Ray's stories, he was sent by Raoul to have a beer—and saw no white Mustang on the street (which fits Ray's second story about being away from the place altogether). Further, a newspaperman supposedly saw Grace and Charley later on April 5, and Charley was too drink-sotted to make sense. All of this leads skeptics to think Charles Stephens may have been encouraged to perjure himself.

There is, too, the suggestive but inconclusive ballistics data: a slug only "consistent with" a .30-'06 (a slug that, despite its mutilation might, according to some theorists, conclusively have been matched to the rifle) allegedly fired from an awkward position. Indeed, a criminologist active in assassination inquiries—Herbert MacDonell—told the Federal Court that it would have been impossible with the 42-inch-long Gamemaster to stand in the tub and get the needed angle on King, that to do so the rifle's butt would have to have been six inches *within* the wall. Impossible, that is, if the rifle made the prosecution's "dent," a semicircular indentation in the bathroom window's inner sill that the state claims was made by the rifle barrel. (Unfortunately for that theory, if you lay either the barrel or the muzzle in the dent, the rifle points straight out or slightly upward, not at the balcony. But unfortunately for MacDonell's idea, you can aim from the tub if you put the rifle far enough out the window.)

The FBI's own documents—made public not long ago—show there are no splinters torn from the sill or powder marks on it as there would have been if the muzzle had rested in the dent. It's conceivable the dent was made by a hammer. It's also been rumored that the window in the sniper's nest was not open at the time of the shot and, furthermore, that an object sat on it which was substantial enough to prevent a rifle from being shoved through the window and knocking a screen to the ground, as the state maintains. If these conjectures are true, the shot simply had to come from elsewhere, according to Ray's advocates (trajectory studies, however, indicate the shot did come from the bathroom).

If such contentions sound like some advanced by doubters of the Warren Report, so do the musings on the weapon itself. Why, for example, was the .243 exchanged for the .30-'06? The .243 is a splendid sniper's weapon, with higher velocity and a flatter trajectory than the .30-'06. The prosecution believes the exchange was made because the .243 had a flaw in the chamber and so couldn't smoothly load the cartridges. Ray's defenders say that's absurd, that anyone as familiar with rifles as the state assumes Ray was could have used an emery board to file off the imperfection. No, the exchange was made because those who were framing Ray were going to use a .30-'06 and so needed a matching weapon. And one loaded with their patsy's fingerprints. Weisberg points out that a .30-'06 Gamemaster was stolen from a Memphis sporting-goods store shortly before the assassination. Others have opined choosing a Gamemaster was not consistent with such a masterful frame-up. Why pick a distinctive pump-action high-powered rifle rather than a more common bolt-action weapon? No, they say, the choice—like Oswald's—was that of a lone and inexperienced killer (some wonder, too, if Raoul's alleged gun-buyers would want pump-action guns for paramilitary use).

The final musings about the weapon and its effects also remind us of the John Kennedy case. Why were there five full-jacketed military .30-'06 rounds found among the hollow-point hunting cartridges in the bundle of evidence? Ignoring the supposition that these mean the Government was involved (military .30-'06 rounds are widely available), we can ask which sort of cartridge killed King. Suits filed under the Freedom of Information Act have unearthed documents that theorists say prove the FBI had covered up or distorted important facts about that. For example, their spectrographic tests, Weisberg claims, show only one metal on King's clothing, whereas hollow points are alloys of several metals. Thus the FBI report is really on a fragment from another kind of round. They have suppressed that information, some think, because it means maybe *two* bullets hit King, one in the throat—an impossibility from the bathroom window. There *was* a throat wound, but Memphis' medical examiner said it was a surgical incision, and that the only bullet hit King up around his right cheek. Obviously, Weisberg thinks that's wrong, and that autopsy records, also suppressed, will prove it. As of today, autopsy physicians continue to say there was only one shot.

Even so, we have peculiarities. Was the assassin so confident—more even than Oswald—that he would have chambered only one round? Many theorists ridicule that suggestion, and claim there was no clip *in* the rifle found at Canipe's, though one was in the box. The state's hypothetical answer is that Ray, the bungling sniper, saw King come suddenly out, was surprised, jammed one round home, ran to the bathroom and shot. The conspiracy folks rebut with questions. Assuming Ray alone did the killing, and assuming he carefully chose his sniper's nest, perhaps by walking down South Main seeking a flophouse overlooking the Lorraine, why would he not have the clip in his rifle? The state says he had been there since 3:30. He'd brought his bag with him. Wouldn't a dedicated racist assassin be *prepared* to kill King? Or, if he were expecting a quick job, one shot, why would his spread, zippered bag and all the rest be with him instead of in the Mustang, ready for escape?

Could he even have packed up all that gear and escaped in the time available? Ray's defenders have long said they didn't see how he could run from the bathroom, put the rifle in the box, wrap it and the overnight bag in the spread, run down the hall and stairs, drop the bundle, get in his car and drive away when there were cops all over the place, many of them in the fire station on the corner, then also serving as a police observation post. Besides, they say, a Lieutenant J. E. Ghormley was on Main Street in time to see Ray escape, if Ray had done it. Before the shot, Ghormley was in the fire station with his crews from three Tactical Action Cruisers. When King fell, policemen rushed toward the Lorraine, but Ghormley was impeded by a bad leg. He decided not to jump down from the wall above Mulberry Street, then thought of the sniper's possible location and walked briskly to South Main, where he found the bundle, questioned Canipe and with his walkie-talkie radioed an alert for the young man in a white car. In a reconstruction for CBS, it was said Ghormley took three minutes to get to Canipe's. Previously, however, he has estimated it could have taken no more than a minute. Defense attorneys have duplicated Ghormley's move in less than a minute. Ray could have escaped in three minutes, but not in one. And whichever time applies, Ghormley saw nothing on the street. No car, no man, only the bundle in the doorway. He also says he saw nothing in the parking lot next to Canipe's. That fact, put next to perplexing and contradictory statements attributed to Mr. Canipe, has led a few of Ray's advocates to an alternate version of what might really have happened.

They hypothesize that the real assassins were in that parking lot. Two of them, a "hit man" and a "wheel man," in another white Mustang. Ray had already been set up by his prints, his gear, his presence in the rooming house, and now he'd been sent down to get a beer. The conspirators could make up the bundle while Ray was gone and he'd be easily caught at the scene. But Jimmy had noticed a tire was low and gone off to get it pumped up, he's such a nice guy, and new witnesses could prove it. But the killers didn't know that, and they're watching the motel, and out comes King, and the hit man says something like "There's the son of a bitch now, go drop the bundle," and the wheel man drops it at Canipe's, but they can't shoot just then because King is with somebody on the balcony, looking straight at them, and they wait a minute and then King is alone, and the hit man blows him away. They peel off in the Mustang. *That* was the car Canipe saw and, a bit later, Jimmy comes back, sees the confusion and takes off, having figured out that he'd been set up. One bit of proof is that Canipe once said the bundle was dropped about five minutes *before* the 6:01 shot. Certainly, Ghormley would say there was nobody in the parking lot. The killers were gone.

Here, then, the outline of a possible defense for Ray. It has never been tried in a court. No jury has heard what Canipe now believes, or decided whether Ghormley's recollections mean the killers could have been in the parking lot or that they couldn't. No jury has probed other stories embedded in the murder of Martin Luther King.

There exists the tale told by a derelict called Harold "Cornbread" Carter, who said he was drinking in the yard behind the rooming house, when he saw a rifleman shoot and run off. Or that of King's chauffeur, Solomon Jones, who, from his position in the courtyard just below the balcony, said in the shot's echoes he'd seen a man, his head cloaked by a white sheet or hood, in the dense bushes facing the Lorraine above Mulberry Street, who then *sans* sheet emerged to disappear into the gathering crowd (people remembering the white sheet said to be found in Ray's car thought that intriguing).

There is an unverifiable report that a mysterious "advance man" visited the Lorraine and arranged for King to stay in a second-floor room instead of the usual ground-floor room, presumably so that the assassination would be facilitated.

There is also what seems to be a third account of where James Earl Ray was during the shooting, this one elicited by a Memphis lawyer and former newspaperman named Wayne Chastain, who, like Harold Weisberg, has done invaluable investigations of the Ray mystery. In this version, Raoul gave Ray $200 and told him to go to a movie (not to Jim's Grill), but he saw the vexing tire and went to have it fixed, and at 6:05 was on his way back when he saw an ambulance pass (presumably with King) and then he saw the mob scene around the motel and rooming house and then he split when a policeman, of all people, told him to "get out of here."

Further fomenting riotous speculation, two older stories suggesting a conspiracy have been joined to another theory, thereby engendering a King-CIA-Cuba-Dallas mongrel reminiscent of John Kennedy. A week after the killing, a man calling himself Tony Benevites told a Memphis attorney that his "roommate" had killed King for money with a .30-caliber rifle from the wall behind the rooming house and then gotten away on a motorbike. The man struck the attorney as believable, especially since, like a real mobster, he knew the best place to conceal a pistol was in the small of the back. The man said he was from New Orleans, but was headed for Brownsville, Tennessee, to meet a Grand Dragon of the Ku Klux Klan. The same day, a man calling himself J. Christ Bonneveche told two ministers that a man named Nick had killed King for $20,000 for a well-known fraternal order, and that he himself worked for the Mafia, was now on the lam over some lost money. He showed the ministers a counterfeit traveler's check, and how his fingerprints had been filed off, and then said he was off for Brownsville. Queer as these stories seemed, they were regarded mostly as more of the "I did it" embroidery with which the unstable decorate well-publicized murders.

Lately it's been suggested that these two sinister men with the similar names may be one sinister man named Jack Youngblood, a former mercenary for Castro, a man alleged to have discussed gunrunning with, of all people, Jack Ruby, and a man whose friends think he had ties to the CIA. Youngblood, it's theorized, participated in the conspiracy, perhaps Raoul's, that killed King. He's reportedly been identified as a man who ordered eggs and sausages at Jim's Grill about 4:30 the afternoon of the murder, then left about 5 P.M. The Memphis police supposedly then questioned Youngblood but released him. One of Ray's former attorneys in Memphis is said to believe Youngblood was the hit man for some agency of the Federal Government. But no one has yet shown that Youngblood-Benevites-Bonneveche are one, or who this multiphasic personality worked for. Not a scintilla of evidence yet points to Youngblood as anything but one of those dark presences hovering around Cuban exiles during the palmy days when the CIA was waging its own little war on Castro.

The Youngblood story, predictably, is not the only farfetched tale. For a time, two of Ray's former attorneys were taken by the story, related in spy-story meetings, of a convicted confidence man named Clifford Holmes Andrews, who said he could say who killed King. A hint: It was two men, hired by four wealthy whites. Fine, except that Clifford Andrews next told CBS it was Raoul and members of the Quebec Liberation Front, again employed by four rich racists. And except that Andrews was in a Canadian jail from March, 1968, until long after King was killed. Then there's another prisoner, a young convicted dope dealer named Robert Byron Watson, who has said he overheard his employers at an Atlanta art gallery plotting King's assassination. It's also been reported that six months before the murder, a group of people visited a jail in Atlanta, looking for inmates to help murder King. Meanwhile, back in Tennessee, a black businessman named John McFerrean came forward right after the killing to say he'd overheard a white man in a produce house in Memphis, at about 5 P.M. April 4, say over the telephone, "You can shoot the son of a bitch on the balcony . . . you can pick up the five thousand bucks from my brother in New Orleans." Still another man said, a day or so before April 4, he'd heard men in Baton Rouge plotting King's death.

It could be that the last two rumors, even if unfounded, are correct geographically. As with John Kennedy, many strands of the Ray yarn knit together in Louisiana, especially in New Orleans. James Earl Ray told Huie he often was there, meeting Raoul, and it's been established he did visit

New Orleans in December, 1967, and again on his way to that fateful appointment in Memphis. He's also reportedly said that's where he headed when fleeing Tennessee, only to turn toward Atlanta when he realized the conspirators might kill him, too. (Not incidentally, it's been asserted the FBI flew some cigarette butts found in Ray's car to New Orleans for analysis, causing some to wonder if, since Ray didn't smoke, Raoul did.)

Further, Ray often has said he gave Percy Foreman two Louisiana telephone numbers, so that the lawyer could contact people, presumably including Raoul, who knew something about the murder. Foreman says he clearly remembers only one number, that in New Orleans, and he found the phone disconnected. A few investigators suspect the building where the phone was installed might yield a clue to King's murderers. In 1973, Ray filed a $500,000 suit against the State of Tennessee, in which he alleged that Foreman had failed to investigate these numbers, while another attorney—then conveniently deceased—had looked up the phones and found one was a Baton Rouge "parish official under the influence of a Teamsters' Union official" and the other was "an agent of a Mideast-oriented organization disturbed because of Dr. Martin Luther King's reported forthcoming, before his death, support of the Palestine Arab Cause." But Ray did not name the individuals or list the numbers. He did not say what connection these people had to the case or where he got his information on union officers and geopolitics (some think his lawyers fed him these data). The suit, typically, created more mystery, as it seemed designed to do. In the meantime, the telephoning went on. Another number—the one Ray, according to Charley Stein, dialed often on their trip to New Orleans in December—was purportedly secured from Stein by a West Coast reporter. Early in 1969, the newsman told Harold Weisberg he called the number and was answered by a voice that identified the location as a Louisiana State Police barracks. The reporter asked for Raoul and, in sheer implausibility, one answered: Raul Esquivel, Sr., a highway patrolman apparently stationed at 12400 Airline Highway, Baton Rouge. However, no connection between this Raul and Ray's shadowy accomplice has ever been found, and the number could have been planted with Stein, or even with Ray.

Baton Rouge is interesting, though, at least to people who believe in a conspiracy. The state capital was a stomping ground for Leander Perez, the legendary Louisiana power broker, who once publicly wished King were dead. Perez had strong allies among organized labor. One reputedly was a former Louisiana Teamsters official who once told Justice Department investigators that Jimmy Hoffa had threatened to have Robert Kennedy killed. And this man, it is rumored, had an associate who closely resembled the man Grace Walden described in the hall at 422½ Main Street: "Small bone built. He had on an Army-colored hunting jacket unfastened and dark pants. He had on a plaid sport shirt. His hair was salt-and-pepper colored." Conspiracy fanciers quickly recall the field jacket supposedly found in Ray's car that, like other items, was too small for him. They seize, too, on rumors that this shrouded figure from Grace Walden's memory hung around Perez' followers and among mafiosi from New Orleans. Yet any role in King's assassination by this unnamed man or the Mob, or Perez, or Partin, or anybody but James Earl Ray remains strictly conjectural.

Still, for those who must believe Ray did not do it, the Teamsters notion is alluring. It was, after all, a labor dispute that brought King to Memphis. A dispute by a black union. Men who drove trucks on their sanitation rounds. It's conceivable that in an atmosphere of hate and turmoil, two or three angry union men could, in a Yablonski reaction, decide to take out this superspade, this Communist, who's leading people who want to get our jobs, worse, get so high on the ladder folks won't judge just by color any more. Yes, that's feasible; but again there is no proof.

No proof, really, of anything. Only rumors, stories, speculations, thick as flies around a battlefield corpse, and as various in their directions. There are even people who believe that Fidel Castro did away with King, in order to foment unrest, maybe even revolution, in this country, and as new reports appear, intimating there is proof that Castro killed John Kennedy (and Robert) to avenge attempts on his life, such ideas gain a frightening ghost-riddled currency. But other citizens point to King's reported association with known Communists, to his pacifism, and suggest that American right-wingers ordered him killed (one Roy E. Frankhouser, a former Government informer on Klan and American Nazi Party activities, alleges that the FBI tried to kill King). Everyone is suspect, and like the echoes from Dealey Plaza, the murder's mad music goes on and on.

Only one note is constant: doubt. At last count, 80 percent of Americans have joined Coretta King and Ralph Abernathy and Jesse Jackson in thinking King fell to a conspiracy. Certainly, there still are worthwhile leads to investigate, witnesses to call, stories to assess, maybe even truths to find. The best witness—James Earl Ray—is available. He seeks a trial, though he's said he won't help solve the crime by naming conspirators. Are there any? Or is he simply another lone American assassin, playing the law like a crazily lit and flip-bumpered game, taking revenge for a life tilted from the outset? One wonders if Ray's various protestations of innocence shouldn't someday be tested in a courtroom, where his advocates and the state's can address the fundamental question: Who killed Martin Luther King?

Nothing less, surely, would satisfy King himself. It was for justice that he lived and died. The wooden casket, shiny in the thin April sunlight, the plain wagon, the brace of plow mules slowly bearing King's body to his grave, should have imbued us with that simple imperative. Apparently, we lost that message in the haze of time's slow burning. Or maybe it was only that we could no longer feel, so many were the blows. Martin Luther King's accused assassin had not even been caught before another American leader was murdered. This time, he was white. Again he was a Kennedy.

VIII

THE FLOURISHING SPIRIT OF VIOLENCE

"We must recognize that this short life can neither be ennobled nor enriched by hatred and revenge. Our lives on this planet are too short and the work to be done too great to let this spirit flourish any longer in our land."

—SENATOR ROBERT F. KENNEDY. April 5, 1968,
on the assassination of Martin Luther King

Robert Francis Kennedy's life was to be short indeed in that flourishing spirit of hatred and violence. Only sixty-two days after Memphis and Martin Luther King, the spirit descended out of Los Angeles' midnight skies into the tawdry confines of a pantry in the Ambassador Hotel, to take form as a Jordanian refugee named Sirhan Sirhan and put a .22 long-rifle slug into Kennedy's brain. He died 25 1/2 hours later, on D-day, the sixth of June, 1968, at age forty-two. With him died his hopes of gaining the Presidency. With Kennedy died, too, any lingering illusion that somehow America had, with the deaths of John Kennedy, Malcolm X and King, been purged of its destructive urges. Indeed, by the end of 1968 it was clear the year had been one of the most violent since the end of World War II. In the burgeoning horror of Vietnam, it began with news of the Tet offensive, then careered through broad-scale campus antiwar revolts, and the decision of President Lyndon Johnson not to seek re-election, through the martyrdom of King and its attendant ghetto riots, on to the murder of Bobby Kennedy and the Walpurgisnacht of the Democratic Convention's police riot, and finally to the election of Richard M. Nixon.

Obviously, 1968 was a year to remember, if only to avoid repeating, for it was certain that the spirit of hatred and revenge which Kennedy had reviled had come to dwell among Americans as seldom before. Yet for Kennedy, in the City of Angels on the evening of his greatest triumph in the vital California primary, it may well have seemed otherwise. It may have seemed that it was again possible to believe, as he said fifteen minutes before he was assassinated: "We can work together [despite] the division,

201

the violence, the disenchantment with our society, the division between age groups or over the war in Vietnam. We are a great country, an unselfish country, a compassionate country."

Sirhan Bishara Sirhan did not, as far as we know, hear Kennedy speak those words. The Senator had ended his short victory speech in the hotel's Embassy Room at about 12:10 A.M., June 5. He could then have moved off the podium to his left, exiting through the mass of jubilant supporters, the lines of radiant Kennedy Girls. His bodyguards thought Bobby would, and started clearing a way. Simultaneously, a hotel man suggested he go toward the right. But Karl Uecker, a maître de, surveyed the crowd and led Kennedy toward the rear through a curtain, in the direction of a nearby service pantry. That seemed a good way to escape the mauling Bobby had taken throughout the campaign from enthusiastic fans, and was a good way to get to his interview with the "pencil press" in another meeting room. In retrospect, it also seemed a random choice, one that might confound a conspiracy's plan.

It didn't confound Sirhan. Near a crude sign saying "THE ONCE AND FUTURE KING," he waited by a steam table in the narrow pantry, and watched as Kennedy moved along, shaking hands with the kitchen help, trailed by his outdistanced bodyguards, surrounded by journalists who had divined the route. Precisely what happened next is debated. But several things seem clear. There is Sirhan in a peculiar half-crouch, smiling, his hand moving to his belt and a little gun coming up in it—like a cap gun, a witness said—and then the gun fires as Sirhan lunges toward Kennedy, almost as though striking at him with a knife, according to one man, and then Kennedy is falling backward toward an ice machine, down to the concrete floor, while the gun keeps firing again and again, even though Uecker has grabbed Sirhan. Then, suddenly, the shooting stops as others mob the Jordanian, throw him over a steam table and try to tear the gun away. All around the screams go up: "My God . . . Oh, no . . . Jesus Christ." A radio announcer blabbers into his recorder and a TV man films the hysteria, both of them dissociated, unbelieving, like all the beholders of all our assassinations. Five others also are wounded, but Bobby draws the most attention. His blood pools as the struggle continues to subdue the slender, unexpectedly strong assassin. Bobby's friends leap in. George Plimpton takes hold of Sirhan. Later, he will remember his "enormously peaceful" eyes. Roosevelt Grier finally secures the gun. He gives it to Rafer Johnson. The two black athletes shout oaths while people call out, "Kill him, kill the bastard." Rafer fights the lynchers off, and Jesse Unruh, characteristically polemical, jumps to the top of the steam table and announces, "We don't want another Dallas. If the system works at all, we are going to try this one." People twist Sirhan's leg, and Grier pins him down while they wait for the cops.

Kennedy, meanwhile, asks, "Am I all right?" Next to his heart, he holds a rosary volunteered by one of the encircling people and twisted around his thumb by Juan Romero, a busboy who has cradled Bobby's head and said, "Come on, Mr. Kennedy, you can make it."

The bystanders wonder about that. Dr. Stanley Abo probes the wound behind Kennedy's right ear with his finger, to relieve the pressure, and Ethel Kennedy, pregnant with their eleventh child, comforts the now comatose victim. It takes seventeen terrible minutes to get Kennedy out of the maddened pantry and into an ambulance. By that time, Sirhan is in custody. The cops have pulled him from under Grier at 12:22, hustled him out, read him his rights and thought he looked remarkably collected, almost "smirky." Hoping he could help prevent another disaster à la Oswald, Jesse Unruh rides to the precinct station with the assassin, who refuses to give his name. Unruh later says the swarthy boy mumbled, "I did it for my country." That's hotly disputed, but it's true that in the hours to come the suspect displayed a canny coolness, a sure knowledge of his rights (like Oswald, he'll ask for an ACLU lawyer—unlike Oswald, he'll get one), an interest in famous murders, and an anonymity broken only when his brothers see his picture in the morning newspaper and tell the police who he is. For now, all the police know is that he probably shot Kennedy with the eight-shot Iver-Johnson .22 revolver Johnson had given them, all eight chambers stuffed with expended cartridge cases. And that he was carrying $409, a clipped David Lawrence column speculating on Kennedy's inconsistency in opposing the Vietnam war while supporting military aid for Israel, two unexpended .22 cartridges, one detached .22 slug, a Kennedy campaign song sheet and an ad inviting the public to an RFK rally at the Ambassador, Sunday, June 2. The police wonder if the ad means he was stalking the Senator.

If so, he succeeded. Kennedy was fatally wounded, although neurosurgeons did all they could to remove the bone shards and lead fragments from the killing shot, which entered the right mastoid—a honeycomb-soft bone—to sever arteries and lacerate cells. Had he lived, Kennedy at best would have been deaf in the right ear and paralyzed in the right face and would have suffered vision and spastic spells. Ted Kennedy and Ethel and Jackie, in from London, looked on as Bobby's life oozed away. His brain died at 6:30 P.M. on June 5, the EEG wave hardening to a line. His body followed at 1:44 A.M. on June 6. Now for Sirhan it was murder and for

America the agony of another Kennedy funeral. After a painstaking autopsy, Bobby's body was flown to New York, where it lay in state at St. Patrick's Cathedral on June 7—the day Sirhan was indicted for the murder. Coretta King, widowed two months before, came to pay her respects. So did Ralph Abernathy, up from Washington, where the Poor People's March that King had hoped to lead now languished by the Mall in a shantytown called Resurrection City, its members hoping moral suasion would bring the stronger antipoverty legislation Robert Kennedy had endorsed.

President Johnson attended the High Requiem Mass of June 8—the day a no-account thief named James Earl Ray was caught in London—and heard Ted Kennedy eulogize his brother: "He should be remembered simply as a good and decent man who saw wrong and tried to right it, saw suffering and tried to heal it, saw war and tried to stop it." Fittingly, only two days before, LBJ had issued a call, doomed as it turned out, for gun-control laws that would prevent mail-order sale of all firearms and their interstate trade. (Such a law wouldn't have stopped Sirhan, however, since he got his $25 gun through his brother, who got it from a man, who'd gotten it from a woman, who'd gotten it for protection after the Watts riots.)

Robert Kennedy's remains were moved in a funeral train all too reminiscent of Lincoln's down the roadbed from New York to Washington. Kennedy's people, the ones he had counted on to help make him President, filled each window and lined the tracks: black and white, men and women, the aged and the children, people rich and poor, offering him homage as best they could.

Kennedy was buried that evening in Arlington Cemetery on a gentle knoll sixty feet from his brother's grave. Unlike his brother's, Robert Kennedy's funeral ceremony was simple, but, like his brother's, rain- and tear-dampened. After the short liturgy, Bobby's son Joseph Kennedy III received the casket's covering flag. He passed it to his mother. The Kennedys, family-strong and ghostly in the light of myriad candles, moved one by one to kneel and kiss the mahogany coffin. Then it was over, again.

Sirhan Bishara Sirhan, for now everyone knew his name, spent June 8 reading and listening to radio music in his jail's infirmary. His leg and finger had been injured in the pantry fracas. He had a few bruises. Otherwise, he was in good health, small (5'3", 120 pounds) but lithe and, according to the New County Jail doctor, "self-satisfied, smug, and unremorseful." That façade would crumble in the months to come, as through his lawyers Sirhan learned of the massive evidence against him, testifying to his act, its motivation, its planning. So much incriminated Sirhan that his lawyers, including the estimable Grant Cooper, decided they could only plead that Sirhan's mental capacity to premeditate the crime was diminished, and so Sirhan was really guilty only of second-degree murder. Certainly their client's behavior, his violent mood swings, suggested that the "diminished capacity" notion might be true.

A consulting psychiatrist, Dr. Bernard Diamond, even suspected that Sirhan may have been in some sort of trance when he shot Kennedy—an idea shared by Robert Blair Kaiser, a writer-sleuth who participated in the defense planning and later published a history of the case. The trance idea was interesting—it jibed with Sirhan's interest in the occult, in thought transference, and Rosicrucian doctrines—but it was hard to sell to a jury. Sirhan's own story wouldn't stand up either. Who would believe, even if it were true, that he'd gone to the Ambassador, gotten drunk on Tom Collinses, decided to drive home but was too drunk, took his gun from the car so it wouldn't be stolen, went into the hotel for coffee and found some in the area behind the Embassy Room stage, and then was somehow in the pantry where he guessed he did shoot Kennedy, but he couldn't remember a thing about it?

No, liquor-induced amnesia might contribute, but it couldn't carry the whole defense burden. Sirhan's attorneys in time agreed on a narrow strategy. He killed Kennedy with that gun in the pantry, but he wasn't in a rational state of mind; was, in fact, rather crazy.

For its part, the prosecution set out to prove that Sirhan assassinated Kennedy with malice aforethought, motivated by Kennedy's pro-Israel statements. They reasoned those statements, particularly after the Six Day War humiliated the Arabs in 1967, had so inflamed the Jordanian that he undertook vengeance, thus becoming the prototypal lone assassin: a paranoiac but legally sane young man with a political fixation and a savior complex. The state's expert psychiatric witnesses would debunk the defense's contention that Sirhan was demented. Of course, the state had plenty of other evidence, too, eventually ten full volumes assembled by the police's investigative team called Special Unit Senator. (Those volumes, although repeatedly sought by interested parties, have remained secret, causing speculation that not everything in them fingers Sirhan as a lone killer.)

The trial began February 17, 1969, and ended two months later with a guilty verdict. Sirhan, the jury decided, had willfully killed Kennedy. The convicted assassin remained insouciant and cocky, even after he was—despite a plea from Ted Kennedy—condemned to death. "But I am fa-

206 Assassination in America

mous," Sirhan said. "I achieved in a day what it took Kennedy all his life to do." Sirhan also asserted, as he had before, that there was no conspiracy and that he was not afraid to die. (In fact, Sirhan's death sentence later was reduced to life imprisonment and he is now eligible for parole in 1986.) For the state, the victory was twofold: Not only had it proved Sirhan was a lone killer but it had protected him and his rights, and at last—after John Kennedy and King—brought an assassin to justice.

Not without considerable help, to be sure. The state had the usual abundance of investigative resources (the trial alone cost $609,702) and the ability to select from the immense bank of data what best suited its case. The press, which otherwise might have published items that questioned the state's developing case, was gagged by a court ruling issued soon after Sirhan's arraignment (still, enterprising newsmen chased down leads, perhaps figuring they couldn't prejudice the case any more than had Mayor Sam Yorty, who, right after the murder, proclaimed that Sirhan was "a sort of loner who harbored Communist inclinations, favored Communists of all types . . . [his diary said] that R.F.K. must be assassinated before June 5, 1968"). Then, too, the defense's decision to say Sirhan was a victim of diminished mental capacity meant the questions of a conspiracy, even important questions of physical evidence, were not deeply probed in Sirhan's behalf. Instead, the trial, like Guiteau's, consisted mostly of psychiatric testimony.

Thus the trial of Sirhan did not solve Kennedy's murder—an outcome to consider for those who believe a trial for James Earl Ray might clear up King's assassination. It's true much was revealed about the sort of man Sirhan is and about facts pointing to his planning and execution of the crime. But much else was slighted, leaving us with speculations that have survived. What do we now know—and what do we still question—about Sirhan and Kennedy?

We know, thanks to Sirhan's notebook and the work of writers like Robert Blair Kaiser, that the convicted assassin was a mightily disturbed young man. In his diary-notebook, snatched up by the police when Sirhan's brothers allowed them to search his room (a seizure of dubious legality), he wrote: "May 18 9:45 A.M.—68 My determination to eliminate R.F.K. is becoming more of an unshakable [sic] obsession . . . please pay to the order . . . R.F.K. must die—RFK must be killed Robert F. Kennedy must be assassinated." There are many such homicidal notes, several juxtaposed with entries about money, which have led some to suspect that Sirhan was paid to kill Kennedy (but no untoward sums were ever discovered—Sirhan worked, and in April, 1968, he got $1,705 in workmen's compensation due after a fall from a horse in 1966, an event to which we'll return). In one place, Sirhan writes that he advocates "the overthrow of the current President of the fucken United States of America," and in another that the solution is to "do away with its leaders." Certainly, it seems Sirhan's attitude fit that of an assassin. His diary, according to the expert Dr. David Rothstein, exhibits the paranoia of those who write threatening letters to U.S. Presidents. (The notebooks *are* his, according to handwriting experts, and not forgeries, a fact which some conspiracy buffs disputes, saying the notebooks, like Arthur Bremer's, were dictated by master plotters to Sirhan.)

What brought Sirhan to this attitude? Perhaps as revealing as any remark he ever made was the one to his mother upon arriving in America in 1957. The twelve-year-old boy asked, "When we become citizens, Momma, will we get blond hair and blue eyes?" His question came out of the miasmic sort of childhood psychiatrists say is common to many of our assassins and accused assassins: one marked by a lack of love from the father (Sirhan's father, people testified, often beat the boy) and by traumatic upset (in Sirhan's case, the barbaric 1948 Jewish-Arab war, much of it carried on in Jerusalem, where the Sirhans lived before the fighting uprooted them). The war also later provided Sirhan with a political cause similar to Booth's Confederacy, Guiteau's Stalwart Republicanism, Czolgosz's anarchy, Oswald's Cuba. Such early experiences can cause anomie, a feeling that one belongs to nothing, and a consequent desire to become —however it's accomplished—someone who does belong. For example, the prototypal blond, blue-eyed American—that, too, a fantasy—who had not been ousted by Jews from his home, who had not seen bombings in Jerusalem, who had not stood around refugee camps at the age of four in a spell cast by the horror of continual maiming and killing. Nor is anomie the only effect on embryonic assassins. Often there is a feeling of impotence (in the early morning of his arrest, Sirhan said, "We're all puppets"), which can spark desires for self-improvement, for secret societies, for anything to enhance self-esteem. That was true of Sirhan.

At Pasadena's John Muir High School, the swarthy foreigner was shy and envious of the white-skinned Americans, with their cars and money and fathers (Sirhan's deserted the family after six months in America to return to Palestine). At Pasadena City College—whence issues the Rose Bowl Queen every year—he amassed F's while flirting with collegiate communism (one leftish fellow student, Walter Crowe, afterward feared he had inspired Sirhan to kill Kennedy by discussing the virtues of terrorism) and Nasserism and Castroism and Rosicrucianism. Sirhan then badly wanted a Mustang and money (awaiting trial, he fantasized blackmailing first Lyndon Johnson, then Richard Nixon, for a pardon and money, and then James Hoffa for $150,000, the threat always the same: they ordered him to kill Kennedy). In lieu of riches, Sirhan experimented with moving objects and people by transmitting thoughts to them. He tried automatic writing and gazed at candles, attempting self-hypnosis. He boasted that he once conjured Kennedy's face in a mirror. Sirhan became excited by the success of black militancy during 1967 (June 2 of that year, he entered in his notebook a "Declaration of War against American Humanity" for injustices visited upon himself). In April, 1968, Kaiser reports, Sirhan was intrigued by the successful escape of King's assassin. Assassination itself interested him and he underlined pertinent passages in history books. And so, Sirhan wandered through his early twenties, among odd doctrines and peoples, a lonely bed-wetting boy who had nightmares about waking in a great darkness, who worried about his food, who was both proud and ashamed of his Arabness and who detested Robert Kennedy's Zionist supporters—he once interrupted coitus when a girl confessed she was Jewish—although thinking with another mind that Bobby was for the underdog, and he was one of those for sure.

Sirhan was also, one defense psychiatrist said, a chronic and deteriorating paranoid (in the top 95 percentile of tests) with persistent systems of "delusional false beliefs." One such belief, incidentally, was the Messianic notion that he had elected Nixon by shooting Kennedy, which in history's cold light seems not so delusional. Dr. Bernard Diamond believed Sirhan's predominant appearance of lucidity came from feigning sanity. That opinion came partly from Diamond's sessions with a hypnotized Sirhan—predictably, he went under easily—during one of which the Jordanian writhed in horror as he melded the bombings of his youth with the Phantom jets Kennedy approved sending to Israel.

Israel, the detested usurper, obsessed Sirhan in both hypnotic and conscious states—a fixation that became fraught with ironies at his trial, where among his defenders he had both a Jewish civil rights attorney and an Arabian-American lawyer (who some thought had been retained by Arab interests to ensure that Sirhan's trial provided maximum airing of Arab grievances). Israel's linkage to Kennedy was obvious. "I hated his guts, sir," Sirhan told Diamond. In one hypnotic session, according to Kaiser, Sirhan re-enacted the murder, reaching for his left hip, muttering "You son of a bitch," pointing his finger and crooking it several times around the imagined trigger. Diamond in time hypothesized that Sirhan was entranced when he shot Kennedy, in a dissociated state brought into his fragmented mind by Kennedy's presence in the hotel, the booze and maybe the bright lights and mirrors of the campaign rooms through which he drifted before the shooting (at the trial, however, testimony was offered that Sirhan had lurked mostly in a dark corridor). Such a trance, some think, could have been induced by a co-conspirator who had programmed Sirhan, perhaps by one of his occultist acquaintances. Special Unit Senator's investigation, though, found no evidence of the numerous meetings many hypnotic-suggestion experts believe would have been necessary to assure control of an assassin. Sirhan himself suggested (and Diamond and Kaiser thought it possible) that he may have killed Kennedy due to autosuggestion, his hatred and lust for vengeance so strong in his subconscious that they took over his body and rational mind. In the end, several questions bubbled out of these psychological swamps. For instance, did Sirhan, in and out of hypnosis, steadfastly deny there was conspiracy because he had been programmed to do so, or because he was schizophrenic, or both? What, then, was the import of his blocking on psychological-test questions asking if he felt people were controlling his mind? Did he block because he was controlled by others or because he felt another of his selves steering him? Or was it all, as some prosecutors felt, a screen erected by a basically sane, cunning man who had planned the crime and executed it alone, in cold blood?

Whatever the answer, Sirhan obviously was not normal. His family, less fancy than the doctors, attributed Sirhan's increasingly bizarre behavior to that fall from the horse. After the college flunkout, Sirhan wanted to be a jockey. He worked a while at Santa Anita, and in 1966 got a job as an exercise boy, actually riding, at a ranch called Granja Vista del Rio, near Corona, California. There, on a foggy September 25 morning, up on a horse named Hy Vera, Sirhan was thrown against a metal post, where he lay crumpled, crying and bleeding. "He never could become a jockey," his boss later said. "He sort of lost his nerve." After the mishap, Sirhan didn't work much, even though his notebook suggested he continued to covet the things America's dream was supposed to bestow on her immigrants. His last job was at an organic-foods store in Pasadena. He quit in the spring of 1968, about the time he got his gun and his workman's compensation check (several of America's other assassins have been unemployed or unsuccessful when they pulled the trigger). From March on, Sirhan moved inexorably toward the Ambassador's pantry, albeit through the half-light of facts and rumors that surrounds assassination reconstructions.

He took to practicing a lot with his gun and he intensified his occult experiments. His notebook entries became more violent and disjointed.

Sirhan watched the gathering California primary campaign and by May 18 (this, too, recreated in hypnosis) had confided those murderous desires to his diary. Then, it seems, he began stalking Robert Kennedy. Witnesses later said they thought they had seen Sirhan at RFK campaign functions on May 20 and 24. On June 1, Sirhan seems to have practiced shooting and bought some ammunition (the salesclerk at first said he was with two other men—co-conspirators?—but he later recanted). Then, in the evening, he watched the key debate between RFK and Eugene McCarthy.

The next day, Sirhan admits, he attended the RFK rally at the Ambassador, enticed by the public invitation and bemused by the notion that a Kennedy, a hated Kennedy, would thus solicit the great unwashed. Sirhan's activities on Monday, June 3, are unclear. He may have driven his '56 pink-and-white De Soto (so unlike the Mustangs he and James Earl Ray preferred) to San Diego to an RFK speech. More likely, he drove around awhile, maybe shot some pool or some targets, then went home to watch TV. But there is a story, admired by conspiracy theorists, that on June 3 Sirhan and a Mexican-looking kid were picked up by a freakish Los Angeles character—minister, gambler and all-around hustler—while hitchhiking in downtown L.A. The preacher said he drove them to a brief sidewalk meeting with a slick dark-haired fellow and a blond girl, then took Sirhan alone to another rendezvous with somebody who worked in the kitchen at the Ambassador. During all this the man said he made a deal to sell Sirhan a horse, a deal to be consummated the next morning. But Sirhan didn't show. Instead, it was the dark-haired fellow, accompanied by the girl and the Mexican, who wanted the horse delivered near the Ambassador that evening of June 4; but no deal was struck, and the preacher went off to Oxnard to sell the Gospel and the next day learned of the Kennedy shooting and so came forward like a good citizen with this story. The police in time decided, mostly based on polygraph tests, that the minister had lied. Anyway, few thought it feasible that conspirators would plan to escape in a horse trailer. But the story didn't die, since it fit with other conspiracy tales, as we'll see.

In any event, most of Sirhan's activities on June 4 are documented. About 11:30 A.M., he was at the San Gabriel Valley Gun Club. There he stayed until it closed at five o'clock, firing almost four hundred rounds of "mini-mags" (uploaded .22 long-rifle cartridges) and standard .22s. When asked by other shooters about his small gun, he said, "It could kill a dog." He also offered expert advice to a housewife about her shooting (her blond hair and fondness for firearms later made her suspect, but the woman was cleared of any role in a conspiracy). Leaving the range, Sirhan went to a hamburger joint, became distressed over two newspaper accounts—one of renewed skirmishing between Jordan and Israel and the other about a Zionist rally on Wilshire Boulevard—visited with some Arabs he'd met at college and then, failing to find the Jewish rally, headed for the Ambassador.

Sirhan arrived there about 8:30. He left his wallet and identification in his car parked two blocks away. Police think he carried his gun in then, stuck in his waistband, but Sirhan's hypnotic reconstructions have him fetching it later. Either way, soon the slight figure in blue velour shirt and denim pants is mixing with the Kennedy crowds. He inquires of an electrician where Kennedy is staying and if he has bodyguards. Then he is seen in the press room, peering at a Teletype tapping out the news of Kennedy's building victory. Next he seems to mingle with the crowd in the Embassy Room, and then he's drinking a Tom Collins and remarking about the heat in the rooms, and then he's seeking entrance to the anteroom behind the stage from which RFK would soon speak, but is rebuffed and returns to the adjoining pantry corridor, where he asks a busboy if Kennedy would be coming through there soon. All around him ascends the hysteria of victory, again somebody *else's* victory, the noise of the mariachi bands, of the campaign song "This Man Is Your Man," of the cheers, "We want Bobby! We want Bobby!" and the applause and laughter as the candidate appears and addresses them, and thanks them, and then comes off the stage and down the corridor toward Sirhan, standing between the table and the ice machine, waiting with those peaceful eyes. Lastly, there is the sound of shots and screams.

Immediately after the murder, the din intensified. Cries about The Girl in the Polka-Dot Dress came first. Sandy Serrano, a campaign follower, said she was on a fire escape escaping the heat when a girl in a white dress with black polka dots came up, along with two young men, a chicano and a hirsute Anglo, one of them maybe Sirhan. Then, a few minutes later, Serrano said the girl and a man came pelting down the fire escape shouting, "We shot him, we shot him." A mystery was born (and one whose cast dovetailed with the minister's story). It deepened later when Thomas Vincent DiPierro, son of an Ambassador maître de, told police he'd seen the smiling assassin, holding on to a tray stand, just before the murder. He seemed to be with a pretty girl in a white dress with black polka dots.

The press at once set out in full cry to find this vanished conspirator. Before long, a go-go dancer named Cathey Fulmer volunteered that she might be the girl, since she was wearing a polka-dot scarf that night at the Ambassador. But that didn't check out as anything except publicity-seeking by a sick girl (Miss Fulmer committed suicide a year later and fanciers of the "dying witnesses" in the JFK assassination mulled the significance). Next Valerie Schulte, a Kennedy Girl who'd been in the pantry, said *she* was the polka-dotted girl, a statement disputed by other witnesses. Eventually, the police concluded that Serrano and DiPierro had "contaminated" each other's stories before giving their statements, and so discounted the tale (they believed DiPierro's account of Sirhan's shooting Kennedy up close, though). Nonetheless, today many still think there was a girl and that she was part of a conspiracy.

Endlessly, the rumors came. A psychotic skyjacker and bad-check artist told the FBI that Castro had Bobby done in to complete vengeance on the Kennedys for their anti-Cuba doings. A French "investigator" and several Americans suggested that Arab terrorists—possibly dispatched by Nasser —had killed Kennedy in retaliation for U.S. friendship with the Zionists. Donald Freed, who collaborated with Mark Lane in a sensational JFK-conspiracy film, lately has revived the programmed assassin idea in a pulpish book which supposes Sirhan was robotized through lurid sex and hypnotism, in order to kill Kennedy for the same right-wingers who had arranged Martin Luther King's death. Another writer previously vouch-safed to police that he had information hinting that the CIA had killed Bobby to keep him, should he become President, from investigating his brother's assassination and discovering that the CIA had arranged it. What's more, this writer boasted, he'd told Jim Garrison of his suspicion, and Big Jim had thundered, *Why not?*

Ludicrous though it was, that last made a weird sort of sense. Garrison and the assassinated Kennedys were, after all, a spectral dance team twirling through America's recent political murders, the adagio ghosts of assassinations past. No wonder that people still mongered rumors tying together the deaths of John and Robert Kennedy via a knotty guilt-by-association skein of Big Labor, Organized Crime, Castro, anti-Castroites, dissident U.S. intelligence agents, Watergaters and even the late famous recluse, Howard Hughes.

Compared with such conjectures, the riddles of the physical evidence weighed heavy as gold. Dr. Thomas Noguchi's thorough autopsy provided the most basic data, which paradoxically gave impetus to several questions about the assassination. (Even so, the autopsy contrasted with the shoddy performance wrought on JFK; to assure proper procedures the Government flew in three observers from the Armed Forces Institute of Pathology, ironically including the much criticized Colonel Pierre Finck, one of JFK's autopsy physicians.) Noguchi found three wounds: the fatal right-mastoid shot, which left a slug too shattered for testing; a nonfatal entry behind the right armpit, the slug exiting at the front of the right shoulder, leaving no testable lead fragments; another wound one-half inch away in the right armpit, this slug coming to rest in the lower rear of the neck, whence it was extracted for ballistic testing. The killing shot, Noguchi established, laid a powder tattoo one inch long on Kennedy, which meant the gun was no farther away than three inches. The other wounding shots also came from within about six inches. An examination of Kennedy's suit jacket showed a fourth bullet had passed through his right shoulder pad, going on to bounce around and wound one of the other five victims—or so the police thought.

Skeptics were not so sure, and their queries clustered around these crucial factors: (1) the assassin's location as deduced from the wounds, versus eyewitness accounts of where Sirhan and Kennedy were; (2) the fate of the missing bullets—indeed, how many shots actually were fired and where did they all go?—and (3) what the testable bullets recovered from Kennedy and two other victims revealed.

Critics of the police investigation first pointed out that several eyewitnesses said Sirhan was never closer to RFK than a foot. In addition, many witnesses (over seventy in the pantry were interviewed) thought Sirhan was in front of Kennedy, and thus could not have shot him from behind, as the autopsy showed. Former U.S. Congressman Allard Lowenstein is one who has believed in a "second gun" and who thinks Sirhan's trial ignored the possibility of a conspiracy. He quotes the maître de, Karl Uecker, who was guiding Kennedy through the pantry, as saying Sirhan's gun was always in front of them and no closer than eighteen inches. Moreover, Uecker believes Sirhan fired only two shots before Uecker knocked him back onto the steam table, so how could Kennedy have been hit by four bullets from Sirhan's gun?

The question is tantalizing. Yet at least two witnesses contradict Uecker's recollection. A security guard named Thane Eugene Cesar, who figures in another speculation, said Kennedy turned just before he was shot. Vincent DiPierro, who was close enough to Kennedy to be splattered with his blood, also says that while it's true Sirhan was to Kennedy's right front, about three feet away before the shooting started, the gunman then lunged forward, coming close to Kennedy, and at the same time Bobby turned leftward to shake more hands. That movement, the witnesses think, brought Kennedy's back to Sirhan. Dr. Noguchi thinks a first shot into the head could have sent Kennedy into a "body spinning," which would bring his back toward Sirhan and account for the additional wounds there. As for the number of shots, DiPierro, again with many others, remembered a first burst of shots, and then several more as during his struggle Sirhan kept firing wildly, throwing bullets all over the narrow pantry.

It's certain Sirhan's eight-shot revolver was empty when the shooting stopped. And six people were hit. Seven bullets or fragments were retrieved from the victims (three of them unmutilated enough for ballistics testing), and the eighth—according to the police the one that transited Kennedy's chest—went upward through ceiling panels and "was lost somewhere in the ceiling interspace." Splendid, the skeptics retort, except that there were at least twelve bullet tracks: four in Kennedy, three in the ceiling panels and one each in Paul Schrade, William Weisel, Irwin Stroll, Ira Goldstein and Elizabeth (née Evans) Young. How can there be so many? Doesn't it mean another gun fired from someplace? It does to Lowenstein and journalist Ted Charach (who made a movie plumping for the "second gun") and to Vincent Bugliosi, who as deputy district attorney in 1970 prosecuted and put away Charles Manson and some of his family.

For their part, the police believe eight shots could indeed have caused all the holes and wounds. One bullet, they say, penetrated a suspended ceiling panel, ricocheted off the concrete beyond it and went down through another panel to strike Elizabeth Young's head. The third hole in the ceiling panels was made by the lost bullet (other wild shots bounced off the floor, they think, to wound people in odd places like the buttocks and lower leg). Critics say that's absurd, and bring forth what they regard as refuting evidence. They contend the bullet that was recovered from Elizabeth Young is this case's "magic bullet," akin to that which wounded John Connally in Dallas, since it's supposed to have done so many things and all without losing more than eight grains of its original 39-grain weight. Furthermore, Young was bending over, they think, when she was struck, so how did the deflected bullet hit her in her forehead? Defenders of the investigation remind us that bullets can do exceedingly peculiar things, and that no one, not even Mrs. Young, knows what position she was in when hit.

Undaunted, those who are skeptical of the official explanation then ask why the ceiling panels in question were destroyed by the police? As part of a "monstrous cover-up" of second-gun evidence? Why, too, when the evidence recently was re-examined was the left sleeve missing from Kennedy's suit coat? Because there were more holes in it? And is the decision not to release the investigative report simply more proof of a whitewash? The police reply that the panels were unfortunately destroyed by a low-ranking officer, a year after the trial, as part of what he thought was "routine." The coat sleeve was removed long ago by physicians at one of the hospitals Kennedy was sent to and, anyway, there were no bullet holes or other evidence connected with it. The report is withheld, authorities say, because it necessarily included interviews with people who might be harmed if what they said about other people or organizations became public. There was no second gunman, the police repeat. None. The bullet holes add up to eight shots.

Bugliosi disagrees and says he has proof to the contrary. He cites photos showing Sergeants Charles Wright and Robert Rozzi by a door frame, pointing at what appeared to them to be bullet holes (the door, be it noted, is a goodly distance from the murder scene). If they were bullet holes, of course, there had to be another gun, since Sirhan's revolver held only eight shots, each already accounted for, however curiously. Though the L.A. District Attorney, like his predecessors, assured Bugliosi that the holes were not made by bullets, the Manson prosecutor obtained a written statement from Sergeant Rozzi that said it looked to him like there was a "small-caliber bullet" lodged inside the hole, and whatever the object was, he thought somebody else had later removed it. Trying to check this story, Bugliosi talked by telephone with Sergeant Wright, who, Bugliosi claims, told him it definitely was a bullet they'd seen and no doubt someone had removed it. But, when Bugliosi met Wright the next day, the officer refused to give a signed deposition and softened his talk, saying that the object just *looked* like a bullet and he had only *assumed* someone had removed it. Lowenstein points out that the police took several door frames as evidence, presumably because they might pertain to the case. The police say the frames revealed no bullet holes (the frames were also routinely destroyed), just as a new search of the pantry area in 1975 revealed no signs of additional shots. Predictably, Lowenstein, Bugliosi *et al.* attack the official findings, claiming that two .22 slugs booked as evidence bear traces of wood though police said they were found in Sirhan's car (precisely how that relates to the door-frame mystery is untold). They maintain other cops and witnesses have said more shots were fired, even that there exists in L.A.P.D. files other clear evidence of a conspiracy, like Sirhan's fingerprints in that minister's pickup truck, proving that the itinerant preacher told the truth about Sirhan, the blonde, a "Las Vegas type" slicker and the horse deal. Yet to this date, unfortunately for the conspiracy theorists, none of these claims has been documented.

Actually, the only second-gun theory with even faint plausibility doesn't much relate to such protestations. Its advocates, notably Charach, believe

Thane Eugene Cesar had the second gun. Certainly, Cesar was armed in the pantry. He was a security guard trailing Kennedy when the fatal shots were fired. Two TV men have said they saw Cesar with his gun drawn after the shooting, and Cesar once was quoted as saying he drew his gun (though he also denied this). So did Cesar shoot Kennedy from behind and up close? Not with his service revolver, which was a .38-caliber weapon. With what then? By the baroque reasoning of second-gun theorists, with a concealed .22, a gun that he later disposed of to a sinister friend, variously reported as residing now in Arkansas, Indiana or other points east. Charach claims he has interviewed this mysterious friend and that, sure enough, he says Cesar sold him a .22 after the assassination, telling him there might be repercussions if it were found among Cesar's possessions. Assuming Charach is right, though, still doesn't mean Cesar was a second assassin (really, anyone in that pantry who owned a .22 might fear repercussions). No one has tied Cesar to Sirhan, and the odds against *two* independent assassins in the pantry are long indeed. As for Cesar's purported motive, it's been suggested he was a right-wing racist who hated Bobby for his support of black civil rights. Again, that may be so, but it doesn't prove anything. At base, none of the Cesar story makes sense, except to those who cannot for whatever reasons—financial, emotional, political— accept that Sirhan did it alone.

Nevertheless, the questioning of that conclusion continues. Most recently, a new ballistics test was made as a result of separate petitions filed in Los Angeles County Superior Court by Paul Schrade (the union leader and Kennedy supporter also wounded in the fusillade) and by CBS (as part of their inquiry into the killing). Both parties wanted another test to determine if Sirhan's pistol fired all the shots. But why? Hadn't the L.A.P.D.'s ballistics man, DeWayne Wolfer, firmly established at the trial that test-fired slugs from Sirhan's gun matched those taken from the victims? Yes and no. The slugs were said to match. But we recall that the ballistics evidence was never challenged in court since his attorney cheerfully admitted Sirhan shot Kennedy. No challenge, that is, despite confusion sown by what Wolfer called "mislabeling" of a trial exhibit. It seems People's Exhibit Number 55, which contained the test slugs, bore a tag, listing the slugs as fired by a revolver with a serial number different from that of Sirhan's gun. Wolfer explained he *had* used another Iver-Johnson for powder-tattoo tests (thus sparing Sirhan's pistol any possible damage), and had by mistake put *its* serial number on the envelope containing what were, really and truly, slugs from Sirhan's pistol. Skeptics doubted this, and began claiming Sirhan's pistol was never test-fired, had maybe even been destroyed (the L.A.P.D. said no, they had only gotten rid of the twin Iver-Johnson).

Soon, skepticism became the rule as two criminalists announced that bullets taken from Kennedy did not match one taken from another victim. William Harper, a respected California expert, first studied the seven recovered bullets. Using a scanning camera rather than the conventional comparison microscope, Harper concluded in 1970 that the bullet taken from Kennedy's neck did not match that taken from the abdomen of William Weisel, primarily because the RFK slug had twenty-three minutes' greater rifling angle than did the Weisel slug (twenty-three minutes is .001 percent of a circle). Harper also decided that the Kennedy bullet had only one cannelure (knurled groove circling the base), while the Weisel bullet had two. This assertion interested Herbert MacDonell, a professor of criminalistics and a frequent defense witness in notorious cases (MacDonell disputed the state's evidence in the James Earl Ray evidentiary hearing in 1974). Appearing in May, 1974, at hearings convened by former L.A. County Supervisor Baxter Ward (who then, like Bugliosi in 1976, was running for district attorney), MacDonell explained that the difference in cannelures meant there probably were two guns. You see, all Sirhan had in his gun, so the cartridge cases prove, were mini-mags manufactured by the Cascade Cartridge Corporation in Lewistown, Idaho—a company that puts two cannelures on all its mini-mags.

With such claims abroad, the pressure for a new ballistics test mounted. It became irresistible after Wolfer testified he couldn't exactly remember the test results other than the positive match of test slugs to Sirhan's gun. He recalled a spectrographic test (which, as in the Kennedy and King cases, would show if all the bullets had the same metallic composition), but the results apparently "had been destroyed." Also, a more sophisticated neutron activation analysis he'd rejected, feeling it would prove unreliable.

In late 1975, Judge Robert Wenke decided the matter needed clearing up once and for all. He ordered retesting of Sirhan's revolver. A panel of seven firearms experts, chosen with the agreement of all concerned, was impaneled. Four test slugs were fired from Sirhan's gun, examined by each expert, and on October 7, 1975, the conclusions were announced.

The experts agreed that there was no evidence showing more than one gun fired the bullets; that all the slugs had two, not one cannelures; that the Kennedy, Stroll, Goldstein, and Weisel slugs had "similar characteristics"; and that there was no significant variation in rifling angles between the Kennedy and Weisel bullets. So much, it would seem, for the second-gun theory. Yet the "moral crusade," as Charach dignifies it, marches on, ever seeking to prove a conspiracy, to get a new trial for Sirhan. It seems the conspiracy advocates would test anything, except the strength of their beliefs against what seems, overwhelmingly, to be the central fact: Sirhan Bishara Sirhan, by himself, killed Robert Kennedy. He may have been drunk, or entranced, or possessed of a rational if murderous hatred, but it seems he did it. At last report—to CBS's Dan Rather—Sirhan said simply that there was no conspiracy, that he can't believe any external force influenced him, that so far as killing Kennedy goes, he just doesn't remember.

But we remember. Perhaps remember too well how we had lost another leader to another assassin, and in the process perhaps lost another irreplaceable piece of our national self. And by 1972—when we knew in full what Vietnam meant, even as Watergate was rising behind its stone wall —we had yet another memory. This one come courtesy of a fat-faced bundle of frustrations named Arthur Herman Bremer.

Bremer's story is not long, nor should it be. He was, after all, a failed assassin, and we've seen how most assassins are failures to begin with. There he was on May 15, 1972, at the Laurel Shopping Plaza in Maryland, blond and resplendent in a red, white and blue shirt all plastered with Wallace buttons, his empty eyes concealed by sunglasses, his perpetual smirky smile flashing from the second row, as he watched George Corley Wallace mumble platitudes, working the crowd, and then Bremer thrust his snub-nosed .38 between a couple named Spiegle, across the rope, and fired five times at point-blank range. Amazingly, Wallace lived, albeit wounded four times and paralyzed from the waist down (three others also were hit in the volley—they recovered). And so Bremer joined historical company with the likes of John Schrank, who tried and failed to kill Teddy Roosevelt. It seems clear Bremer dreamed of himself as a great figure in history. "I am one three-billionth of the world's history," the twenty-one-year-old wrote in his hundred-page journal, filled elsewhere with his admiration of Oswald and Sirhan, and with a corresponding hatred for Richard Nixon, for George Wallace, for the haves of the world. "I Am A Hamlet," he wrote, while complaining about headaches and pains in his chest. On another occasion, he confided he'd like to see his name in the history books and, after his arrest, he told a cop, "Just stay with me and you'll be a star, just like I am."

Whether or not such sentiments motivated Bremer's attack is a moot question, though they strongly suggest megalomania, that flip side of the schizoid-paranoid personality a psychiatrist detected after the attempt on Wallace. But it's far from moot that Bremer's childhood in Milwaukee provided the psycho-environment we've learned is conducive to creating assassins. His father he perceived as weak, unsuccessful, a nonentity. His mother, he said, was lazy, inattentive, and cruel—given to frequent beatings of Arthur and his brothers (one of whom became a confidence man who once was indicted for bilking fat ladies in a weight-salon scam). An indifferent student (I.Q. of 106), the young Bremer grew withdrawn, friendless, invisibly moving into and through an adolescence apparently made bearable by the fantasies he drew from *Playboy, Gun Digest,* various soft-core sex comics (these publications were later found in his messy bachelor apartment).

In his pre-Wallace life, Bremer had one girlfriend, a fifteen-year-old named Joan Permich, who worked as a monitor in the elementary school where Bremer was a janitor. Arthur took the affair very seriously, pursuing Joan with sweaty earnestness. She did not reciprocate the feverish feelings. Their breakup in January, 1972, helped turn Bremer's mind toward political murder, or so some think. Certainly by April, when he began his diary, Bremer's eye was on a compensation beyond mortal love—he would achieve fame through assassination. That is, it's certain if the diary is his work and not E. Howard Hunt's, as Gore Vidal has speculated. Samples of Bremer's handwriting seem to confirm that he wrote the journal, a fact that doesn't, as we'll see, unknot an interesting tie to Hunt, Nixon and the Watergate contretemps.

Anyway, by April Arthur had his gun. Two guns, in fact—the .38 and a 9mm Browning automatic.

They weren't his first weapons. In November, 1971—a few months after he'd bought a car and moved out of his folks' house into an apartment— he was arrested while parked in a fashionable residential area with a .38 (the police relieved him of this one) and two boxes of ammunition. No one can say what, if anything, he intended, though a psychiatrist has said Arthur was out target-practicing that day—like Sirhan, Guiteau, Oswald —and had then resolved to rob some houses. Also about this time, the doctor says, Bremer thought about shooting his boss, a woman, at the Milwaukee Athletic Club, where he worked at a second plebeian job. Thus Bremer seemingly had violent urges before his trauma with Joan Permich, which did, however, derail him enough to make him shave his head and, like Sirhan, quit his jobs.

Bremer wasn't quite finished working though. He soon signed on as a Wallace volunteer, probably as much for the free meals as for the ideology (oddly, one supposition has Bremer shooting Wallace out of an identification with oppressed blacks, a contention that the diary's right-wing rantings refute). Cadging free meals was consistent with Arthur's personality. Everyone agreed he was frugal, a fact that hasn't dampened conjecture about where he got the money to follow around Nixon and Wallace, some thinking it came from a conspiracy's masterminds. But Bremer had made about $9,000 before he quit and he had only about two dollars on him when he was arrested. He recorded money worries in his journal. There were few luxuries. His battered 1968 Rambler cost only $795. Aside from a fling at New York's Waldorf-Astoria he stayed in modest lodgings. (One sad extravagance was a New York massage parlor, where a comely masseuse jerked him off while ripping him off for $48.)

The chronicle of his days is that of a mind slipping from control, as he trails Nixon to New York, Canada, Washington. He writes: "This will be one of the most closely read pages since the Scrolls in those caves. . . . My fuse is about burnt. There's gona be an explosion soon." He wants to kill millions, especially "Nixy." But the President, he finds, is too closely guarded, although he brags he got within twelve feet of Nixon's car in Ottawa. Then in May he writes, "I've decided Wallace will have the honor of—what would you call it?" Characteristically, he frets that "editors won't care" if Wallace is assassinated. Around then, too, Arthur began observing and commenting on himself going mad. "NURSE! GET THE JACKET!" he scrawled. Following the string of Wallace's "send 'em a message" campaign, Bremer yo-yoed through Wisconsin and Michigan, appearing at rallies, even being photographed in plastic Wallace boaters (afterward, Wallace workers said, sure, they recognized the little creep—police even questioned him once). Bremer gleefully noted the many lapses in Wallace's security, particularly delighting in chatting with Secret Service men.

Finally, down and almost out after driving to Maryland on May 14, Bremer's last best chance came.

Wallace now lies, like all the political victims before him, in his own pooling blood. A bullet has severed nerve ganglia near the twelfth thoracic vertebra. He will never walk again, or control his bowels, or be elected President—something that the convincing primary victories in Michigan and Maryland, coming after the shooting, had made seem quite possible.

As with many of our acts of political violence, the reverberations are unexpected, savagely ironic. We realized no outraged black had shot Wallace, the man who stood in the schoolhouse door. A white had. And Wallace, the law-an'-order (and pro-gun) candidate, fell prey to an armed criminal. What was more, a criminal whose study of Oswald and Sirhan demonstrated a domino effect more devastating to Wallace than the one he feared and excoriated in Southeast Asia. And just as the deaths of King and Robert Kennedy brought legislative efforts for civil rights and against guns, so Wallace's crippling brought on calls for harsher, swifter justice—especially from Richard Nixon and Spiro Agnew.

Other effects were, however, to be expected. A trial for the accused, the contention that he was sane enough to know what he was doing, and the eventual guilty verdict and sentence—in Bremer's case, to sixty-three years. Predictable, too, were the rumors of conspiracies.

Wallace to this day believes Bremer was an agent, a belief perhaps dyed by an ingrained sense that no lone gunman could get *him*. He also doubts that Arthur wrote the diary. Other conspiracy lovers suppose, yes, a second gunman lurking somehow undetected in the crowd. Nearly half of all Americans are disbelievers and smell conspiracy just as they do about the murders of Lincoln and Cermak and the Kennedys and King. Arthur Bremer's father thinks his son needed to be directed to his act, not being much of a self-starter and never before in much trouble. Bremer's mother allows it was something he ate, or maybe "one of those false cigarettes" that drove her son mad (Bremer seems not to have used drugs). Even the Federal Government, while the investigation went on, kept open the question of a conspiracy. But to date, only one truly curious set of occurrences suggests anyone besides Bremer was involved.

Enter the infamous E. Howard Hunt, Watergate burglar, spy-book author and one-time CIA spook. In testimony before the Senate committee investigating Watergate, Hunt said that the now devout Charles Colson had dropped lacy hints that Hunt might want to "review the contents of Bremer's apartment." Colson was acting, it's reported, on Nixon's direct order, and though Colson denies having made any such suggestion to Hunt, the questions persist: Why would the plumbers be interested in Bremer? Would White House tapes thus far withheld reveal the reason? What about the curiously complete amount of background information about Bremer that was found in his apartment? Was the reportorial treasure trove obligingly planted by the FBI and Secret Service men who preceded newsmen there? Did they at the same time remove anything which might have implicated the Committee to Re-elect the President (Nixon, that was)?

It's possible, if not enlightening, to envision Bremer as part of a "dirty tricks" campaign, maybe being manipulated to scare Wallace out of the race so that the incumbent President and his men could take over the law-and-order issue. Or, if the imagination runs riot, theorists of a certain cast could fantasize Bremer as the ultimate dirty trick, a directed killer, maybe even as a psychotic who was suddenly, madly, out of his employer's control. Frightening and bizarre as such speculations are, it's true that a confessed dirty-trickster—Donald Segretti—was asked by the Senate's Watergate committee if he knew Bremer. Segretti firmly said no. That's where the question rests, as it probably should.

We don't have evidence of anyone's contacts with possible conspirators. Or evidence of payoffs. Or evidence of anything except the smiling Bremer, his blond hair and his blue revolver glittering in the May sunshine. That, and the paralyzed Wallace—who has suffered indignities like the taunts of students wearing Bremer masks and pushing wheelchairs—musing over and over that it just couldn't have been that simple.

It just couldn't have been that simple. Yet we are left with that, whether or not conspiracies exist. Booth, Guiteau, Czolgosz, Schrank, Zangara, Weiss, Oswald, Ray, Sirhan, Bremer. They have lock-stepped through our history with guns and scarred psyches, with real ills and imagined causes that became excuses to kill. Not long ago Lynette (Squeaky) Fromme and Sara Jane Moore brought femininity for the first time to the roster of those who would bypass the democratic process and kill our leaders. We tried to explain them as we have tried to explain the others.

It's said the one is Manson-mad, acting out of a soul diseased by her despicable guru. The other describes herself as a woman with three lives, who as mother, FBI informant and convert to the violent doctrines of far-left urban guerrillas decided on assassination as a way to awaken Americans as to who their leaders really were, to make us realize that Ford, Rockefeller *et al.* were "enemies of the people."

But does that, or any explanation for any contemplated assassination, really mean anything? Is there any answer to the riddle of why assassins always are with us? No sociology, no political analysis, no psychology, no bemoaning of a declining morality, no commission or committee has yet found an answer or devised a cure. No judge, jury or executioner has yet stayed an assassin's hand. Perhaps that is impossible. Perhaps there is a Cain deep in some of us, an ineradicable mark on us, an urge pulsing in our hearts to kill the chief, to extinguish forever another's authority over us—an urge as primal, as implacable as evil itself. If so—and it seems that way—the question is not if another American assassin will strike.

It is when.

EPILOGUE

One hesitates to say it for fear of giving substance to the words, yet it is true. If American assassins continue the trend described here, they will kill or seriously menace a prominent American by 1984 at the latest. It could well be sooner, especially if the current pandemic of political terrorism fully infects the United States, giving our native tradition a chance to convert terrorism from indiscriminate group activity to broad-scale personal political murder.

Can anything be done to prevent the giddying, sickening upset of assassination? Has our history taught us anything? Certainly we can think that the President and other indispensable politicians could be better protected, as much as anything by refusing silly excursions into unscreened crowds, by keeping their precise movements unannounced, by cooperating fully with Secret Service procedures. We might, since psychologists have limned the profile of the typical assassin, try to locate and segregate the Oswalds and Sirhans and Bremers and Frommes and Moores when our leaders visit their environs. Political campaigns could be conducted more via the media and less by pressing the flesh.

Unfortunately, practicing such precautions soon reaches a critical point of diminishing returns—and that is when the leaders of a democracy are so isolated from their constituents, become so much, to themselves and their supporters, mere cathode-ray figures rather than flesh-and-blood that the democratic process breaks down for want of genuine communication and fellow feeling. Many think we have already reached this point, but in any event that effect, if attained, would make for a powerful irony. Our assassins, who so many times have killed for their peculiar vision of liberty, would have split a cornerstone of the nation's true freedom.

Indeed, perhaps our only firm conclusion is that political murder has the most awful results in a democracy. That we become undone when guns speak and not voters. That when politics by assassination becomes common, our institutions may turn away from democracy and, like totalitarian states, we may begin to think of murder as a legitimate instrument of policy. That we become sick in our national soul.

Saddest of all, there seems to be no absolute cure. Yes, we know much about what creates assassins. A Freudian desire to kill the father. A genuine political idealism. A physical or mental illness. A bestial nature which permits homicidal hack work for money. But it is precisely because assassins are so variously motivated that there is no cure for assassination. No security plan or socio-politico-psycho understanding can forever deflect every potential killer.

It seems we are left, then, with assassins gestating in America. We might find cold comfort in that it is the unique richness of our society as much as any other factor that engenders the peculiarly American assassin. Only a nation that promises its citizens so much can disappoint a few so greatly that they become addled killers acting to restore the Eden all Americans are supposed to inhabit. But realizing the American Dream is a nightmare for some Americans is small recompense for the sorrow our assassins have brought us through the years, and even less for the sorrow they continue to bring.

As this book was being prepared for publication, several new shades of our past political murders rose to haunt us. One whispers that the truth is, two John Birchers—a general and a congressman—conceived and directed the murder of John Kennedy to keep America from going Red, and that there is positive proof of this. Another spectral voice husks that it was, as suspected, the CIA and the Mob who killed JFK, perhaps to avenge the Cuban fiasco, perhaps to regain the casinos for, say, a senior don like Santo Traficante. We hear from every side, notably Marguerite Oswald's, that her son was a federal agent, a supposition recently bolstered by the CIA's admission that the agency did have an interest in Oswald—contrary to prior testimony—as a source of information, at least about Russia. Evidence seems to mount that the CIA, Howard Hughes, Watergate, the Mob and Castro have been wandering in diabolic labyrinths which intersect at crucial points, perhaps in Dealey Plaza. We learn that James Earl Ray probably escaped from prison in Missouri not from cunning or with outside help, but because he caught wind of another inmate's escape plan and got there first. We are told that Edward Kennedy has been the object—would-be assassins say—of a plot to kill him in the alleged interests of "New York Mafia" figures, maybe some related by rumor to the murder of his brothers. All this we hear, so incessantly it does not surprise us that the current Congress includes a special committee to reassess the investigations of the assassinations of John Kennedy and Martin Luther King, and to recommend whether a full-scale reinvestigation should be made of the killings. Doubtless such a new probe will ensue. One can only hope it lays, once and for all, our ghosts to rest—whatever the conclusions of the investigation or however much the nation may suffer emotionally.

Of course, we know it would be nicer to believe these emotional upheavals are behind us. Our history tells us they probably are not. To our dismay, new assassins will hatch. We can only hope against hope they fail and leave America's history in the hands of kinder fates.

A SELECTED BIBLIOGRAPHY

Agee, Philip. *Inside the Company.* New York: Straight Arrow, 1975.

Anson, Robert Sam. *"They've Killed the President."* New York: Bantam Books, 1975.

Beals, Carleton. *The Story of Huey P. Long.* Westport, Conn.: Greenwood Press, 1971.

Belin, David. *November 22, 1963: You Are the Jury.* New York: Quadrangle Books, 1973.

Bishop, Jim. *The Day Kennedy Was Shot.* New York: Funk & Wagnalls, 1968.

———. *The Day Lincoln Was Shot.* New York: Harper & Brothers, 1955.

Bloomgarden, Henry S. *The Gun: A "Biography" of the Gun That Killed John F. Kennedy.* New York: Grossman, 1975.

Blumenthal, Sid, and Yazijian, Harvey, eds. *Government by Gunplay: Assassination Conspiracy Theories from Dallas to Today.* New York: Signet, 1976.

Bornstein, J. *The Politics of Murder.* New York: William Sloane, 1950.

Bremer, Arthur H. *An Assassin's Diary.* New York: Harper's Magazine Press, 1973.

Buchanan, Thomas. *Who Killed Kennedy?* New York: Putnam's, 1964.

Canfield, Michael, and Weberman, Alan J. *Coup d'Etat in America: The C.I.A. and the Assassination of John F. Kennedy.* New York: Third Press, 1975.

Columbia Broadcasting System. *CBS News Extra: "November 22 and the Warren Report."* Broadcast over CBS Television Network, September 27, 1964.

———. *CBS News Inquiry: "The Warren Report."* Parts I–IV, broadcast over CBS Television Network, June 25–28, 1967.

———. *CBS Reports Inquiry: "The American Assassins."* Parts I–IV, broadcast over CBS Television Network, November 25 and 26, 1975, and January 2 and 5, 1976.

Cottrell, John. *Anatomy of an Assassination.* New York: Funk & Wagnalls, 1966.

Cowles and UPI. *Assassination, Robert F. Kennedy, 1925–1968.* New York: Cowles Education Corporation, 1968.

Crotty, William J., ed. *Assassinations and the Political Order.* New York: Harper & Row, 1971.

Curry, Jesse; *Personal JFK Assassination File.* Dallas: American Poster and Printing Co., Inc., 1969.

Cuthbert, Norma B. *Lincoln and the Baltimore Plot 1861.* San Marino, Calif.: Huntington Library, 1949.

Cutler, R. B. *The Flight of CE 399: Evidence of Conspiracy.* Manchester, Mass.: R. B. Cutler, 1969.

Demaris, Ovid. *America the Violent.* New York: Cowles Book Company, Inc., 1970.

_____. *Captive City: Chicago in Chains.* New York: Lyle Stuart, 1969.

Dethloff, Henry C., ed. *Huey P. Long.* Problems in American Civilization Series. New York: Heath & Co., 1967.

Deutsch, Hermann B. *The Huey Long Murder Case.* New York: Doubleday, 1969.

Dewitt, David Miller. *The Assassination of Abraham Lincoln and Its Expiation.* Plainview, N.Y.: Books for Libraries, 1970.

Donovan, Robert J. *The Assassins.* New York: Harper & Brothers, 1955.

Eisenschiml, Otto. *Why Was Lincoln Murdered?* New York: Little, Brown, 1937.

_____. *In the Shadow of Lincoln's Death.* New York: Wilfred Funk, 1940.

Epstein, Edward J. *Counterplot.* New York: Viking Press, 1969.

_____. *Inquest.* New York: Viking Press, 1966.

Flammonde, Paris. *The Kennedy Conspiracy.* New York: Meredith Press, 1969.

Ford, Gerald, and Stiles, John. *Portrait of the Assassin.* New York: Simon and Schuster, 1965.

Frank, Gerold. *An American Death: The True Story of the Assassination of Dr. Martin Luther King, Jr. and the Greatest Manhunt of Our Time.* Garden City, New York: Doubleday, 1972.

Freed, Donald. *The Killing of RFK.* New York: Dell Books, 1975.

Garrison, Jim. *A Heritage of Stone.* New York: Putnam's, 1970.

Gottfried, Alex. *Boss Cermak of Chicago; A Study of Political Leadership.* Seattle: University of Washington Press, 1962.

Graham, Hugh Davis, ed. *Huey Long.* Great Lives Observed Series. Englewood Cliffs, N.J.: Prentice-Hall, 1970.

Greenberg, Bradley S., and Parker, Edwin B., eds. *The Kennedy Assassination and the American Public: Social Communication in Crisis.* Stanford, Cal.: Stanford University Press, 1965.

Harris, Thomas O. *The Kingfish: Huey P. Long, Dictator.* Baton Rouge, La: Baton Rouge Clator's Publishing Division, 1938.

Havens, Murray; Leiden, Carl; and Schmitt, Karl. *The Politics of Assassination.* Englewood Cliffs, N.J.: Prentice-Hall, 1970.

Hepburn, James. *Farewell America.* Vaduz, Liechtenstein: Frontiers Publishing Company, 1968.

Hofstadter, Richard, and Wallace, Michael. *American Violence: A Documentary History.* New York: Knopf, 1970.

Houghton, Robert A. *Special Unit Senator.* New York: Random House, 1970.

Howard, Robert P. *Illinois: A History of the Prairie State.* Grand Rapids, Mich.: William B. Ferdman's, 1972.

Huie, William Bradford. *He Slew the Dreamer.* New York: Delacorte Press, 1970.

Hyams, Edward. *Killing No Murder: A Study of Assassination as a Political Means.* London. Thomas Nelson and Sons Ltd., 1969.

Jansen, Godfrey. *Why Robert Kennedy Was Killed: The Story of Two Victims.* New York: The Third Press, 1970.

Joesten, Joachim. *Oswald: Assassin or Fall Guy?* New York: Marzani and Munsell, 1964.

Jones, Penn, Jr. *Forgive My Grief I.* Midlothian, Tex.: Midlothian Mirror, 1966.

———. *Forgive My Grief II.* Midlothian, Tex.: Midlothian Mirror, 1967.

———. *Forgive My Grief III.* Midlothian, Tex.: Midlothian Mirror, 1969.

———. *Forgive My Grief IV.* Midlothian, Tex.: Midlothian Mirror, 1974.

Kaiser, Robert Blair. *RFK Must Die!* New York: Dutton, 1970.

Kane, Harnett T. *Louisiana Hayride.* Gretna, La.: Pelican, 1971.

Kennedy, Robert F. *The Enemy Within.* New York: Harper & Row, 1960.

Kimmel, Stanley. *The Mad Booths of Maryland.* Indianapolis, Ind.: Bobbs-Merrill, 1940.

Kirkham, James F.; Levy, Sheldon G.; and Crotty, William J. *Assassination and Political Violence.* New York: Praeger, 1970.

Kirkwood, James. *An American Grotesque.* New York: Simon and Schuster, 1970.

Lane, Mark. *A Citizen's Dissent.* New York: Holt, Rinehart and Winston, 1968.

———. *Rush To Judgment.* New York: Holt, Rinehart and Winston, 1966.

Lasky, Victor. *Robert F. Kennedy: The Myth and the Man.* New York: Trident Press, 1968.

Leech, Margaret. *In the Days of McKinley.* New York: Harper & Brothers, 1959.

———. *Reveille in Washington.* New York: Time, Inc., 1962.

Leonardi, Dell. *The Reincarnation of John Wilkes Booth.* Old Greenwich, Conn.: Devin-Adair, 1975.

Lewis, Lloyd. *Myths After Lincoln.* New York: Harcourt Brace, 1911.

Lewis, Richard, and Schiller, Lawrence. *The Scavengers and Critics of the Warren Report.* New York: Dell Books, 1967.

McDonald, Hugh C., and Bocca, Geoffrey. *Appointment in Dallas: The Final Solution to the Assassination of JFK.* New York: Hugh McDonald Publishing Corp., 1975.

McGinnis, Joe. *The Selling of the President, 1968.* New York: Pocket Books, 1968.

Manchester, William. *The Death of a President.* New York: Harper & Row, 1967.

Marchetti, Victor, and Marks, John D. *The CIA and the Cult of Intelligence.* New York: Knopf, 1974.

Meagher, Sylvia. *Accessories After the Fact.* New York: Bobbs-Merrill, 1967.

———. *Subject Index to the Warren Report and Hearings and Exhibits.* New York: Scarecrow Press, 1966.

Mitgang, Herbert. *Lincoln as They Saw Him.* New York: Rinehart, 1956.

Model, F. Peter, and Groden, Robert J. *JFK: The Case for Conspiracy.* New York: Manor Books, 1976.

National Broadcasting Company. *There Was a President.* New York: Random House, 1966.

Newfield, Jack. *Robert Kennedy: A Memoir.* New York: E.P. Dutton, 1969.

Noyes, Peter. *Legacy of Doubt.* New York: Pinnacle Books, 1963.

O'Connor, Lynn. *Clout: Mayor Daley and His City.* Chicago: Henry Regnery, 1974.

O'Toole, George. *The Assassination Tapes: An Electronic Probe into the Murder of John F. Kennedy and the Dallas Cover-up.* New York: Penthouse Press, 1975.

Poore, Ben Perley. *Reminiscences of Sixty Years in the National Metropolis.* 2 vols. Washington, D.C.: Hubbard Bros., 1866.

Popkin, Richard. *The Second Oswald.* New York: Avon Books, 1966.

Rapoport, David C. *Assassination and Terrorism.* Ottawa: Canadian Broadcasting Corp., 1971.

Reid, Ed. *The Grim Reapers.* Chicago: Henry Regnery, 1969.

Roberts, Charles. *The Truth About the Assassination.* New York: Grosset and Dunlap, 1967.

Roffman, Howard. *Presumed Guilty.* Cranbury, N.J.: A. S. Barnes, 1976.

Roscoe, Theodore. *The Web of Conspiracy.* Englewood Cliffs, N.J.: Prentice-Hall, 1960.

Rosenberry, Charles E. *The Trial of Assassin Guiteau.* Chicago: University of Chicago Press, 1968.

Sandburg, Carl. *Carl Sandburg's Abraham Lincoln.* 3 vols. New York: Dell, 1954.

Scott, Peter Dale, *et al.*, eds. *The Assassinations: Dallas and Beyond—A Guide to Cover-ups and Investigations.* New York: Random House, 1976.

Sheridan, Walter. *The Rise and Fall of Jimmy Hoffa.* New York: Saturday Review Press, 1973.

Sindler, Allan P. *Huey Long's Louisiana.* Baltimore: Johns Hopkins, 1956.

Smith, Merriman, *et al. Four Days.* New York: United Press International and American Heritage, 1964.

Stern, Phillip Van Doren. *The Man Who Killed Lincoln.* New York: Literary Guild of America, 1939.

Stuart, William H. *The Twenty Incredible Years.* Chicago: M. A. Donohue, 1935.

Thompson, Josiah. *Six Seconds in Dallas.* New York: Bernard Geis Associates, 1967.

Toch, Hans. *Violent Men: An Inquiry into the Psychology of Violence.* Chicago: Aldine Publishing Company, 1969.

Townsend, George Alfred. *The Life, Crime and Capture of John Wilkes Booth.* New York: Dick & Fitzgerald, 1865.

Townsend, G. W. *A Memorial Life of William McKinley.* New York: Thompson & Thomas, 1902.

Warren, Earl, *et al. Report of the President's Commission on the Assassination of President Kennedy.* Washington, D.C.: Government Printing Office, 1964.

————. *Hearings Before the President's Commission on the Assassination of President Kennedy.* 26 vols. Washington, D.C.: Government Printing Office, 1964.

Weichmann, Louis J. *A True History of the Assassination of Abraham Lincoln and of the Conspiracy of 1865.* New York: Knopf, 1975.

Weisberg, Harold. *Whitewash: The Report on the Warren Report.* Hyattstown, Md.: Harold Weisberg, 1965.

————. *Whitewash II: The FBI–Secret Service Cover-up.* Hyattstown, Md.: Harold Weisberg, 1966.

————. *Photographic Whitewash: Suppressed Kennedy Assassination Pictures.* Hyattstown, Md.: Harold Weisberg, 1967.

————. *Oswald in New Orleans.* New York: Canyon Books, 1967.

————. *Post Mortem.* Frederick, Md.: Harold Weisberg, 1971.

————. *Frame-Up: The King/Ray Case.* New York: Outerbridge and Dienstfrey, 1971.

White, Stephen. *Should We Now Believe the Warren Report?.* New York: Macmillan, 1968.

Williams, T. Harry. *Huey Long: A Biography.* New York: Knopf, 1969.

Zapruder, Abraham. Copy of 8 mm. film of assassination of John F. Kennedy.

Zinman, David H. *The Day Huey Long Was Shot.* New York: Ivan Obolensky, 1963.

Contemporary newspapers, magazines, pamphlets and—in the more recent cases—radio and TV accounts were also consulted extensively in the preparation of this work.

INDEX

364.1   copy 1
Ma
          McKinley
               Assassination in America

DATE DUE
